ABSENT
FATHER
LOST GENERATION

ABSENT
FATHER
LOST GENERATION

JONATHAN C. STAFFORD

TATE PUBLISHING
AND ENTERPRISES, LLC

Published by Tate Publishing & Enterprises, LLC
127 E. Trade Center Terrace | Mustang, Oklahoma 73064 USA
1.888.361.9473 | www.tatepublishing.com

Tate Publishing is committed to excellence in the publishing industry. The company reflects the philosophy established by the founders, based on Psalm 68:11,
"The Lord gave the word and great was the company of those who published it."

Book design copyright © 2015 by Tate Publishing, LLC. All rights reserved.
Cover design by Nikolai Purpura
Interior design by Gram Telen

Published in the United States of America

ISBN: 978-1-63306-592-5
Psychology / Developmental / Child
15.01.27

To my father, James "Jimmy Hicks" Stafford, who did the best he could with the hand he was dealt.

To my three sons, Tyler, Jonathan, and Nathaniel.

Last, but certainly not least, to each one of my young readers being raised by a single mom. My sons were my inspiration for writing this book; however, you guys are my purpose for writing this book.

Acknowledgments

There are so many people I would like to thank for their contribution to this project. Without these people, this dream of mine would not have come true. First of all, I would like to thank my Lord and Savior Jesus Christ, for the encouragement, the strength, and the opportunity, to finally finish this project.

I would like to thank my lovely wife, not only for her patience with all the long nights it took for me to finish this book, but also for her help with the editing process.

I would like to thank my mother, Edith Anne Stafford; my sister, Shannon Moore; my brother-in-law, Richard Moore; my nephew, RJ Moore; and my niece, Shalena Moore, who have always encouraged me and stood by me from day one.

I would like to thank my Big Moma, Isalena Thompson, because I just love her. I would like to thank my eighth-grade teacher, Mrs. Collins, who saw something in me when no one else was even looking. I've always credited Mrs. Collins with being instrumental in helping me turn my life around.

I would like to thank my fill-in fathers Bobby Carter, and Terry Adams. Thank you guys, for your support during my high school years. And last, but not least, I would like to thank Tate Publishing Co. for giving me this opportunity to have my first book published.

Contents

Who's My Daddy?

A father of the fatherless, and a judge of the widows.

—Psalm 68:5

Who's my daddy? Wow, I can remember the very first time I heard my dad ask that question to my grandmother. The year was 1983, I was thirteen years old, and our entire family was at my grandmother's house for Thanksgiving dinner. There was me, my dad, my older brother, my younger sister, my favorite aunt, my three uncles, my grandfather, and my grandmother; and we were all sitting in the dining room watching a football game on television. Being allowed to sit in the dining room was major for us kids, simply because the dining room was totally off-limits to the grandkids! The dining room was sort of a sacred room. Guess you could say For Adults Only! So when the grandkids got an opportunity to dine in the dining room, it was a huge deal. Inside my grandmother's dining room, one would find a complete dining room furniture set covered in plastic, very thick plastic. I think the idea behind this was to keep the furniture looking new, and feeling new, for as long as she could. It worked. My grandmother still has the furniture, and it's still covered in plastic, thirty-five years later. One also may find in my grandmother's dining room some very nice and expensive china dishes—inside a very rare, and expensive, china cabinet, which was totally off limits to the grandkids to touch, or even go near, without the supervision of a parent. Last, but not least, the dining room had two sets of runners in it. One runner ran from the hallway to the dining room, and the other ran from the kitchen to the dining room; and when you entered or exited the sacred dining room, you must use one of the two runners.

Now that I'm older, when I think back on my childhood, I realize that the thing I liked most about being in my grandmother's dining room was the awesome pictures. She had the best pictures—not wall pictures, but pictures of my father. She had his childhood pictures, graduation pictures, and even his wedding pictures—none of which we had at our house. The only pictures of my dad we had at our house were of him as a grown man. We didn't have any of his baby pictures, toddler pictures, adolescent pictures, or even teenage pictures. So when the old folks used to tell me all the time that I looked just like my father, I could never see it. I mean, I didn't have a beard, a mustache, or an Afro; but, of course, they meant I looked like he did as a young man.

The old folks were right. Whenever I would go to my grandmother's house and look at my father's high school pictures, I was always amazed at how much I really did favor my dad. I loved to look at the pictures. This particular Thanksgiving I remember quite well. It was very cold and windy outside, but inside, the temperature was about to rise! We had just finished a delicious Thanksgiving feast of turkey, ham, potato salad, green beans, dressing, cornbread, corn, pecan pie, chocolate cake, and my grandmother's world-famous sweet potato pie. Well, it's really not world famous, but it really should be. It's the bomb! As I said, we were all sitting around watching television, letting that feast of a meal digest, when all of a sudden, my dad turned to his mother and asked the question, "Who's my Daddy?"

The room got very quiet—so much so you could hear a pin drop. At first my grandmother acted as though she didn't hear my dad; so he asked again, this time even louder, and with more authority. "Who's my daddy!"

My grandmother cut her eyes at him, as if to say, *Don't you get nothing started in here!* My dad asked a third time, and my grandmother replied, "Don't ask me that question. You know who your daddy is!"

"No! I don't know! Now tell me, who's my daddy? And you need to tell me right now!"

My grandmother looked him square in the eye and said, "You know who your daddy is. Now don't ask me no more!"

My dad said, "Fine. We're leaving!"

And we left! My daddy knew very well how to ruin a perfectly good Thanksgiving dinner.

· · · · · · · · · · · · · ·

The truth is, my dad never met his biological father. He had heard rumors of who he might be, but he never could get his mother to confirm, or deny, them. I believe the reason my dad wanted to know his father was because he was really trying to figure out who he was! The reason I believe this is that at this time, my dad was in his mid-thirties; it was not like he wanted to start a father-son relationship with the man. Instead, I believe my father was looking for answers to questions he may have had about himself. Questions such as, "Why am I a deacon in my church, respected in my community, and having extramarital affairs (that would lead to child born out of wedlock)?"

Is it possible that my dad was a man of God? Is it possible that my dad was respected in his community? And is it possible that my dad had an extramarital affair that would lead to a child born out of wedlock? Could this be?

· · · · · · · · · · · · · ·

There's an old saying that goes like this: "The apple doesn't fall far from the tree." There is a movie from the mid-eighties called *Teen*

Wolf, starring Michael J. Fox. I love it! It's about a young man who turns into a wolf when he gets frustrated or upset. There's a scene when Michael J. Fox's character is playing basketball at school and the weirdest thing happens to him. While dribbling the basketball down the court, his hands begin to transform into paws, his legs begin to grow animal-like hair—not only his legs but also his chest, his arms, his face, and every inch of his body begin to take on these animal-like features. The young man has turned from a sweet, innocent little boy into a wolf right before the spectators' eyes! Of course, this young man has no idea what's going on with him, so he freaks out and runs out of the gym, straight to his house, up the steps to his bedroom, slamming the door.

Minutes later, his dad knocks on the door, but the boy refuses to answer it because he's sitting in his room looking like a full-blown wolf, and he's sure his dad will not understand what's going on with him. His dad keeps knocking, so the boy finally comes to the door. His dad looks at him and says, "I guess I should have told you about this before." The dad proceeds to tell his son he knows what's going on with him.

The son says, "Dad, you cannot know what's going on with me right now. Look at me, I'm a werewolf!"

His dad looks at him and says, "Son, so am I."

Wow, the dad had the same problem as the son, and the son never knew it. All the son's hurt, shame, and embarrassment could have been avoided if only the dad had sat his son down and explained to him the issue he had, and the possibility of that issue being an issue for his son! Again, the apple doesn't fall far from the tree. For example, at a certain age, he could have sat down with his son and told him, "Look, it may or may not be a struggle for you, but if it is, don't freak out because Dad has had the same struggle for years, and this is how I deal with it, and this is how we're going to deal with it."

Wouldn't it be awesome if a dad could sit down with his son and have a serious father-son talk? A talk that would go something like this:

"Hey son, I know you're only eleven years old, but I think it's time we had our first real father-son talk. When I was your age, I was introduced to pornography for the first time. I stumbled across a *Playboy* magazine between the mattresses on my dad's side of the bed. I remember that even at such a young age, I would think to myself every time I would sneak into my parents' room to look at the magazines, *This cannot be good. Something has to be wrong with what I'm doing right about now.* By the time I became a teenager I was into XXX-rated movies, which resulted in premarital sex, which resulted in a child out of wedlock. Son, I'm telling you this because I don't want you to make the same mistakes I made. Truth is, if it was a struggle with me, it could possibly manifest itself in your life as a stronghold!"

The Bible talks about sexual sins, how they're passed down from generation to generation, becoming drastically worse from person to person. Let's look at the life of David and his son Solomon. The Bible tells us that David had seven wives and three concubines, but his son Solomon had seven hundred wives and three hundred concubines. Wow! Dads, can you imagine an issue that you're struggling with manifest itself a hundred times over and popping up in your son's life? Something that may have been controllable for you may manifest itself in your son's life as something uncontrollable!

So I say to all dads reading this book, "Deal with your issue *today*, because if you don't, your issue could deal with your sons tomorrow! I'm reminded of an interview I once saw of the notorious killer Jeffrey Dahmer and his father. In the interview, Jeffrey's father confessed that he often thought about killing people. Not only did his son go out and commit the act of murder, he went a step farther and ate his prey. Sometimes I wonder if the killing spree of Jeffrey Dahmer could have been avoided if only his father had had an open and honest relationship with his son. If he had been honest about his thoughts, fears, and his wicked desires, could this have possibly opened up an avenue for Jeffery to escape his own wicked desires?

. . . .

In 2004, I founded God's Posse Ministries. This is a ministry for young men between the ages twelve and eighteen. The sole purpose of this ministry is to literally take these young men (most of whom are without fathers in their homes) by the hand and walk them out of boyhood into manhood. In the ten years since we started the ministry, I've had the opportunity to counsel quite a few young men, most of whom came from a single-parent home. Some of the sessions I'll never forget, especially the one with this young man we'll call Ray. Now my friend Ray was considered at this time to be one of the biggest drug dealers in the state where he lived—and he was only sixteen years old!

I remember it as if it were yesterday. We had just finished a meeting one Saturday morning; and while everyone was getting ready to leave, I noticed this guy just kind of hanging around. Finally, he came up to me and said, "Sir, do you mind if I talk to you for a minute?"

I said not at all. "What's up?"

As we sat down and began to talk, the first question he asked me was, "Do you know who I am?"

I said, "No, I don't think so."

He said, "I'm the biggest drug dealer in the state. If you need some dope of any kind, in this state, I'm your man."

"Okay, that's all good, but I don't need no dope, so what's up?"

He said, "Don't get me wrong, I got it made. I got money, I got women, I got cars, and I got *power!*"

"Okay, why are you here?"

The young man then broke down and said, "Sir, I'm afraid for my life! I can't sleep at night. I'm constantly looking over my shoulders, and the things I thought would make me are the very things that are destroying me. Could you please pray for me?"

"Sure, I can do that. But before you leave, can I ask you a couple of questions?"

"Yes, sir."

It didn't take long for me to see how my new friend got into the shape he was in. I asked him what his earliest memory of his father was. His response, somehow, didn't surprise me at all: "I never knew my father growing up. I was introduced to my daddy when I was twelve years old. My mother said I was out of control, and she was sending me to live with my father. I was hanging out with the wrong crowd—smoking, drinking, doing drugs, and getting laid."

"At the age of twelve?"

"Shoot. Yeah," he replied. "So my mother said, 'Either you're going to jail, or you're going to live with your father.' Needless to say, I took the latter of the two and went to stay with my good old daddy. When I first arrived at my dad's apartment, which he shared with his girlfriend, he made it perfectly clear the reason I had been raised by my mother was he didn't want me then, and didn't want me now! I remember thinking to myself, *Wow, what a warm welcome!* He showed me to my room, and said, 'Now you stay the heck out of my way, or I'm going to beat the crap out of you, send your little bad butt to jail!' I guess you could say my first impression of my daddy was not a very good one. As a matter of fact, the two most painful rejections I've ever experienced in my life came from my dad. The first, of course, was when he abandoned me at birth and didn't want to have anything to do with me, and the second was on the day I finally met him.

"But to answer your question, the earliest memory I have of my daddy is of him selling dope out of his one-bedroom apartment. Every weekend, it was like our apartment was transformed into a dope house, and there was always lots of people coming and going. Friday nights were the worst. I remember coming home on

Fridays and having to literally go through a war zone just to get to my bedroom. There would be people everywhere—the living room, the bedroom, the dining room, and even the bathroom. As a matter of fact, the bathroom was the busiest room in the house. And to this day, I still don't understand why! Eventually, I would learn to just stay in my room the entire weekend, and after a while, I really began to feel like a stranger in my own home.

"As soon as I turned fourteen, I moved out of my father's house and begin an adult life that would turn out to be full of more rejections, more disappointments, and, of course, more crime. I'll never forget what my father told me the day I left his house. He said, 'Boy, you're a hustler, your granddaddy was a hustler, I'm a hustler, and you're a hustler. It's in your blood, so you might as well get used to it!'"

My new friend went on to say, "But I don't want to be a hustler anymore. It's not all that it's cracked up to be. And honestly, I want out of the game."

I said to him, "Ray, your father lied to you. You don't have to be a hustler just because it runs in your family. There's something called free will that each human being has. This simply means you have the right on this day, or any other day, to choose the direction you want to take the rest of your life." I asked my new friend, did he mind if I prayed for him?

He said, "Please do."

So I prayed for my friend, he left, and I never saw him again. I often think about Ray, and how the lifestyle that was passed down to him did not fit the person he was.

· · · · · · · · · · · · ·

About six years ago, I became the happiest man on earth. No, I did not win the $50 million jackpot—it was even better than that. About six years ago, my beautiful wife gave me something I'd been wanting all my adult life. A son! My son is the most wonderful thing that ever happened to me, and I love him more than anything in this entire world. The coolest thing about having a son is they think we are the ultimate superhero. They think there's nothing their dads cannot do. For that very reason, I cannot wait for the day when I can sit down with my son, who thinks his daddy is the bomb, and tell him, "Jonathan, Daddy's not a superhero."

Or "Hey, Jonathan, Daddy doesn't know everything."

Or how about this one: "Hey man, Daddy struggled with pornography too!"

As a father, I know you're probably thinking, *Why in the world would I want to open up to my son about who I really am when he's totally convinced of who I'm not.*

Here's the deal: It's okay to let your son believe that you're some type of superhero as long as it's Superman. See, the thing I like about Superman is this: Even though he picks up cars, knocks down buildings, flies through the air, and could whip any villain on earth, he understands that there's something more powerful than he is—*Kryptonite.* If he is exposed to it on any given day, it could destroy him!

Fathers, if we were honest with ourselves, we know there is a Kryptonite in our lives—something that, if we are exposed to it on any given day, could destroy us! What could be your Kryptonite, you ask? Well, if you struggle with drug abuse, then drugs could be your Kryptonite. If you struggle with alcoholism, then alcohol could be your Kryptonite. And if you struggle with pornography, the porn industry could be your Kryptonite. The fact is, there's something out there for every man that, if he's exposed to it at the right time, under the right circumstance, could totally destroy him!

I believe our sons need to know this, because the truth is, the more you allow your son to know about you, the more he will allow you to know about him. The more you open up to him, the more he'll open up to you. I believe it's just that simple. The reason we don't really know our sons is they don't really know us. Now don't get me wrong, I'm not saying you need to go into details concerning your struggle; but I'm saying this: he needs to know that you struggle with something, and that you're not perfect. For example, if your son is struggling with pornography, he doesn't have to know that you struggle with pornography, but if he knew you struggled with something, he would feel more comfortable coming to you for help and advice.

How about this scenario: What if a son struggled with pornography and so did his father, and they confessed their struggle to each other and vowed to help each other. What a powerful father-and-son ministry this could be—to go through a struggle such as that together and come out on the other side victorious. How close do you think this father-and-son relationship would be?

• • • • • • • • • • • • • •

Earlier in this chapter, I asked the question: is it possible my granddaddy was a man of God, respected in his community, and fathered a child out of wedlock? The answers to those three questions are yes, yes, and yes. My granddaddy was a man of God, (he was a pastor); he was respected in his community (a community leader), and he fathered a child (my dad) out of wedlock.

My father was born November 3, 1944, in a small town about thirty-two miles south of Atlanta. His parents met while my grandmother was away at school living with my granddaddy (who was a prominent pastor of a very large African American church) and his wife. Story has it, an affair took place, my grandmother got pregnant, gave her child to her mom to raise, and then left town. Not only was my father raised without a dad, he was also raised without a mom. I often wonder how my life would have been if the two people I loved the most had rejected, and abandoned me at birth. I'm sure I wouldn't be sitting here writing this book today. As I said before, my father was raised by his grandmother, the woman who, up until the day she died, he referred to as Mom. My father absolutely adored his grandmother, and for good reason—she was an amazing woman. There was absolutely nothing she could not do, except teach my father how to be a man!

Growing up, my father was Mr. Popular. His athletic abilities made him popular in sports, his good looks made him popular with the ladies, and his charm, well, that made him popular with everyone else. People just loved to be around him. At the age of sixteen, my father smoked his first cigarettes, a habit that he would have until the day he died; and by the age of eighteen, he had his first drink (this would be the habit that would eventually take his life). By the time he hit twenties, his life was slowly, but surely, spiraling out of control!

My father's first cry for initiation came in 1962, when he was eighteen years old. He woke one morning, got out of bed, got dressed, and marched down town to register for the armed forces, following in the footsteps of his uncle. My father may not have been the brightest person on earth, but he realized there wasn't a man around to initiate him from boyhood to manhood. There was no one around to say to him, "Look, this is what boys do, and this is what men do!" His uncle had the same problem, so he joined the army and decided to let Uncle Sam initiate him; so my father, knowing that if someone did not step into his life to teach him how to grow up and become a man, he would continue to self-destruct, followed in his uncle's footsteps.

His plan was to enroll in the United States Army for four years, and then possibly make a career out of it like his uncle was doing. However, upon arriving at the recruiting center, he was asked to take a physical, which revealed he had high blood pressure. In so many words, Uncle Sam told my dad, "Uncle Sam wants everybody, but you! I don't want you; neither can I use you. Rejection number 3. Remember rejection number 1 was his mother leaving him, and number 2 was his father abandoning him; so here we are again, with Uncle Sam saying to my father, "James, you're not good enough to be in our family either." Remember his mom left him with his grandmother and fled town to start a new life for herself. She was saying to him in not so many words, "Look, Jimmy, you're not good enough to go with me to start a new family, so I'll just leave you here with your grandmother." And his father may as well have told him in not so many words, "Look, dude, you're not good enough for me to take you home, so I must reject you also. After all, I have a family, and you're not worth me losing everything I've worked very hard for. Neither are you good enough to bring into the perfect family I already have, so I'm just going to act like you don't exist, like everyone else does." And now here was Uncle Sam, who takes everybody, and anybody, telling my father, "You're not even good enough to be in our family!"

I can only imagine the devastation my father must have felt. After this last rejection by Uncle Sam, he just gave up on trying to be a man. I guess he finally decided he would do the best he could with what he had, and that was what he did. However, it wasn't until my father's grandmother passed away that he really began to hit rock bottom. She was his heart, she was his life, she was his everything, and he never really recovered from her passing away.

After Uncle Sam rejected my father, he really began to focus on his first love—basketball. He loved basketball; he ate, slept, drank, and lived for basketball. Most of the old folks around town, even to this day, say my father was the best basketball player they had ever seen play. So it came as no surprise that when the local professional basketball team had an open tryout, my dad's name was at the top of the list. Things were looking pretty dog gone good for Pops. But, I guess as fate would have it, later that same year, before the tryouts, my dad found out he was about to be a father for the first time. He told my mom he did not want to be a part-time father, so he gave up his dream of becoming a professional basketball player to start a family. I'm not sure if that was fate, because I often wonder how differently my father's life would have been if he had been accepted in the army, or if he played in the NBA.

• • • • • • • • • • • • • •

Let's back up just a little. My mom and my dad were married June 7, 1963. The following year, on December 28, 1964, they would welcome their first child—a baby boy. Everything seemed perfect for my father: he had a good job, a beautiful wife, and an awesome little baby boy. However, it wouldn't take long for that womanizing spirit that was passed down from his biological father to fall heavily upon him. Shortly after the birth of their first child, my mother began to notice a sudden and drastic change in my father. By this time, my father was a heavy smoker and a weekend drinker, but the thing that bothered her the most was that my father had begun staying out all night long gambling and womanizing. He would leave the house on Friday nights, and sometimes she wouldn't see him again until Sunday afternoon. My mother always suspected he was doing something more than just gambling all weekend long. For someone to spend as much time gambling as my father did, he never quite figured out the art of the sport.

What I mean is this: my father would start gambling (playing cards) at about 9:30 p.m., and at about midnight, he would be $500 to the good. Now my father knew how to win money; he just didn't know how to leave with it! Even Kenny Rogers understood you've got to know when to hold 'em, know when to fold 'em, know when to walk away, and know when to run. Yeah, my father never quite figured that out! He would win, win, win; then he would lose, lose, lose. And before he left he would owe, owe, owe everybody.

Three years and seven months later, on July 18, 1968, my parents would welcome their second child—another baby boy—

into this world. The same year, my father's wandering eye would finally catch up with him. He would have an affair, which would lead to a baby out of wedlock, this time a baby girl. On June 18, 1969, my father would welcome his first baby girl into this world with his mistress; and unlike his father, he took full responsibility for his daughter. He supported her financially, and every chance he got, to spent time with her; he took advantage of it. My mom and my dad would have one more child together on March 9, 1971, exactly two years and seven months after the birth of their second son. They would welcome their first and only little girl into this world. After my younger sister was born, my father—already having a drinking problem, a gambling problem, and a womanizing problem—added yet another problem to his jacked-up résumé: spousal abuse. My dad began to physically and verbally abuse my mom regularly. Most of the abuse took place on the weekends after he'd been out partying and gambling, but there were times when he came home during the week after a bad day at work and took his frustrations out on my mom. I can honestly say that by this time, my dad was totally out of control.

In 1976, my dad did something that shocked everyone who knew him. He bought a brand-new house. Up until this point, our family had always lived with my grandparents. I remember my siblings and I were so happy to be getting out of my grandmother's house and into a house of our own. Don't get me wrong, we loved our grandparents—they were very good to us and treated us very well, but seven people in a two-bedroom house was a little cramped!

I remember our new house quite well. It was beautiful. It was like our mini mansion. It was a two-story home with three bedrooms, a basement, and a huge backyard with a tree house in it. The tree house, of course, was our favorite part of the house; we would literally spend hours upon hours out there playing. My dad was truly the man right about now; all his friends envied him. He had a beautiful wife, a beautiful family, a good-paying job, a nice car, and a brand-new house. But of course, as his luck would have it, it did not last long. About a year after we got the house, we lost it; so now we were back to where we started—living with my grandparents.

After my dad lost the house, he would soon lose his good-paying job as well. His drinking problem really escalated during this time. He would literally go to work drunk every day, until finally, his supervisor couldn't cover for him anymore and had to fire him. My dad was a good worker and went to work every day; but the influence of the liquor bottle in his life was more powerful than the almighty dollar itself. Everything would go downhill from there.

Since my dad didn't have a job, or a place to stay, things grew very tense around the house; and the beatings became more often and more violent. This abuse would go on for another two years or so, until my brother and I decided enough was enough. In 1978, we evicted our father from the house for good! It's funny, because I can remember the day quite vividly. It was one of the scariest days of my life, and also one of the happiest. It was a Saturday morning. My dad, my brother, and I had just returned from one of my football games. As we were pulling into the driveway, my dad began to lay into me about how terrible I played. I think I rushed for over a hundred yards and a couple of touchdowns. For me and my brother, that was a pretty good ball game; but for my dad, as always, it wasn't enough.

After my brother stopped the car, my dad reached over the car seat and grabbed me by my shirt, trying to pull me over the seat. My brother got out of the driver side, walked over to the passenger's side, opened the door, grabbed Dad, pulled him from the car, picked him up, and slammed him down and proceeded to whup my dad's—you get the picture, right there in the middle of the front yard. I had never ever seen my brother that upset before, or since. To be honest with you, I didn't think he had it in him! It takes a lot to get my brother to the point of explosion, but once he gets there, you better *watch out!*

After Dad got up from the ground, and got over the shock of what just happened, he started walking toward the house; and my brother and I knew exactly where he was going. He went into the house, grabbed his favorite toy (a 12-gauge pump shotgun), and came back out. Now you have to understand the history of this shotgun. Anytime Dad wanted to scare us or intimidate us, he would grab his shotgun and pump it twice. Dad stood on the front porch, with his shotgun loaded and pumped, and then suddenly my mom came out and screamed, "Jimmy, what's wrong with you? Is your life so miserable that you want to shoot your own son?" After a standoff that lasted a couple of minutes, Dad finally put the shotgun down and left the house. When he returned, all his things were in the front yard, waiting for him; and that was the last time my father would live under the same roof with the rest of us.

• • • • • • • • • • • • • •

From about 1978 to 1997, the year Dad passed away, he would continue to get jobs, lose jobs, drink, gamble, chase women, get women, abuse women, and lose women. He was homeless on more than one occasion, but this one particular time I will never forget. It was the winter of 1984. I was fifteen, and we had not seen Dad in about two or three weeks. During this time in his life, it was not uncommon for us not to see our dad for weeks at a time, because he was always moving from house to house, place to place, or even room to room. I remember one morning waking up earlier than normal for school to our guard dog, Bear, barking. He was having a fit, so I looked outside to see what all the fuss was about. I didn't see anything but since I was already up, I went ahead and started getting ready for school.

After I washed my face, brushed my teeth, and got dressed, I sat down to watch the news; and he started barking again. This time I got up and went to the kitchen door and looked out into the carport. I saw Bear sitting on top of the vacant car he normally slept inside. I thought to myself, *What's going on? Why is he on top of the car?* I opened the door and said, "Bear, what are you doing on top of the car?" As I approached the car, I looked in and saw my dad cramped in the backseat sleeping. I knocked on the window and woke him up. "Dad, what are you doing back there?"

He said, "For the last week, I've been living in the backseat of this car." He went on to explain how during the day he would go out and find him a hustle, and then at night, he would sneak back into the car. He looked at me and said, "Son, please don't tell nobody."

"Okay," I said.

"Look, while I got you here, can you do me a favor?"

"Sure."

"Can you go into the house and get me a toothbrush and some toothpaste so I can brush my teeth, and a warm rag to wash my face with?"

"Yeah." Even to this day, I get teary-eyed thinking about my dad cramped into the backseat of that car, brushing his teeth, and washing himself. I mean, really, how could something like this happen to a man like him? My dad was Mr. Popular. He was good-looking, he was charming, he had a beautiful wife, a good job, and a house on the hill. There was nothing he wanted that he couldn't have, so how in the world did a man with everything lose it all and end up sharing an abandoned 1972 Chevrolet Vega with a ninety-five-pound Chow by the name of Bear? I'll tell you how: because of all the wrong decisions he made in his life, especially the one he made as a young man, to start drinking alcohol. I truly believe alcohol destroyed my father's life.

Life is full of decisions—from the time we wake up until the time we go to bed, we are constantly making decisions. As a matter of fact, when it's all said and done and we look back over our lives, we're going to see that most of the bad things that happened in our lives came on the heels of a bad decision, and most of the goods things that happened in our lives came on the heels of a good decision. My dad made a lot of bad decisions, no one will argue that; but the life that he led and the decisions he made were not one hundred percent his fault. In the book *Is There a Man in the House*, Dr. Charles Stanley wrote,

> "The Bible teaches that as fathers we are responsible for helping our families avoid the experiences that will lead them astray or to fall into sin, causing them pain and loss. Even though there will be suffering in every family, fathers still have the responsibility of setting moral boundaries for their families."

This makes a lot of sense to me, because it seems my father lived a life without boundaries. He did what he wanted to do, when he wanted to do it, because there was no one there to set them for him. You will hear me say this on more than one occasion throughout this book: "It is the father's responsibility to set boundaries for his son." So without Dad in the house to set the boundaries, oftentimes the boundaries are never set. As result of this, we see a lot of our young men running the streets, out of control and doing things we never thought we would see our kids doing. Now, don't get me wrong, I know some very strong mothers who are able to raise amazing young men (one of whom is the mother of our current president, Barack Obama). I once saw an interview with the president, and he said something like, "It was my father's absence that shaped me rather than his presence."

I remember thinking to myself, *Wow, what a powerful statement that was!* However, I'm not talking in this book about the exceptions to the rule. I'm talking about norm. In the book of John 5:19, Jesus puts it like this: "Truly truly, I say to you, the son can do nothing of Himself, unless it is something He sees the Father doing; for whatever the father does, these things the Son also does in like manner."

Do I believe my father's life would have turned out differently had he had a father in it? Absolutely! Would he have made mistakes? Sure. Would he have made the mistakes he made? Probably not. Proverbs 22:6 reads, "Train up a child the way he should go; and when he is old, he will not depart from it."

This is one of my favorite scriptures in the entire Bible; however, I believe it should read something like this: "Fathers," train your son in the way they should go; and when he is old, he will not depart from it. I believe it's the father's job to train, teach, and instruct his sons in the way in which they should go. I also believe it's the father's job to shape and mold them into the men they would have them to be! For years I considered my dad as the biggest failure at being a father I'd ever met, until I got saved and the Lord spoke to me and said, "Your father did the best he could with what he had to work with. My father had no one in his life to lead, guide, and instruct him on how to be a man; so how in the world was he supposed to lead, guide, and instruct me on how to be one?

My mother-in-law once told me about a corn maze she and my father-in-law went to while on vacation one year. She said the instructor would blindfold you and then take you in the middle of the cornfield, remove the blindfold, give you a set of instructions, and leave you out there. It was up to you to find your way back on your own.

She said, "For hours it seemed like we we're going in circles, seeing the same corn over and over and over again."

Eventually, though, they would find their way out. After she shared this story with me, I thought about the young men in our society being raised by single moms and how we pretty much do the same thing with them. Although, it's a little different. We let our boys sit around the house blindfolded until they turn eighteen years old, and then we open the door and say, " Al right, you're a man now. Go out and be one!" I can see our young men, as they leave the house, looking back with their hands thrown up in the air, saying, "Okay, but how in the world do I do that!"

In most cases, I believe we as Americans blindfold our young men for eighteen years, open the front door on their eighteenth birthday, take the blindfold off, and shove them out into the world with the instruction, "Now go out and be a man." When they respond, "I don't know how," we respond with, "You're a man, you'll figure it out." Then after seeing the same corn over and over and over again, and making the same mistakes over and over and over again, and going down the same wrong road over and over and over again, and after making all the same wrong choices over and over and over again, eventually they will figure this being-a-man thing out; but in the meantime, look at all the hell and heartache they had to go through to do so! My father passed away on March 9 1997. He was fifty-three years old.

The Wonder Years

Train up a child in the way he should go; and when he is old, he will not depart from it.

—(Proverbs 22:6)

As I have said before, this is one of my favorite scriptures in the entire Bible; but now that I'm saved and have sons of my own, I do believe the scripture should read something like this: Men train up your children in the way they should go, and when they are old, they will not depart from it. In my own opinion, it's the father's responsibility, as well as his duty, to train his children in the way in which they should go. Statistics have shown that 75 percent of all families where the fathers are born again Christians have children who are strong Christians. Compared to 23 percent when the mother is the born again Christian. Fathers, this just goes to reinforce what I said early about how powerful the life we live before our children is, and how influential we are as fathers in their lives. According to Dr. James Dobson, in his book *Bringing Up Boys*, "Most American children receive no spiritual training whatsoever. They are left to make it up as they go along, which leads to meaningless existence."

Making it up as they go along, or should I say just trying to figure it out, as they go through life. This is what I see happening to over 70 percent of all black babies, and 19 percent of all white babies that are born to single parents in the United States. Most will never know their father, or experience what it means to be loved by them. Making it up as they go along, and trying to figure it out on their own, is what this chapter is all about. The word *train*, according to Webster, means to undergo, discipline, and instruction, drill, etc. So if the word *train* means to discipline and instruct, and it's the father's job to train, then would it be safe to say it's the father's job to discipline, and instruct his children in the way they should go? Absolutely. That's why it's so very important for dads not only to be there for their sons but also to understand their roles in their lives. This is why the absence of the father in the house is so devastating to the children, especially to the males, because there is no one in the house to discipline and instruct them—no one to teach them, lead them, and guide them out of boyhood into manhood.

Moms, please don't get me wrong. I know situations have caused some of you to have to try and wear both hats as the mom and the dad, and you've done a great job; but the truth of the matter is, God has not called you to father your son! It takes a man to initiate another man! I realize in this day and time that women can be anything they want to be. We have female doctors, dentist, lawyers, astronauts, politicians, judges, wardens, boxers, golfers, pastors, lieutenants, presidents and CEOs of large companies, and the list goes on and on. As I said before, the list seems to be endless as to all the things women are able to be in this day and time; however, there's one thing a woman will never be able to be—a father.

A woman is not mentally, physically, or spiritually equipped to be a father. One of the craziest things I've ever heard come out of a woman's mouth was when a friend of mine once told me, "I am my son's mama and his daddy."

I looked at her and said, "Not only is that not spiritually possible, but it's not even physically possible!" I had known this friend for years. We actually grew up together. Her story is a sad one, but I would like to share it with you, if you don't mind.

• • • • • • • • • • • • • •

She was one of the most popular girls in the county growing up. She had it all—the looks, the charm, the personality, the brains; and could get any guy she wanted. So it was no surprise when this handsome Romeo swept her off her feet at a ripe old age of eighteen; and two years later, she would be married. A year and a half after she was married, she would give birth to her first and only child—a baby boy. Soon after the birth of their child, their marriage began to crumble; and the following year, they would get a divorce. My friend was never the type who would settle for a kid out of wedlock, and now she had one. She went from living the American dream, married to the perfect husband, having a nice house, good job, beautiful baby boy to living the life of a single mom. She learned to move on with her life somewhat, but she never could get over the devastating hurt and embarrassment caused by the divorce, which led her not to trust men and to stay away from serious relationships. This resulted in her having multiple partners throughout her young son's life.

In the beginning, everything was fine. From about the age of one to eight, everything was perfect. His mama taught him how to cut the grass, build doghouses, fix things around the house, and even change oil and work on the car—all the things that a man would normally do; and of course, he was in church every time the doors opened! However, all that would change by the time he hit ten years old.

My friend said the first change she noticed in him was his passion for God. She said before he turned ten, he was so involved in the church. He was on the youth usher board, he sang in the choir, and he even led devotion from time to time. But after he turned ten years old, it seemed as though he had lost all interest in church. Not only did he not want to participate in anything anymore, he didn't even want to go anymore. It was during this time that he would constantly ask me about his father, whom he'd only met once. He often wanted to go see him, and spend time with him, and I often had to tell him that was not possible, because his father didn't want to have anything to do with him.

"The truth of the matter is, it wasn't his father's fault that he couldn't see him. It was mine. After the divorce, things got so bad between us I forbade him to see his son anymore, and he didn't! By the time he was twelve, he was totally out of church, and running with the wrong crowd. He began to stay out later and later, until before we knew it, he was staying out all night long without so much as a call to let us know if he was still alive. By the time he was thirteen, he started coming home with gang-affiliated tattoos all over his body, I asked him on more than one occasion, 'Son, are you in a gang?' And he would always say, 'No, Mom. I just thought the tats looked cool.' Finally, on his fifteenth birthday, he confessed to being in a gang. He told me he had been in it since he was twelve, and he couldn't get out now even if he wanted to. Of course, he really did not want to, because his gang family treated him with acceptance, love, and respect—three things he so desperately needed from a male influence.

"By the time my son turned seventeen, he had a baby out of wedlock. And later that year, he would get shot in the buttocks. I hardly ever saw him anymore, and when I did, he was high. The next year of my son's life would be spent in the streets, and in and out of jail, until the inevitable happened. Two days before his eighteenth birthday, he was gunned down in the parking lot of a gas station by a local gang rival. And just like that, my baby was gone! And just like that, I would never be the same. A huge part of me died that day. My son was my life, and I had built my life around him. He was, simply put, my everything! The following day, I would have to do the hardest thing I would ever do in my life—go down to the morgue and identify my one and only child."

• • • • • • • • • • • • • •

I shared my friend's story with you to show how devastating the absence of a father in a boy's life can be. It takes a woman and a man to make a child. This is true, regardless of what you may have heard, or what you think you may be seeing. It's not physically possible for two women to produce what's needed to make a child; neither is it physically possible for two men to produce what's needed to make a child. It takes a woman and a man to make a child, period! Now, since this is true, why would we not think it would take a woman and a man to raise a child! There are certain things that a mom brings to a boy's life that a dad can't bring, and certain things a dad brings to a boy's life that a mom can't bring; and one is just as important as the other to produce and raise a well-balanced child. As far as I'm concerned mothers and fathers, respectively, are responsible for the following ten functions:

Mothers

1. Love unconditionally (painless).
2. Set no boundaries for her son.
3. Be BBFs (best friends forever) with the boy.
4. Build her life around the boy.
5. Spare the rod spoil the boy.
6. Submit to the boy.
7. Worship the boy.
8. Comfort the boy.
9. Let the boy be irresponsible.
10. Get the boy in the church.

Fathers

1. Love unconditionally (painful).

2. Set boundaries for his son.

3. Be a father to the boy.

4. Build the boy's life around the parents.

5. Exercise the rod and spare the boy.

6. Teach the boy to submit.

7. Teach the boy to worship.

8. Counsel the boy.

9. Teach the boy to be responsible.

10. Get the church in the boy.

There you have it, ten functions of a mother and a father in a boy's life.

. . . .

For the rest of this chapter, I would like to talk about the wonder years. What are the wonder years, you ask? The wonder years are the years for young males between the ages of twelve and eighteen, when they stumble from day to day wondering, *How in the world do I figure out this thing called life!* If the father is absent during this very crucial period of their lives, they're going to spend a lot of time in a daze, and totally confused. It is during this time that the young boy is as clay in the potter's hand. What I mean by that is that they are very formable during these years. The ages of twelve to fourteen are the three most important years of a boy's life. I believe from the age of eight to eleven, a young man is being formed (whether it's by parents, friends, mentors, or by life itself) into the man he shall become. From the age of twelve to fourteen, the young man is being shaped into the man he shall become; and from the age of fifteen to eighteen, the young man is being molded into the man he shall become. For this very reason, when single moms ask me when they should get their sons a male mentor, I always say the sooner, the better.

Please don't wait until he's a teenager and have already made up his mind about who he is and what he wants to do with his life, because to be honest with you, by that time, it's too late.

My friend with the troubled teen I mentioned earlier in the chapter called me when her son was about fifteen years old and said, "Craig, I think my son is in a gang, and I was wondering if you could take him under your wing and mentor him?"

I told her I would talk to him. "But honestly, I don't know how much good it would do since you already suspect he's in a gang. The truth of the matter is, unless the Lord grabs hold of his heart and saves him, there is nothing I can tell him that's going to change him."

We'll talk more about this in the chapter "The Initiation."

• • • • • • • • • • • • • •

The Three Big Ps: Peer Pressure

Also during these wonder years, there is something called the three big Ps your son is going to have to deal with. The first of the three big Ps is Peer Pressure. We all know what peer pressure is, but here's my definition: it's when their peers' opinion of them means more than anyone else's. They would rather please their peers more than please Mom, Dad, or even God. Being in the *in* group is the most important thing to them during these years. We've all, at one time or another, let our peers and what they thought of us determine decisions we've made.

I'm reminded of a time in the eighth grade when I let peer pressure get the best of me. Now, growing up, we were very poor, and early on, I was not the most popular guy with the ladies. As a matter of fact, before the eighth grade, I don't think I'd ever had a girl show me any attention at all! However, that would change once I hit the eighth grade. Maybe it was because I was one of the stars on the eighth-grade basketball team, and we happened to do pretty well that year (13–0). County champs. It seemed as though I gained popularity overnight. Anyway, there was this sixth grader who liked me, and I liked her, so we started talking. That's what we called it back then. Since I didn't have a license to actually take her out, we were just talking.

My best friend at the time was a six-foot-one freshman in high school, and when I introduced him to my new girlfriend, he seemed to like her a lot! Later that week, I asked him, "What do you think about my new girlfriend?"

He said, "To be honest with you, man, she's too young, and too short for you. You guys look really funny together."

Now keep in mind I'm about five feet seven, he's six feet one, and she was about four feet eleven. I thought about what my best friend said and thought to myself, *Man I don't want to be looking funny with my lady.* So the very next day, I broke up with my girlfriend, whom I liked a whole lot! As a matter of fact, when I broke up with her, she said, "What happened? I thought we really liked each other?"

I lied and said, "I never really liked you, and besides that, I think you're too short for me."

Wow, there it was—following the advice of my best friend who thought my new girlfriend was too short and too young for me. I had broken it off with my first and only true love; and to be honest with you, I was really sad. However, things would get a lot worse the following week when I saw none other than my best friend walking down the hall with my ex-girlfriend—hand and hand, all smiles. Now remember, I was too tall and too old for her according to him, but there he was—a year older and five inches taller than I was, and he had stolen my lady. I had been got by a smooth operator.

Needless to say, I never listened to him again, because with friends like that, you don't need enemies! That was a minor example of how peer pressure caused me to make a decision I would later regret. Unfortunately, in this day and time, the decision the peers are causing our kids to make are more severe than mine—even causing them, in some cases, to lose their lives! Now we know all about the old school peer pressure—peers pressuring peers to drink, do drugs, and have sex; but in the twenty-first century, we have more dangerous pressure that's on the rise: peers pressuring peers to kill themselves. This is known as bullying.

Eric Mohat, seventeen, was harassed so mercilessly in high school that when one bully said in class, "Why don't you go home and shoot yourself, no one will miss you," he did. Now his parents, William and Janis Mohat of Mentor, Ohio, have filed a lawsuit in federal court saying their son endured name calling, teasing, constant pushing, and shoving and hitting in front of school officials who should have protected him. The lawsuit—filed March 27, 2009—alleges that the quiet but likable boy, who was involved in theater and music, was called "gay", "fag", "queer" and "homo" and often in front of teachers. The Mohats also claimed that bullying was a "significant factor" in the deaths of three other students in Eric Mohat's class in 2007. Just days before his suicide, Eric Mohat told his mother, "I get picked on every day, and I've got a whole nine weeks left. I can't do this anymore."

The National Youth Violence Prevention Resource Center estimates that nearly 30 percent of American youth are either a bully or a target of bullying. Bullying, in my opinion, is just an escalated form of peer pressure. I call it peer pressure to the tenth power, the most extreme form. If you think about it, all that the bullies are doing is trying to impress their peers.

• • • • • • • • • • • • • •

It is during this time in boys' lives when they are literally attacked from every side by everything. They're being pressured with drugs, alcohol, sex, and even gangs. Statistics have shown that kids as young as eleven years old are being jumped into gangs all over America each year. You know what that tells me? If the devil is recruiting our young men at the age of eleven for destruction, we need to be recruiting them by the age of nine for the Kingdom of

God. We must always stay at least one step ahead of the enemy. It is much easier to lead a young man to Christ at the age of nine than to try to recover one from the clutches of the devil at the age of fourteen.

So how do you deal with bullying? This is a really good question, and honestly, I believe there's one of two ways to deal with this kind of behavior. We can allow the bully to control us with their words and actions, ruining our days, months, years, and eventually our lives; or we could flip the script on the bully, such as I did in the sixth grade.

As I said before, when I was growing up, we were very poor. Oftentimes, I had to wear clothes that did not fit properly. For example, I had this one pair of jeans that were hand-me-downs from a friend who was about four to five inches too short. However, it was my favorite pair of jeans. I wore these jeans every Friday, and every Friday I got picked on by this eighth grader we'll call Egghead. Every Friday, at lunchtime, I had to walk directly in front of this guy to get to my table, and every Friday he would look at his buddies, laugh, and say, "Here comes the nigger with the high water pants."

At first, I acted as though I didn't hear him; but every week, as he grew in strength from his buddies, he seemed to get louder and louder, until it finally began to take its toll on me. I'd never been in a position like this before, having someone call me a nigger to my face; and because of fear, I felt there was absolutely nothing I could do about it. So I simply stopped going to lunch. Sometime later, while talking to my grandmother, my best friend at the time, I told her about my situation, and she said, "Hun, the only way to fight that kind of battle is with love. You should never let someone like that steal your joy."

Now I loved my grandmother to death, but I was not, in any way, feeling what she was saying about loving this guy. As a matter of fact, I despised this guy, I hated this guy, and I actually wanted to kill this guy. Love him? No way! However, I did take one thing my grandmother said to heart: I was not going to let this loser steal my joy! That night, I decided that the next day I was going to smile as big as I could, walk right into that lunchroom, and have lunch like nothing ever happened.

When my bully saw me walk into the lunchroom that morning, he was somewhat shocked. He had not seen me in a while, and to see me back in the lunchroom smiling, full of joy, blew his little simple mind. Soon as I walked by, he started right up again as if nothing had changed, and in his mind, nothing had. But in my mind, I was a new, stronger, and more determined person. He looked at his buddies, started laughing, and said, "Here comes the nigger with the high water pants."

I just stuck my chest out, lifted my head up, smiled, and kept right on walking. I didn't even look at him. This would go on for another month or so, until finally he realized two things. First of all, since it was no longer affecting me, his friends no longer thought it was funny. After all, it was through them that he got his power. Second, since his friends didn't think it was funny anymore, and since it had no power over me anymore, he begin to look very foolish; and before long, the joke was on him. He would eventually stop altogether, and I would have peace in the lunchroom.

I saw this guy at a gas station about five years after I graduated. I was pulling up in my car, and he was walking into the store. I thought, *I'm not a kid anymore. I should go in there and knock this joker's teeth right out of his mouth. All that time he made my life a living hell. It's my turn now.* I walked into the store, and of course, he was over in the beer section, grabbing a 99¢ quart of beer. I walked right up to him, and he turned around and looked at me. He knew who I was, and of course, I knew who he was—and the teeth I was going to knock out of his mouth were already gone.

I thought, *Wow, life had already whupped this guy way worse than I ever could have.* I turned around and walked out of the store. As I got back into my car and watched him climb onto his bicycle and ride off, two emotions came over me. The first was joy. I was so happy I didn't let this guy cause me to drop out of school and ruin my life. The second was sorrow. This guy had no teeth, no car, and no money—and really no life. How could I not feel sorry for him? My advice for anyone reading this book who maybe going through a time of being bullied would be this, keep your head up, keep a smile on your face, and keep moving forward, never let them see you sweat, never let them steal your joy, and never let them steal your dreams!

· · · · · · · · · · · · · ·

The Three Big Ps: Puberty

The second of the three big Ps is Puberty. Puberty is "the period of life during which the genital organs mature, secondary sex characteristics develop, and the individual becomes capable of sexual reproduction." There are certain signs that are consistent with a young man going through puberty, such as good old pimples. They begin to pop up all over his face. Then there's the change in the voice. It usually gets deeper. They also begin to grow hair—underarm, facial, and pubic. But the most powerful thing I believe happens to a young man when he begins to go through puberty is becoming sexually aroused. This sexual arousal is due to the fact that the body is now capable of sexual reproduction, which means that physically, this boy is now a man.

Sexual arousal can be a scary experience for a young man who does not understand what his body is doing. That's why it's very important for dads to step up to the plate and explain this whole process of manhood to their son. And if Dad's not around, the youngster will have to figure it out on his own, such as I had to! I remember the first time I got an erection caused by sexual arousal. I was in the sixth grade. It was caused by my sixth-grade science teacher, who we will call Mrs. P. I had always thought Mrs. P. was the cutest little lady I'd ever seen in my life, and to be honest with you, I had a huge crush on her; but that was all it was—a huge crush and nothing else. Until about halfway through the school year.

I remember the day as if it was yesterday. It was just like any other day. I was running late to class, so I snuck in the door; went straight to my desk, which was on the second to the last row; and sat down. I begin to go through my book bag looking for my homework; then all of a sudden, I looked up, and Mrs. P. was writing something on the blackboard. Now I'd seen her with her back toward me plenty of times before throughout the year, but this time, something was different. I remember she had on her favorite pair of blue slacks (which was also my favorite), and they were fitting quite well, as they always did. I remember staring at her buttocks as she wrote on the blackboard and feeling my temperature rise and thinking, *Is it getting hot in here, or is it just me?* I was burning up and could not sit still for nothing. I was twisting, shaking, rocking back and forth in my desk; then all of a sudden, it happened. I begin to get an erection, and it freaked me out! I remember thinking, *What is really going on up in here?* It seemed to me at the time that the erection lasted for days. I remember science class coming to an end, and I was thinking, *How in the world am I going to get to my next class without everyone seeing this freak of nature taking place in my body?*

Somehow, I made it through the day and got home without my secret being exposed. I remember later that night wanting so badly to mention it to my older brother, since my dad wasn't around; but honestly, I truly did not think my brother would have understood. I always looked at my brother as the good seed, and I was the bad one. I always thought my brother got everything good and positive from my dad, and I got everything bad and negative. So when this happened to me, I just knew it had something to do with the bad seed; and my perfect brother— well, he just wouldn't understand.

The erections would continue for quite some time until one night, I accidentally discovered my body, and the erection went away. Oh, how I wish I had someone there to explain to me that what I was going through was perfectly normal—and not only normal but necessary for me to make the transition from boyhood to manhood. To all the moms, dads, and grandmothers reading this book, please sit down with your sons before they go through puberty and explain the process to them so they won't have the same embarrassing moment I had as a child. Let them know that not only is puberty normal, it's necessary in order for them to become the men that God has called them to be.

God blessed them, saying, "Be fruitful and multiply and fill the waters in the seas, and let birds multiply on the earth" (Genesis 26–28). It is a direct command from God himself to every man to be fruitful and multiply, and the only way we're going to be able to do this is for us to go through puberty; so I say to all my young male readers, don't be ashamed of this time in your life. Instead, embrace it, because without it, you will never become a man! How are we as males supposed to deal with puberty? First of all, as I said before, we must understand that puberty is not only normal, it is very necessary in order for us to become the men God has called us to be. Second, don't be afraid to talk to another male about it. Chances are, if they are of age, they've been through the big P, and they can help you through yours!

• • • • • • • • • • • • • •

The Three Big Ps: Pornography

The last of the three big Ps is Pornography. The word itself comes to us from the Greek word *porneia*, which means "writings, photographs, movies, etc., intended to arouse sexual excitement, especially such material considered as having little or no artistic merit." Most men have never seen, or have any idea, what the word *pornography* means. To most of us, it consists of either one of two things—dirty magazines or dirty movies, period. When I say dirty, I mean XXX-rated magazines, with naked people performing sexual acts with one another, or the XXX-rated movies with naked people performing sexual acts with one another—neither of which you buy over the counter at your local grocery store. Now we know *Playboy*, *Penthouse*, and *Hustler* are considered to be porn magazines; but by the definition of the word *pornography*, could magazines such as *Maxim*, *Sports Illustrated* (swimsuit edition), *Allure*, and even *GQ*, also be considered porn magazines? Just a little something for you to think about. And if they could, then I can see how the porn industry has become one of the most powerful and most profitable industries in the world. I know you're probably thinking that the women on the cover of the magazines I just mentioned are only scantily clad, not completely naked, which means it's not full-blown pornography.

This is what I say to you: A tumor does not start out the size of a football. No, it starts out as something small and innocent, and it grows to something massive and destructive! We'll talk more about pornography later, but for now, I would like to talk specifically to the moms, dads, and grandmothers raising little boys. Here are five things you can look for to help determine if your boy may be addicted to porn.

1. Does he lock the door when he goes to his room?
2. Does he spend a lot of time on his computer late at night unsupervised?
3. Does he have any porn magazines that you are aware of?
4. Does he seem distant from you and others at times?
5. Does he very seldom talk about girls?

From the age of twelve to fourteen, the young male has to deal with the three big Ps—peer pressure, puberty, and pornography. However, from the age of fifteen to eighteen, they'll have to deal with another big three—the big three W's, the Who, the What, and the Where. That's it, guys. As you make the crucial transition from boyhood to manhood you're going to have to know at one point or another, Who am I? What am I doing here? And where am I going? I believe this is one of the major problems we're having with our young men in our society today. They have no idea who they are, why they're here, and where they're going in life. As a result, we're going to spend the rest of this chapter talking about the who, the what, and the where.

· · · · · · · · · · · · · · ·

Who Am I? (Identity)

That's a tough question for most men, because we're often identified by what we do rather than by who we are. For example, if you asked a pastor, "Who are you?," they may reply with, "My name is Pastor Such and Such." But is that who they are, or is that simply a title they hold? Same thing with a doctor. "My name is Dr. Such and Such." Again, he's associating what he does with who he is.

I believe in order for us to understand who we are, we must first understand *whose* we are. The Bible clearly states we are all God's creations. Genesis 2–7 reads, "And the Lord God formed man of the dust of the ground, and breathed into his nostrils the breath of life and man became a living soul." God created you, and has given you an identity in him. Not only that, but the Bible tells us in Psalm 139:14), "I will give thanks to You, for I am fearfully and wonderfully made; Wonderful are your works, And my soul knows it very well."

Fearfully, wonderfully, and uniquely made. This explains why out of literally billions of people here on earth, no two people have the same fingerprint, footprint, or DNA. Only God could create a being with such uniqueness! So to truly understand who you are, you must first understand who God is, since it's him who gives you your true identity.

Who is God? The Bible tells us in Genesis 2:1–3,

> God is our Creator, thus the heavens and the earth were completed, and all their host. By the seventh day, God completed His work which He had done, and He rested on the seventh day from all His work which he had done. Then God blessed the seventh day and sanctified it, because in it He rested from all His work which God had created and made.

The Bible also tells us in Matthew 14:16–20) that God is our Provider. But Jesus said to them,

> "They do not need to go away; you give them something to eat!" They said to Him, "We have here only five loaves and two fish." And He said, "Bring them to Me." Ordering the people to sit down on the grass, He took the five loaves and two fish, and looking towards heaven, He blessed the food, and breaking the loaves He gave to them to the disciples, and the disciples gave them to the crowd, and they ate and were satisfied. They picked up what was left over of the broken pieces, twelve full baskets.

In the book of Mark 5:25–34, God is described as our Healer.

> A woman who had a hemorrhage for twelve years, and had endured much at the hands of many physicians, and had spent all that she had and was not helped at all, but rather had grown worse-after hearing about Jesus, she came up in the crowd behind Him and touched His cloak. For she thought "If I just touch His garments, I will get well." Immediately Jesus perceiving in Himself that the power proceeding had gone forth, turned around to see the woman who had done this. But the woman fearing and trembling, aware of what had happened to her, came and fell down before Him and told Him the whole truth. And he said to her, "Daughter your faith has made you well; go in peace and be healed of your afflictions."

God is also our deliverer, as is indicated in Mark 5:1–13.

> They came to the other side of the sea, into the country of the Gerasenes. When He got out of the boat, immediately a man from the tombs with an unclean spirit met Him, and he had his dwelling among the tombs. And no one was able to bind him anymore even with a chain; because he had often been bound with shackles and chains, and the chains had been torn apart by him and the shackles broken in pieces, and no one was strong enough to subdue him. Constantly, night and day, he was screaming among the tombs and in the mountains, and gashing himself with stones. Seeing Jesus from a distance, he ran up and bowed before Him; and shouting with a loud voice he said, "What business do we have with each other, Jesus, Son of the Most High God? I implore you by God, do not torment me!" For he had been saying to him, "Come out of the man, you unclean spirit!" And He was asking him, "What is your name?" And he said to Him, "My name is Legion; for we are many." And he began to implore Him earnestly not to send them out of the country. Now there was a large herd of swine feeding nearby on the mountain. The demons implored Him saying, "Send us into the swine that we may enter them." Jesus gave them permission. And coming out, the unclean spirit entered the swine; and the herd rushed down the steep bank into the sea, about two thousands of them; and they were drowned in the sea.

Last but not least, God is described in the book of Revelations 1–8) as the Alpha and the Omega, the beginning and the end. "I am the Alpha and the Omega," says the Lord God, "who is and who was and who is to come, the Almighty." To put it plain and simple, Jesus is the beginning of your identity, meaning your identity begins with him; and he's the ending of your identity, meaning your identity ends with him.

I remember, in the early eighties, there was an episode of *The Cosby Show* where the character Theo was trying to find himself. He turned to his friends, his environment, and even his family; but not once did he turn to God, the creator of his very existence. It's like buying a new BMW, and the first time you have a problem with it, you take it to a Honda dealership. Now the guy at the Honda dealership may be able to fix it, but if he's honest with you, he's going to say, "Sir, you really need to take this automobile back to the people that made it, because to be honest with you, they know way more about this vehicle than I do. After all, they created it, and they know it better than anyone else."

So when the time comes in your life when the question of "Who am I?" begins to burn in your spirit, and believe me it will, I suggest you go to your creator himself and ask him, "God, who am I really?" God will answer that question for you because it's his will that you know your true identity in him. After all, if you know the truth about who you are, then you won't believe the lie about who you're not!

• • • • • • • • • • • • • •

What Am I Doing Here? (Purpose)

Every time I think of this question, one word automatically pops into my mind. *Purpose!* Purpose is "the reason for which something exists or is done, made, etc." One day, if you live long enough, you will ask yourself this question: "Why in the world am I here on God's green earth?" I've got a saying that goes something like this: "Life doesn't begin until purpose kicks in." I truly believe that until you begin to live a life of purpose, you are simply existing here on earth. Jesus said in John 10:10, "The thief comes only to steal, kill, and destroy; I came that they might have life, and have it more abundantly." I truly believe the abundantly lived life in which Jesus speaks of will only be experienced by us once we know our purpose, understand our purpose, and begin living out our purpose here on earth.

Asked the question once of a group of young men between the ages of twelve and eighteen, What is your purpose here on earth?"

Out of about a hundred in attendance that day, 85 percent of them said their purpose had something to do with sports, 10 percent said it had something to do with music, 2 percent said their purpose had something to do with entertainment, and 3 percent had no idea what their purpose was. I found it interesting that such a large percentage would say their purpose had something to do with sports, so I begin to dig a little deeper.

I walked up to this one guy. He was about six feet four, and about two hundred and eighty pounds, a defensive end on his high school football team, college bound, and, I'm sure, would one day play in the NFL. I said, "Hey man, you were one of the ones who said your purpose in life has something to do with sports. Why do you think that?"

He said, "First of all, I eat, drink, sleep, and live for football. Besides, look at me, I'm six foot four, two hundred and eighty pounds. I've already committed to the U, and I'm positive I'll play in the NFL one day!"

I said to the young man, "I definitely hear your passion for the game of football, but just because football is your passion in life does not necessarily make it your purpose in life. I get this all the time—people confusing their passion in life for their purpose in life. Again, the word *purpose* means "the reason for which something exists, or is done, made, etc." And the word *passion* means "compelling emotion." As you can see, these are two totally different things: one has to do with the reason you exist, and the other has to do with feelings and emotions. Now can God use something that you're passionate about as part of your purpose in life? Absolutely!

Former Atlanta Falcon running back Warrick Dunn has a foundation called Homes for the Holidays, which he started in honor of his late mother, who was brutally slain while on duty as a police officer. As a result of this tragedy, he developed a passion for helping single moms obtain housing. His foundation Home for the Holidays was established in 1997, and since then, it has rewarded single parents and children who have reached the American Dream of first-time homeownership in Atlanta, Georgia, Baton Rouge, Louisiana, and Tampa and Tallahassee, Florida.

In 1998, Homes for the Holidays began to enhance home ownership in Dunn's hometown of Baton Rouge, Louisiana. Although the Homes for the Holidays program has existed since 1997, the Warrick Dunn Foundation wasn't established until 2002, as a way to grow programs for single-parent families. Homes for the Holidays not only provides uplifting support for these communities, it is also a way for Dunn to share his mother's dream with single parents who have reached the goal of home ownership. The Home for the Holidays program positively impacts the lives of single-parent families by rewarding hard work and recognizing individuals who are actively improving their lives by achieving first-time home ownership.

The desired outcome of Homes for the Holidays is to give single parents an opportunity to establish a positive home environment where their children can thrive educationally, socially, and economically. I'm sure Mr. Dunn uses his money and influence from his passion (football) to help fund his foundation. The reason I believe this is a prime example of God using someone's passion in life as part of their purpose in life is I truly believe what Mr. Dunn is doing glorifies the Lord. Helping single moms house not only themselves but also their kids has to bring God glory. And it's not only Mr. Dunn. Tiger Woods once said something to the effect that golf is a job that happens to pay well enough for him to embark on his real purpose in life—the Tiger Woods Foundation, which he founded with his father, Earl Woods, in 1996.

The Tiger Woods Foundation was established to create and support community-based programs that improve the health, education, and welfare of all children in America. Currently, the foundation has established several programs and events such as the Tiger Woods Learning Center, Start Something (which was renamed Tiger's Action Plan on April 1, 2008), Tiger's Block Party, Chevron World Challenge, AT&T National, and Tiger Jam—all of which benefit millions of children. Again, do I believe God has taken Mr. Wood's passion for golf and used it as part of his purpose in life? In the book of (Matthew 19:13,) Jesus says, "Let the children alone, and do not hinder them from coming to me; for the kingdom of heaven belong to such these."

In my opinion, anything positive done for children in our society today will bring God glory, and if it brings God glory it could very well be your purpose here on earth! If you ever want to know if your passion in life is indeed your purpose in life, ask yourself this one simply question: "Does what I'm passionate about bring God glory?" For example, if you are a singer, ask yourself, "Do the lyrics I write and the songs I sing bring glory to God?" If you're an athlete, you might want to ask yourself, "Does the way I carry myself on and off the field or the basketball court glorify God?" If you're confused about what it means to bring glory to God, it simply means this: Is what you're doing pleasing to God? Would God be happy with it? If the answer is yes, then that may very well be your purpose in life. After all, it's God who gives us purpose, so wouldn't it only make sense for our purpose to give him glory? If the answer is no, then it's only a passion.

• • • • • • • • • • • • •

Growing up, I always felt there were angels watching over and protecting me. Even though I didn't grow up as a believer I always felt God's presence and favor in my life. Like the time when I was about nine or ten and I stole a brownie from the local drugstore. The store manager looked right at me as I picked up the brownie and put it in my pocket, but for some reason, he didn't call the police. God spared me, and I had no idea why.

Or the time when I was twelve years old and my best friend and I broke into the city hall and jumped on the tractors and drove them around until the alarm went off. We jumped off the tractor, leaped over the fence, and darted back to my house, knowing all the time that they had a pretty good idea it was my friend and I who committed the crime. God spared me, and I had no idea why.

Or the time when I was nineteen and working at a department store in my neighborhood while in college trying to make a little extra money. At this particular department store, we would work overnight once a month, unsupervised. At first, there was no temptation for me at all to do anything illegal. Like I said, I was in college trying to make something out of my life. I wasn't about to do anything stupid. Or so I thought.

After about two months of watching my friends walk through the store on the nights we worked overnight and load up their carts full of whatever they wanted and simply rolling the carts out to their cars and loading them up, I began to think, *Wow, that's like stealing from a baby.* Then one of my friends came up to me and said, "Man, what are you waiting on? I know there's something in here you need."

And before I knew it, I had a cart and was walking around the store loading up anything and everything. I remember stealing Halloween costumes for my niece and my nephew, Thanksgiving gifts. I was even doing my entire Christmas shopping right there in that department store. So as you can see, this went on for quite some time until one day, I was on my way to work, and as I approached the parking lot of the department store, I noticed it was full of police cars and detectives. Even though I didn't know exactly what was going on, my first thought was to turn around and go back home. Then I thought, *No I can't do that, because if I don't report to work today, I'm going to look suspicious.*

So I walked into the department store, and as soon as I walked in, a detective came up to me and said, "Are you Jonathan Stafford?"

I said, "Yes, sir."

He said, "Good. I need to talk to you for a minute."

I said, "Sure." I was so nervous I thought I was literally going to wet my pants. I'd never had a police officer need to talk to me about anything. As we made our way back to the office, I thought, *I'm going to jail today.* Just then, I saw my friend being escorted in handcuffs to a police car, and my heart stopped, for what felt like days!

Once I got inside the office, the detective said, "You know why you're here, don't you?"

Of course I said, no.

"He said. "You and your friends have been under surveillance for about four months. I've got a confession from them, both of whom are on their way to jail, that you were in on the crime of theft by taking with them."

I said, "Well, I wasn't."

He said, "Not only do I have a confession, but we also have a videotape of you in the act of the crime. Would you like to see it? If I have to show you this video and you don't confess on your own, then you're going to be on your way to jail with your buddies."

To this day, I still don't believe they had a video of me stealing from that department store, but I was young, so I took the bluff and broke down and told them everything I had stolen—well, almost everything. The detective would ask me if that was all, and I would say, "I think so." Then I would remember something else and tell him about it.

Then finally, he asked, "Is that all?"

"Yes, sir."

"Are you sure?"

"Yes, sir."

"There better not be anything else that you're not telling me about."

I said, "That's all, sir."

He said, "Because your employer says you're a really good worker with a great attitude, I'm going to give you a break. Here's what I'm going to do: If you can go home and bring everything you stole back to the store, I'll let you go, and it will be up to the department whether they're going to press charges or not. I had to go to relatives' houses, my girlfriend's house, and anybody else who got a Christmas present from me that year; and the hardest part, of course, was explaining to them why I had to retrieve their gifts. After I brought back everything I could recover, they told me to go home and sit tight; and within the next week, I would know whether I was going to be facing charges. That was the longest and most stressful week of my entire life. I think I lost about twenty pounds during that time! A week, a month, and then a year would go by, and I would never hear back from them. Again, God had spared me, and I had no idea why.

Finally, there was the time when I was twenty-five years old and I got caught up in a very bad situation. It was a cold and windy December night, and my best friend and I had just gotten back from a double date. His girlfriend had set me up with one of her friends for a night on the town. We got back to her apartment got situated and settled in for the night. At about two o'clock, I got up, left the apartment to go to my car to get some more beer. I made it to the car okay, but on the way back, I made a wrong turn and ended up at the wrong apartment. I knocked on the door of the apartment I thought was my friend's girlfriends' with a loud bang. Someone from inside said, "Who is it?"

"Open the door, fool!" I said, thinking it was my boy.

All of a sudden, the door swings open; and needless to say, it wasn't my boy at all. I had walked into the middle of a drug deal! When the door swung open, I could see dope and semiautomatic weapons on the table, and this huge guy looked at me and said, "Nigga, you five-0?"

I said, "No! I'm sorry. I got the wrong apartment." I took off running and didn't look back, but I could hear them saying "Five-0, five-0, five-0" as they pursued me. Terror gripped me, and I ran down the stairs as fast as I could, found my car, opened the door, jumped in the backseat, got as low as I could on the floor, and prayed for dear life. I could hear them outside looking for me, saying, "Man, he was five-0. We better get out of here before the rest of them come!" I had never before or since been that close to death, and I never want to again!

However, God saw fit to spare me once again, and again, I didn't know why. Truth is, from day one, God has always had a plan and a purpose for my life. That's why he continued to spare it time after time after time again. The same is true with you. It's no coincidence why you haven't caught a life-threatening STD, or gone to jail for fifteen years to life, or, even worse, dead. No, it's no coincidence. It's God saying, "I'll let you go so far, for so long, but I'll always have you in my sight, my hand, and in my plan."

• • • • • • • • • • • • • •

September 20, 2004, is a day I will never forget because it's the day God revealed to me my purpose here on earth; and my life, as I knew it, has never been the same since. I remember it quite vividly. Our congregation was getting ready to start an eight-week study based on a best-selling book called *The Purpose-Driven Life* by Pastor Rick Warren. This book is designed to help you fulfill your God-given purpose. Rick Warren is the founding pastor of Saddleback Church in Lake Forrest, California, one of America's largest. In this best-selling book, Rick Warren shows you how to obtain purpose in a unique way. Often, self-help books suggest that you can discover purpose in life by looking inside yourself. Not so in *The Purpose-Driven Life*.

Warren's thesis is that you must begin with God, who created you for a purpose. It is only when you understand that you were made by God and for God that you can unlock your purpose here on earth. The book itself is one of the best-selling books of all time; so that alone should tell you how important it must be for a lot of people to know their purpose here on earth. As I said before, we were getting ready to start our journey into a life of purpose the preceding day, but our charge for that night was to go home and, in our prayer time, ask God, "What is my purpose here on earth? Why am I here?" So I did. That day I went home, and that night I asked God, with a sincere heart, "What is my purpose here on earth? I mean, Why did you save me, Lord?"

Now you've got to understand, at this point in my life, I'd been saved for about a decade and had no idea what it was God wanted from me. At one time, I thought my calling in life was to become a pastor, just like everyone else who receives a calling from the Lord, and this would be almost confirmed by God when he led me from my first church to my second one. Now my first church was more of a salvation church. It was great at getting you saved. Most of the messages were aimed toward persuading you to receive Jesus Christ as your Lord and Savior, which was fine with me at first because I was totally lost. But after I got saved and had begun to grow in God's Word, my spirit began to desire more.

It was also around this time that I felt God calling me into the ministry on a more full-time basis, so I began to pray. It didn't take long for him to lead me to my second church, which happened to be a church planting ministry. From my understanding of this ministry, all they did was plant a new church somewhere in the United States every three to five years and take a pastor from within to pastor that particular church. So as you can see, I totally thought I was headed in the right direction, and certainly in the right place, at the right time to do what God had called me to do.

However, that would not be the case. I stayed at this church for five years and watched two churches be planted, and was not chosen to pastor either one, so I begin to pray again. Now, to be totally honest with you, I really was not feeling the whole pasturing a church thing. I knew God had called me into the ministry, but I wasn't quite sure where or what. So that night, when I prayed, I asked the Lord to speak to me in a very unusual way concerning my purpose. I asked the Lord to show me my purpose in a dream. This was unusual for me because the whole time I'd been saved, God had never spoken to me in a dream. I'd heard of people talking about visions and dreams, but I had never had one from God. And for some reason, I thought if he showed me in a vision or in a dream, I would believe it, and it would be plainer to me.

Be careful what you ask God for, because I asked him to do something, and he did just that. That night, sometime before I awoke, God showed me exactly what he wanted me to do with the rest of my life. He told me in a dream that he wanted me to start a ministry for young men, for the sole purpose of leading these young men off the streets and into the kingdom of heaven. It was so detailed that the following day, he even told me exactly how to set up the recruiting, as well as the order in which he wanted the meetings to be carried out. I was ecstatic. Now this felt right to me because I'd always loved talking to young men about young men issues. This was right up my alley!

Later that day, I began to pray to the Lord. *I need an awesome name for this awesome ministry that you have given to me.* At about two forty-five on September 20, 2004, the Lord gave me a name for my new ministry: God's Posse Ministries. There it was—my purpose in life was to oversee God's Posse Ministries.

The ministry has been great—great feedback from single moms, great attendance from the young men themselves, and a great 3-on-3 basketball tournament in which the Lord has blessed us to host for the past ten years. Each year, God's Posse

Ministries host an annual "Calling all ballers 3-on-3 basketball tournament," which, to date, has seen almost one hundred and fifty teams come through, and somewhere in the area of ninety-plus new converts for Christ. I am so very proud of these stats, especially the ninety-plus new converts because 95 percent of those lost ballers had never set foot in a church, and probably never would. However, they would travel halfway across the country to play basketball. Each year, when I get the opportunity to minister to these young men and impart wisdom into their lives, I receive such an amazing rush. I'm 100 percent positive this is what I was created to do! This is why God kept me, this is why he saved me, this is what he ordained me for, and this is why I'm alive! What an awesome feeling to know my purpose here on earth. I once heard someone say, "The worst thing you can do is to live your entire life here on earth and never tap into your purpose."

• • • • • • • • • • • • • •

Now that we know our purpose, the next step in this process is to understand our purpose in life. This consists of three parts. First, we must understand that we were created for a purpose; second, we must understand we were created with purpose; and lastly, we must understand we were created on purpose. We as human beings must understand that God had a divine purpose for our lives on this earth long before we were ever even thought of. Our purpose has awaited our arrival since the beginning of time. Let's take a look at Genesis 1:26–28. Then God said,

> Let Us make man in Our image, according to Our likeness;
> and let them rule over the fish of the sea and over the birds
> of the sky and over the cattle and over all the earth, and
> every creeping thing that creeps on the earth." God created
> man in His own image, in the image of God he created
> him; male and female he created them. God blessed them;
> and God said to them, "Be fruitful and multiply, and fill

the earth, and subdue it; and rule over the fish of the sea and over the birds in the sky and over every living thing that moves on the earth.

Now it seems to me that in the book of Genesis 1:25, God was creating a purpose for the man he had not yet created. In verse 1:6 God created day and night, in verse 6:10 God created the heavens and the earth, in verse 11:13, God created vegetation, in verse 14:19 God created seasons and the stars, in verse 20:25 God created the birds of the air, the great sea monster, and every living creature that move, and the act of reproduction; and finally, after all this, God said, "Let us create a man to subdue, rule over, and take care of, all of this that I've created."

The purpose came long before the person. The same is still true today. I think about great men such as Dr. Martin Luther King Jr., and how his purpose awaited his arrival here on earth. For years, I'm sure the Southern Christian Leadership Conference (SCLC) had been looking for someone who could step into a leadership role and engineer a movement that would change the course of our world forever, but not just anybody would do. I believe God created Dr. King for such a purpose even before the beginning of time, and that's why he fit the job perfectly. It wasn't anything he went to school for, nor was it anything he was trained for, and neither was it anything he particularly wanted to do. It just dropped itself right in his lap. That's the funny thing about purpose: you don't have to go looking for it. It will find you, and when it does, it will wake you up early in the morning, motivate you throughout the entire day, and keep you up late at night!

Second, we must understand that we were created with purpose (see Genesis 2:18–24).

Then the Lord God said, "It is not good for the man to be alone; I will make him a helper suitable for him."

Let's skip down to verse 21:

So the Lord caused a deep sleep to fall upon the man, and he slept; then he took one of his ribs and closed up the flesh at that place. The Lord God fashioned into a woman the rib which He had taken from the man, and brought her to the man. The man said, "This is now bone of my bone, And flesh of my flesh; She shall be called Woman, Because she was taken out of Man." For this reason man shall leave his father and his mother, and be joined to his wife; and they shall become one flesh.

The Bible clearly states that Eve, Adam's wife, was created with a specific purpose: to be a suitable helper for her husband. I also believe that each one of us was created by God with a specific purpose in mind, which is to serve him with all our heart, mind, body, and soul.

Lastly, we must understand we were created on purpose. The word *on* means "attached to, in contact with," so to say that we were created on purpose is the same as saying that we were created with a purpose attached to us, or as a part of us. For this very reason, I am against abortion, because not only are you aborting a child, but you're also aborting a God-given purpose. For every young man reading this book whose parents were not married when you were conceived, or maybe they weren't even dating and you are the product of a one-night stand, and your mom has told you on more than one occasion you were an accident and nobody wants you, nobody loves you, and that she wishes you were never born, I've got good news for you: God wants you, he loves you, and he has this awesome purpose for your life. Believe that!

This also explains why no one on this planet can do what God has called you to do! Your purpose is your purpose, and no one else can fulfill your purpose on this earth except you. Why? Because God has created you, saved you, ordained you, anointed you, and kept you for this very reason. Now I'm not saying if God called you to preach and you run from your calling he won't find someone else to preach, because he will; but I am also saying

61

this: no one will ever preach a message exactly the way God has anointed you to preach it. Have you ever noticed that out of the literally hundreds of different denominations, and the literally thousands, maybe even hundreds of thousands of different preachers, pastors, bishops, reverends, rabbis, apostles, prophets, doctors, etc., there are no two whose anointing, deliverance, and preaching style are exactly the same?

I've never been at home watching a preacher on television, thinking, *He preaches just like such and such.* As a matter of fact, I've seen the same message preached by two different pastors, and each time I heard it, I got a different message from it. The bottom line is this: your purpose is one with you, and you are one with it; and until you realize this and embrace it, you're never going to achieve the greatness God has planned for you here on earth.

• • • • • • • • • • • • • •

Now that we know our purpose, and understand our purpose, there is only one thing left to do: live it out! For most young men, this is the most difficult part of the process, because they feel that if they totally commit to their purpose, they're going to have to give up this wonderful thing called *life.* We think to ourselves, *Man, if I take heed to the calling of God in my life, I won't be able to party anymore, hang out with my criminal-minded friends, or have sex with my underage girlfriend. Man, I am only seventeen, and I can't see myself not being cool anymore. Besides that, if I did commit to this God thing, I can see it now: all my friends would totally clown around with me and call me all kinds of names and pick on me? I cannot take that right now, God, I'll just wait till I'm older. Then I'll give my life to you.*

I have a good friend who told God just that when he was in high school. My friend was a big-time football player, with hopes of playing on the pros one day. But when he was seventeen years old, God called him into the ministry, and my friend "ran from his calling for almost a decade." Here was his problem; he knew he was about to go to a division one school; he knew he was going to be the star of the football team; and as a result of that, he knew he was going to be Mr. Popular and would probably get whatever and whomever he wanted, so he said, *Lord, I'm not even going to kid with you. I'll take a rain check.* My friend went on to a D1 school, excelled on and off the field, and even led his team to a national title his senior year; and during that time, he partied, he drank, and he played as hard as he could; and everything was cool. Or so he thought. He went on to graduate, and after graduation, he begin to get serious about his calling. At the age of twenty-six, he gave his life to the Lord and said, "Lord, use me as you see fit."

God immediately began to use him, preaching all over the state; and life was good for my friend, until one day God showed him something that would change his life forever. He said that one night, while he was praying, he asked God to show him souls that were lost so that he could get busy trying to save them; and God did just that. The only thing was, every soul God showed him was someone from his past—more specifically, from the age of seventeen to twenty-six, the time when he was, as he said, running from his calling. God showed him why he called him into the ministry at such an early age—because there were people in his high school and college who needed to be saved; and my friend, because he wasn't ready to do what God had called him to do at the time, had totally missed out on what God was trying to do in his life. Now can God restore you and still use you? Of course. But if you don't understand why God is calling you into the ministry at such a young age, it may be because your peers need you now!

Don't be afraid. Accept the calling because what God has for you is a hundred times greater than anything you think you'll have to give up to receive it, I promise you.

. . . .

Where Am I Going? (Destiny)

Now that you know who you are (identity), and you know what you're doing here (purpose), there is only one thing left to discover: where are you going (destiny)? Do you have any idea where your life will take you, or where will you end up in this world? The word destiny means the predetermined, inevitable, or irresistible course of events. The truth is, when God looks at our life, he looks at it from the end to the beginning, instead of from the beginning to the end. God does this because he knows something we don't—our destiny. And he knew it even before the beginning of time.

Have you ever taken a trip and used a GPS system to get from one place to another? I remember the first time my family and I took a vacation to Myrtle Beach, South Carolina. We didn't exactly know where we were going, so we relied on the handy dandy GPS system. We used the GPS system to get us from Georgia to Myrtle Beach, word for word, turn for turn, until we reached our destination. Once we finally arrived at our condo, I looked at my wife, she looked at me, and we both begin to explain to one another how we could have taken this road and gotten off on that road and got here much quicker. Or how we could have continued straight down such and such and gotten off at such, and could have avoided all that excess traffic we had to go through. My point is this: even though the handy-dandy GPS system gave us one way to reach our destination, as we found out upon arrival, there was at least one other way we could have reached the same destination without going through all the stress caused by the excess traffic, and, we could have gotten there a lot quicker. So it is with life. I believe there is more than one way for us to reach our God-given destiny here on earth. As a matter of fact, I believe there's at least two ways we can arrive at that place.

The first would be our way, and the second, of course, would be God's way.

One of the best examples in the Bible of a man reaching his God's-given destiny his way comes to us in the book of Jonah, starting in chapter 1:

> The word of the Lord came to Jonah, son of Amittai: "Go to the city of Nineveh and preach against it, because its wickedness has come up before me."
>
> But Jonah ran away from the Lord and headed to Tarshish. He went down to Joppa, where he found a ship bound for that port. After paying the fare, he went aboard and sailed for Tarshish to flee from the Lord. Here's what's happening here: The Lord told Jonah, "I want you to go to a city that is evil, dangerous, and as sinful as a city can be, and preach about me." Now Jonah thought, If I do what the Lord is asking me to do, I would more than likely be killed instantly." So he ran from the word of the Lord. Instead of going to Nineveh as the Lord told him, he went in the opposite direction to Tarshish.
>
> Then the Lord sent a great wind on the sea, and such a violent storm arose that the ship threatened to break up. All the sailors were afraid and each cried out to his own god. And they threw the cargo into the sea to lighten the ship.
>
> Then the sailors said to each other, "Come, let us cast lots to find out who's responsible for this calamity." They cast lots, and all the lots fell on Jonah.
>
> The sea was getting rougher and rougher. So they asked him, "What should we do to you to make the sea calm for us?"
>
> "Pick me up and throw me into the sea," he replied, "and it will be calm. I know that it is my fault that this great storm has come upon you."

Eventually, they would throw Jonah overboard, but the lord provided a big fish to swallow him up and from the belly of the fish Jonah prayed this prayer:

> In my distress I called to the Lord, and he answered me. From the depth of the grave I called for help, and you listened to my cry.
>
> You hurled me into the deep, into the very heart of the seas, and the currents swirled about me; all your waves and breakers swept over me
>
> I said, "I have been banished from your sight; yet I will look again towards your holy temple."
>
> The engulfing waters threatened me, the deep surrounded me; seaweed was wrapped around my head.
>
> To the roots of the mountains I sank down; the earth beneath barred me in forever. But you brought my life up from the pits, O Lord my God.
>
> When my life was ebbing away, I remembered you Lord, and my prayer rose to you, to your holy temple.
>
> Those who cling to worthless idols forfeit the grace that could be theirs.
>
> But I, with a song of thanksgiving, will sacrifice to you. What I have vowed I will make good. Salvation comes from the Lord."
>
> And the Lord commanded the fish, and it vomited Jonah onto dry land.
>
> (Jonah 2:2–10)

We continue with Jonah 3:1–4.

> Then the word of the Lord came to Jonah a second time. "Go to the great city of Nineveh and proclaim to it the message I give you." Jonah obeyed the word of the Lord and went to Nineveh. Now Nineveh was a very important city-a visit required three days. On the first day, Jonah started into the city.

This is one of my favorite stories in the entire Bible. The Lord speaks to Jonah and tells him exactly what he wants him to do, and Jonah says no. The Lord sends a big fish to detain Jonah while he thinks about what the Lord has told him to do. Finally, Jonah gives in and decides to do what the Lord has told him to do. He makes the three-day journey to Nineveh in one day flat and preaches the exact same message that the Lord commanded him to preach from the start, and the word did exactly what the Lord had planned for it to do: it saved the city of Nineveh. Even though Jonah took the long and hard road to his destiny, he still ended up exactly where God predestined him to be from the beginning of time—in Nineveh!

My boy Jonah is a prime example of a man reaching his God-given destiny his way. Now, I would like to look at a man who reached his God-given destiny God's way: his name was Saul, a name that was later changed to *Paul.*

> As he neared Damascus on his journey, suddenly a light from heaven flashed around him. He fell on the ground and heard a voice say to him, "Saul, Saul, why do you persecute me?" "Who are you, Lord?" Saul asked. "I am Jesus, whom you are persecuting," he replied. "Now get up and go into the city, and you will be told what you must do."

• • • • • • • • • • • • •

> In Damascus there was a disciple named Ananias. The Lord called to him in a vision, "Ananias!" Jesus goes on to tell Ananias I want you to go to Judas house there you find a man named Saul.

• • • • • • • • • • • • •

> Then Ananias went to the house and entered it. Placing his hands on Saul, he said, "Brother Saul, the Lord-Jesus

who appeared to you on the road as you were coming here-has sent me so that you may see again and be filled with the Holy Spirit." Immediately, something like scales fell from Saul's eyes, and he could see again. He got up and was baptized, and after taking some food, he regained his strength. Saul spent several days with the disciples in Damascus. At once he begin to preach in the synagogues that Jesus is the Son of God.

(Acts 9:3–5, 9:10, 9:17–19)

• • • • • • • • • • • • • •

Now the story of Saul and Jonah are somewhat different. Jonah heard the Lord tell him exactly what his destiny was, and he ran from it. On the other hand, Saul heard the Lord speak to him concerning his destiny, and without hesitation, he received it and began to fulfill it. This is my $64,000 question for you: How will you respond when your destiny finds you? Will you be like Jonah, (and most Christians I know), and try to run from it, or will you be like Saul and embrace it? Will you be like Jonah and say, "Lord, I would like to do what you've called me to do, but honestly, I'm afraid. I'm afraid I'm going to lose my girlfriend, my friends, my social status, and, of course, my reputation. Honestly, Lord, I'm afraid I'm going to lose everything I have and worked so hard to gain if I follow you!"

Or will you be like Saul and say, "Lord, I'll leave everything and everybody to follow you, because I got a feeling everything I'll have to give up will not come close in comparison to everything I shall gain from you!"

The choice is yours, but if I can help, I'd tell you to travel God's way. It's a lot easier, and the rewards are much greater!

So whether you're twelve through fourteen and you're facing the three big Ps (peer pressure, puberty, and pornography), or you're fourteen through eighteen and you're facing the three big W (who, what, and where), without a father, or a strong positive male influence in your life, these years can be a very difficult time for you. I hope this chapter has shed some light on issues you may be facing, and provide possible solutions for problems that may have come your way.

The Initiation

I will instruct thee, and teach thee, in the way which thou shalt go.

—Psalm 32:8

I was once asked the question, "What in the world is going on with our young men today?" I pondered that question for years, until one day it came to me: It's not our young men who have a problem, it's their fathers—or should I say their lack of a father? The fact that our young men in America are falling victim to such vices as drug abuse, alcoholism, gangs, and pornography at such an alarming rate is partly their fault, but largely their fathers', or as I said before, the lack of.

The scripture above (Psalm 32:8) reads, "I will instruct thee, and teach thee, the way which thou shalt go." Who is I? Who is responsible for instructing and teaching our young men how to be honest, respectable, responsible, hardworking, and God-fearing, men? I tell you who I is. I is the father. However, the problem with that is that somewhere in the area of 70 to 75 percent of all babies born in American are born to single moms, with dear old dad nowhere to be found. I do believe it is the father's responsibility to initiate their son into manhood. Not only that, but I believe they're the only ones who could take on such a task and be successful at it. I've said it once, and I'll probably say it a thousand times over: it takes a man to initiate another man. Author John Eldredge puts it like this in his book *Wild at Heart*: "Femininity can never bestow masculinity."

The word *initiate*, or *initiation*—exactly what does it mean? The definitions of the *word* are 1) a formal admission or acceptance into an organization or group, and 2) the ceremonies or rites of admission. The definition of *initiation* brings up another interesting word: *rite*. The definition of *rite* is "a ceremony to facilitate or mark a person's change of status on a significant occasion, such as the onset of puberty or upon entry into a select group." A rite of passage is a designed way to initiate our sons into manhood. There are several groups of people who have mastered this art of initiation and we're going to take a look at two such groups in this chapter. The Africans, and the Jews.

• • • • • • • • • • • • •

Becoming a man in Africa consists of five major initiation rites, which are fundamental to human growth and development. The first is the rite of birth, the second is the rite of adulthood, the third is the rite of marriage, the fourth is the rite of eldership, and the fifth is the rite of ancestorship. And then there is the ever so popular Jewish rite of passage bar mitzvah. The term bar mitzvah means "son of the commandment" and bat mitzvah can be translated as daughter of the commandment.

• • • • • • • • • • • • •

Now that we've looked at how, African, and Jewish boys are initiated into manhood, let's look at how most American boys make that crucial transition from childhood to manhood. According to Dr. James Dobson, this process of initiation for boys does not happen in America. In his best-selling book *Bringing up Boys* he says,

In the two decades from the time our sons are born until they are about twenty or so as fathers we are to transform them from immature and flighty youngsters into honest, caring men who will be respectful of women, loyal and faithful in marriage, keepers of commitments, strong and decisive leaders, good workers, and secure in their masculinity. And of course, the ultimate goal for people of faith is to give each child an understanding of scripture and a lifelong passion for Christ.

As we can see, the father's presence in his son's life is very important, and he plays such a crucial role in the boy's development into manhood. The only problem is when Dad is absent, there's no one around to literally take this young man by the hand and guide him out of childhood into manhood. This is what we're seeing way too much of in our society today—absent fathers, lost sons. Certain things will come naturally for a young man once he hits a certain age such as becoming a man, but most things will definitely have to be taught. John Eldredge states,

> The deepest search in life, it seems to me, the thing that is one way or another was central to all living was man's search to find a father, not merely the father of his flesh, not merely the father of his youth, but the image of a strength and wisdom external to his need and superior to his hunger, to which the belief and power of his own life could be united. "Where does a man go to learn an answer like that- to learn his true name that can never be taken away from him? That deep heart knowledge comes only through a process of initiation.

He goes on to say,

> Most men have never been initiated into manhood. They have never had anyone to show them how to do it, and especially how to fight for their hearts. The failure of so many fathers, the emasculating culture and the passive church have left men without direction.

Look at it like this: I'm not great with computers. As a matter of fact, I'm not good with them at all, so if you sat me down in front of one and asked me to program it, I'd pretty much be right where you left me twenty-four hours later, scratching my head. Why? Because I've never had any type of computer programming training. On the other hand, I have a cousin who can program any computer any way you ask him. Why? Because he's been trained to do so. We as males are doing a terrible job at training our sons to be men. Why? Because most of us ourselves have had absolutely no training at all in that department. What we normally do in our society is let our sons lie around the house being irresponsible, disrespectful, and lazy, from the time they are born until the time they reach eighteen, which is when we tell them, "Now go out and be a man!" I can see them as they leave the house looking back, saying, "Okay, but how in the world do I do that?" So they're pretty much left to figure out this thing called manhood on their own.

Now our women have this initiation thing down pat. When it's time for a young woman to make the crucial transition from girlhood to womanhood, our women's process of initiation is awesome! I remember when my younger sister hit puberty, my mom made an entire day out of the initiation process. She took her out to lunch at her favorite restaurant, then to see a movie of her choice, then after that, she sat her down and explained to her exactly what was going on with her body. She explained the whole menstrual cycle process to her, and told her not only was she going through a beautiful change, but that it was very necessary in order for her to become a woman. When was the last time we as men took our sons at the onset of puberty out for a day of enjoyment, and then at the end of the day, sat them down and explained to them the entire puberty process? When was the last time we told our sons not only is it a good thing for them to go through puberty but that it was very necessary in order for them to become the man that God had called them to be?

As a matter of fact, we cannot fulfill one of the most important commandments that God has given us as men, which is to be fruitful and multiply, without going through puberty. Most young men love to hear this because they think, *Now that I'm physically a man, I'm able to go out and be fruitful and multiply, or better yet, able to go out and have sex!* How many of you guys realize there is so much more to being a man than just having the ability to reproduce? Biblically, before God released Adam to go out and be fruitful and multiply, or to have sex, he gave him three things: He gave him a purpose, responsibility, and a wife.

First God gave Adam a purpose:

> And the Lord God formed man of the dust of the ground, and breathed into his nostrils the breath of life; and man became a living soul. And the Lord God planted a garden eastward in Eden; and there he put man whom he had formed.

. . . .

> And the Lord God took man, and put him into the garden of Eden to dress it and keep it.
>
> (Genesis 2:7–8, 2:15)

Second, God gave Adam a responsibility:

> And the Lord God commanded the man, saying, of every tree of the Garden thou mayest eat freely: But of the tree of knowledge and good and evil. Thou shalt not eat of it: for in the day that thou eatest thereof thou shalt surely die.
>
> (Genesis 2:16–17)

Third, God gave Adam a wife:

> And the Lord caused a deep sleep to fall upon Adam, and he slept: and he took one of his ribs, and closed up the flesh instead thereof; And the rib, which the Lord God had taken from the man, made he woman, and brought her

unto the man. And Adam said, " This is now bone of my bones, and flesh of my flesh: she shall be called Woman, because she was taken out of Man. Therefore shall a man leave his father and his mother, and shall cleave unto his wife; and they shall be one flesh.

(Genesis 2:21–24)

Look, before God released Adam into manhood, he gave him a purpose (a reason for being), a responsibility (a job), and a wife. Then, and only then, did the he release him to be fruitful and multiply, or to have sex.

And Adam knew Eve his wife; and she conceived, and bare Cain, and said I have gotten a man from the lord And she again bare his brother Abel. And Abel was a keeper of the sheep, but Cain was a tiller of the ground.

(Genesis 4:1–2)

In our culture today, we as men have it backward. We have sex, conceive, have a baby, look for a job, think about getting married, and, lastly, some ten, fifteen, and even twenty years after we get married, we ask ourselves the question, "What in the world am I doing here on earth?"

See, in God's plan, purpose is first. In our plan, purpose is last. I believe if we as men did this thing the way God has ordained for us to do it, these disturbing stats here would slowly but surely disappear: Men commit 90 percent of all major crimes, 100 percent of all rapes, 95 percent of burglaries, 94 percent of drunk driving, 70 percent of all suicides, and 91 percent of offenses against family and children. Why do I believe this? Because if we did it God's way, we would, first of all, know our purpose in life. Second, we would have a job. And third, we would be married. All before we start having sex and having kids. And quite honestly, I probably would not be writing this book. Furthermore, if a man is focused, because he knows his purpose in life, has a job, possibly a career, and is married, he is considerably less likely to commit these violent crimes.

I remember growing up with my dad in and out of the house—mostly out—I would always hear my older friends tell me, "Boy, if you want to be a real man, you need to go out and get all the sex you can, because the more sex you have, the more manly you will become. That's the way it was, growing up in the hood. The more money you had, the more power you had; the more power you had, the more women you had; the more women you had; the more sex you had; the more sex you had, the more you were considered to be "the man." That was the ultimate goal in the hood, to be "the man."

The one thing about initiation is it's going to come from someone, or somewhere; one way or another, something will teach us about life. With Dad not around to teach us who we are, then we are fair game for someone else to teach us who we're not. In rapper Tupac Shakur's number one hit song "Dear Mama," he sings,

> No love from my daddy cause the coward wasn't there
> He passed away and I didn't cry, cause my anger
> wouldn't let me feel for a stranger
> They say I'm wrong and I'm heartless, but all along
> I was looking for father he was gone
> I hung around with the Thugs, and even though they sold
> drugs
> They showed a young brother love.

In Tupac's case, it was the streets that had the privilege of raising him. I did say privilege. I believe it is a privilege, indeed, to raise any man, if it's done correctly. Think about it: when you're able to take a baby from the cradle and help guide, instruct, and teach him how to grow and mature into a respectable, responsible, productive, God-fearing young man, what could be better than that! It seems to me Tupac was looking for the same thing that most young men are looking for today—love, acceptance, and to belong. This is why organizations such as fraternities, gangs, and even cults, are so popular in our society today, because if nothing else, they offer all three of the above. They offer unconditional love, unconditional acceptance, and a bond of brotherhood that lasts until death.

· · · · · · · · · · · · · · ·

Let's look at this love thing for a minute. How important do you think the love of a father is to a young man? Massive! There is something about a father's love that just cannot be replaced, or ignored; and when we try to replace a healthy love from a loving father with an unhealthy love from another man, we can end up in a homosexual relationship. Most of us in this age and time know at least one homosexual that we come in contact with on a daily basis, or are maybe even friends with. I myself know two that I'm friends with, and before starting this book, I sat down with them and asked them what kind of relationship they had with their fathers growing up.

Each one said either they never knew their father, or the relationship they had with him was very cold and distant. I asked one of the young men, "Did your father ever hug you and tell you he loved you?"

"Absolutely not!"

"Hugging another man and telling him you love him—that was the gayest thing you could do as a man, my father would say."

What happens when we do not receive that healthy love from our fathers that we so desperately yearn for is we seek the unhealthy love from another in the form of an unhealthy relationship. I myself grew up with a father who never hugged me or ever told me he loved me. It was just one of those things in our household where you knew Dad loved you, whether he said it or not. It was just understood.

Homosexuality was not my thing. I loved women too much for that, but I can understand how someone could get caught up in that lifestyle if they're not careful, because the love of the father is so very important to us men, and if we're not receiving it, then I can understand how a young man might seek it out in an unhealthy relationship with another man.

In *Wild at Heart*, John Eldredge writes about homosexuals:

> They know that what is missing in their hearts is masculine love. The problem is they've sexualized it. It doesn't work that why so many gay relationships don't work and men hop from man to man trying to find that natural masculine love they so desperately need that would normally be received from their father.

I remember when I first got saved. I went to this Christian men's group one Friday night. Soon as I walked in, this big husky brother grabbed me and hugged me and said, "Brother, I love you!" I totally freaked out. No one, not even my own brother, had ever embraced me like that before and told me he loved me. I didn't know how to respond, but I was not going to tell him I loved him too!

Over the years, I've grown to understand that there is nothing wrong with hugging and telling a brother you love him, as long as it's a healthy, godly love. I have a six year-old myself, and I hug and kiss and love him every chance I get, because I realize there's nothing wrong with the healthy love of the father—the same type of love Jesus shows his sons and daughters.

Now let's look at this acceptance thing. Just how important is it for a young man to feel accepted by his father? Hugely important! Matthew 17:5 tells us, "While he was still speaking a bright cloud enveloped them, and a voice from the cloud said, 'This is my Son, whom I love; with him I am well pleased. Listen to him!'"

Even Jesus himself received the acceptance of his father before starting his ministry, so why would we not think the acceptance of our father wouldn't be important to us? I was twenty-six years old the first, and only time, my father ever told me he was proud of me; and it came at the most unexpected time in my life. Growing up, I wanted to be just like my father. I wanted to do everything just like he did. As a matter of fact, the only reason I played basketball was because it was my father's favorite sport, and not necessarily mine. I thought if I could excel at something he had such a love and passion for, he would accept me, so I played sports, chased women, and even became an alcoholic—all to gain the acceptance of my father.

I remember one time during football season: I was named Player of the Month, and they did a big write-up on me in the local newspaper. All of my friends and family were calling me up and saying, "Man, you're all over the front page of the newspaper!" So I jetted out of the house, ran up to the local convenience store to purchase a newspaper, and there I was—front and center! I'd never been in the newspaper before, so this was huge for me. Without a doubt the proudest day of my life. I bought two copies—one for me and one for my father. I grabbed the newspaper and ran straight to my father's house, and as soon as he opened the door, I said, "Look, Dad, I made the newspaper in a positive way!"

My father looked at me, intoxicated, and said, "What do you want?"

I said, "I just wanted to show you my picture in the newspaper."

He took the newspaper and shut he door. Honestly, I don't think he ever even looked at the article. If he did, he never said anything to me about it. That was certainly not the response I had hoped to receive from the person I lived to impress.

• • • • • • • • • • • •

When I was eight years old, my father came to a little league basketball game of mine intoxicated. He yelled at me and put me down in front of all my friends." That day, I told my father I never wanted to see him again at any more of my basketball games; and from that day until I was a grown man, my father never saw me play basketball again.

One day, when I was about twenty-one or twenty-two years old, I was down at the flat playing a pickup basketball game with the fellows, and my father walked up out of nowhere. I will never forget what I felt when I saw him standing under a shade tree watching me play his favorite sport. Now you've got to understand the last time my father saw me play basketball was some thirteen or fourteen years ago, and on that faithful morning, he called me everything but a child of God. Even though I often hoped and prayed my father would show up at an eighth-grade, high school, or even a college game, he never did. So when I saw him walk up to that basketball court that afternoon, I didn't know what to think or feel. At first I was extremely nervous, but then I thought, *Hey, I'm not a bad ball player, and this is the perfect opportunity to prove to my father that I'm not.* There was something so powerful and emotional about performing for the audience of my father on that particular day. Needless to say, I had the best pickup game of my life. After the game, my father looked at me, and then he smiled as he walked away. Now knowing my father the way I do, that smile spoke volumes!

• • • • • • • • • • • • • •

As I said before, I was twenty-six years old the first, and only time, my father ever told me he was proud of me; and it just happened to be at my baptism. I went to my father's house two weeks before I got baptized. I said, "Dad, I'm getting baptized in two weeks, and I really would like for you to be there, if you could." I told him, "I'll come and pick you up if you like." See, my dad was an alcoholic, and he never drove outside of the town where we lived. He knew all the police officers there, and they knew him; they pretty much let him drive around drunk without really bothering him, most of the time. Anyway, that's why I offered to pick him up for my baptism; and of course, he said, "That's okay." It really didn't surprise me at all, because I knew he wasn't coming.

So the weeks went by, and I didn't hear a word from my father. The Sunday morning of my baptism started just like any other Sunday. I went to church, I led devotion, my pastor preached a sermon, and then I went back to prepare for the most important day of my life. When I came out, I sat at the front of the church waiting for my turn to be baptized. As I looked out over the congregation, I saw my mother, and my sister, my brother-in-law, and their two kids, all of whom came with me. But as I stepped into the water, I looked up again, and to my surprise, I saw my father walk in the door and sit in the back of the church. I remember thinking, *Wow, he made it all by himself!*

My pastor performed the baptism. He took me down and brought me up, and when I came up, the first person I looked for was my father. He gave me the thumbs-up, and at that point, I knew I had done something right. After the church service, I went to the back of the church to talk to my father, and the first thing he said was, "Son, I'm proud of you!"

Wow! There it was. I'd been waiting twenty-six years to hear my father say those words to me, and all I had to do was give my heart to Jesus! The funny thing was, on the same day my father was most proud of me, I was most proud of him! I said to him, "Man, I can't believe you made it all the way up here by yourself."

He replied, "I stayed sober all day yesterday and today for your baptism."

I began to weep, because my father never stayed sober for anybody, or anything. All the times I wished he would have shown up for something and he didn't meant nothing compared to the one time I didn't expect him to show up and he did.

• • • • • • • • • • • • •

To belong—how important is it for a young man to feel that he belongs to something? Very! Again, this is why I believe organizations such as fraternities, gangs, cults, and even sports, are so popular with men. We as men like to feel that we belong to something bigger than ourselves, and where our input is important to whatever it is we're involved in. If you look at the game of football, there are twenty-two players on the field— eleven on offense and eleven on defense. The objective of each player on offense is to do their job to the best of their ability to get the ball into the end zone and score a touchdown. You have blockers who have to block, running backs who have to run the ball, receivers who have to catch the ball, and a quarterback who has to be able to throw the ball, and even kickers who have to kick the ball.

Now, when all these elements click at the same time, you'll usually end up with a touchdown. There are also eleven players on defense, and their objective is to keep the offense out of the end zone. Again, when each player on defense does his job to the best of his ability, it usually ends up in a defensive stand, or a stop. Now, whether you throw the ball for a touchdown, or you run it in, everyone from the blockers to the running backs has to do his job in order to achieve the ultimate goal as a team, which is to score a touchdown! I played football myself in high school, and when everything comes together on that football field and you leave at the end of the game, victorious, you recognize everybody on the team because you realize that even the bench warmers play a part in the victory when they stop warming the bench and become cheerleaders. Being a part of a team, a brotherhood, or something bigger than ourselves dwells in the heart of every man; and until we find something to connect with, we will forever be seeking to belong.

It seems as though, in our society today, we initiate our sons in one of two ways—either through *verbal* or through *visual* initiation.

. . . .

Verbal initiation

One of the most powerful verbal initiations I've ever heard came from one of my all-time favorite movies, *John Q.* In the movie, a distraught father already dealing with serious financial difficulties takes the staff of a hospital emergency room hostage to force the hospital administrators to allow his dying son to have the heart transplant he desperately needs to live. After a several-hour standoff, John Q (Denzel Washington) decides the only way his son is going to live is for him to commit suicide and give his son his heart. After the final preparations have been made, John Q walks into his son's room to verbally initiate him, and this is what he said: "Hi, Mike…Mike, how you doing, bud? I just need to tell you a few things. Always listen to your mother, understand, do what she tells you to do. She's your best friend. Tell her you love her every day. You're too young for the girls right now, but there is going to come a time, when it does, you treat them like a princess—that's what they are. When you say you're going to do something"— fights back tears—"when you say you're going to do something, you do it, because your word is your bond, son. That's all you have, and money. You…you make money when you get a chance even if you have to sell out every once and a while. Don't be stupid like your father. Everything is so much easier with money, son. Don't smoke, be kind to people, if someone chooses you. You know me, and you talk about this. You stand up, you be a man. Stay away from the bad things, son. Don't get caught up in the bad things. There are a lot of great things out there for you." And now tears are flowing down his face. "I'll never leave you. I'm always with you. I love you, son!"

Now, do I agree with everything he told his son? No. However, I do agree with the fact that he understood it was his responsibility as his father to initiate his son into manhood.

The truth of the matter is, if we don't teach our sons how to be responsible, respectable, productive, and, for the believers, God-fearing men, then who will?

Another one of my all-time favorite verbal initiations came from one of my least favorite movies—*Talladega Nights*, starring Will Ferrell. The star of the show is a character by the name of Ricky Bobby. When Ricky Bobby was a kid of about ten or twelve years old, he saw his dad for the first time in years at his school for career day. His dad got kicked out of school, but before he left, he said to his son, "Son, always remember this: either you're first or you're last!"

Some twenty years later, he would see his father again; and during an argument, he would remind his father of the comment he made to him over twenty years ago. Hey, Dad, don't you remember when you told me either you're first or you're last?"

His dad looked at him and said, "Son, that doesn't make any sense. I mean you could be second, third, or fourth!"

Ricky Bobby said, "What do you mean? I've built my whole life around that!"

Now this is a prime example of how powerful a father's words can be to his son, whether they're true of false. Ricky Bobby took the words of his father and built his entire life around those words. I'm thinking at one point and time in his life he had to have known that what his father told him was wrong; but because he was in his formative years when his father told him, Ricky Bobby believed that anything that came out of his father's mouth was more powerful than an atomic bomb.

Proverbs 18:21 reads, "The tongue has the power of life and death." Now this verse doesn't literally mean you can talk someone to death, or talk someone back to life; although my grandmother would totally disagree with that. She used to always say to me, "Boy, you gone talk me to death." Even though you can't literally talk someone to death, you can talk the life right out of them. What I'm saying is this: we as parents have the power in the words we speak to our sons to either encourage them, build them up, and bring life to their situation, or to discourage them, tear them down, and bring death to their situation. So we must speak positive things to our sons if we want to produce positive men; and if we can't say something good about them, in the words of my late grandmother, then don't say nothing at all!

I'm reminded of a young lady on the six o'clock news one evening being interviewed about her son's involvement in a double murder. They asked her, "Do you know how your son may have gotten involved with this double murder?"

She responded, "He aint no good, he aint never been no good, and he aint never been hitting on nothing. I used to tell him all the time he was going to end up just like his no-good daddy, so it doesn't surprise me at all that he's about to go to jail for life!"

After I saw this interview, it didn't surprise me at all how this young man as an adult would end up sentenced to life without parole. His mother actually sentenced him when he was a child!

• • • • • • • • • • • • • •

I remember that when I was growing up, my father gave me two pieces of advice. The first was, "Boy, don't ever do drugs. They'll make you crazy!" One rainy Saturday morning, my father and I were on our way to McDonald's for breakfast when we passed one of his drinking buddies, who also happened to be on drugs. At first we did not even recognize him. He had been beaten so badly. It looked as though someone had taken a sledgehammer and had literally rearranged his face. Of course, my father had already heard what happened to him, because bad news travels fast in the hood. My dad stopped and talked for a minute, and then we proceeded on to Macdonald's.

As soon as we got out of earshot, I had to ask, "Dad, what happened to Rick?"

He said, "Mr. Watson caught him breaking into his house last night trying to steal his television to sell for some dope money, and as you can see, he tried to kill him! Son, that's why I tell you, don't ever do drugs. They'll make you crazy!"

Now, it wasn't just because my father told me not to do drugs that kept me drug free all my life; rather, it was the combination of me seeing firsthand the devastation of drug abuse and the fact that I'd never seen my father do any type of illegal drugs, that kept me straight. I thank my father every day of my life for this valuable piece of advice; however, he failed to warn me about smoking and drinking (because he did those things himself), which would lead to me becoming a smoker and an alcoholic.

I was around thirteen years old, and had started dating a little bit, when my father gave me my second, and final, piece of advice: "Boy, always have at least two women. One you want to marry and one you want to do everything with but marry." This he said with a grin. Just like I built my life around the first piece of advice my father gave me, unfortunately, I also did the same with this piece of advice. Again, the only reason I built my entire life around this piece of advice is that not only did my father talk the talk, but he also walked the walk. He had several affairs, one leading to a child out of wedlock. So from the age of thirteen to about thirty-five, I had a serious problem with being faithful in relationships, even so much so that I'd stop making commitments and just started having friends. I think they call them friends with benefits nowadays. I remember once when I was in the ninth-grade, I started dating this girl I'd had a crush on for years. The way we got together was so funny. One day we both were at a local club, and I was shooting pool with my best friend, Charles. I remember bending over to take a shot and feeling someone pinch my butt. But when I looked behind me, no one was there, so I didn't think anything of it. So once again, I bent over to attempt a shot; and once again, I felt someone grab my butt.

This time I looked at my best friend and said, "Is somebody grabbing my butt?"

He said, "Yeah, it's Marie."

I said, "No."

"Yeah."

And I was like, cool! See, you must understand I'd been wanting to get with Marie for years. We actually played little league basketball together, but I never ever dreamed she would give a guy like me a chance. Marie's parents had money, and they lived on the other side of the tracks; and the only guy she had ever dated before lived on the same side of the tracks. As a matter of fact, the only time Marie came to our side of the tracks was to see her grandmother, who happened to live right across the street from me. So when I heard she was on our side of tracks, in a club, grabbing and pinching my butt, I got a little excited!

My friend and I were finishing up our game of pool when she suddenly did it again; and this time, when I turned around, she was still standing there smiling. That would be the beginning of a four-year love affair. At first, I know our relationship was built on the fact that I was totally infatuated with her. Later, I begin to love her as a friend; and finally, I begin to fall in love with her. About three years into our relationship, my father's words would begin to haunt me. Things were going great. She was totally into me, and I was totally into her. Until one day I was approached by another lifelong crush of mine—a girl named Stacy.

I had been in love with Stacy longer than I had been in love with Marie. Stacy was the total package: she had the looks, the brains, she was athletic like me, and last but certainly not least, she was a total sweetheart; and now, all of a sudden, she had an interest in little old me. As a freshman, I made the varsity basketball squad where Stacey was a cheerleader. I remember one night, on our way home from a long away game, we stopped to eat at a restaurant; and upon reentering the bus, I sat down, and before I knew it, Stacy was right behind me, asking if she could sit with me. And of course, I said, sure!

From that night on, we would sit together on all away games; not only that, but we would conduct ourselves at the away games as if we were boyfriend and girlfriend. I didn't have to worry about my girlfriend finding out because she couldn't come to all the away games, and I knew no one on the team was going to tell her about Stacy and me, so this went on for the entire basketball season. Now Stacy knew about my girlfriend, but my girlfriend didn't know about Stacy; until one day I made the biggest mistake of my young life—I gave a love letter written to Stacy to my girlfriend, Marie, and all heck broke loose!

Because I was so shy in high school, I relied heavily on my ability to write love letters. What I couldn't say with words, I could definitely say with a pen and a piece of paper. I would write my girlfriend at least two five-page love letters a day, and I would write Stacy at least one a day.

I remember that faithful day as if it was yesterday. I had written both of my girlfriends love letters the night before. I put Marie's in the right back pocket and Stacy's in the left back pocket. I arrived to school late that day, and somewhat in a rush; and honestly, I wasn't thinking when I saw my girlfriend before first period. I reached into my left back pocket, grabbed the letter, and gave it to her.

Everything was good until the beginning of third period, when I saw my girlfriend again. She walked up to me bawling her eyes out.

"What's wrong? Did you not like the letter?"

She struck me in the chest and said, "The letter was beautiful. Only, my name's not Stacy! You wrote her the same exact letter you write me every day. The only thing you changed was the name. I hate you!"

We did get back together after that terrible incident, but it was not for long. She eventually broke up with me because, she said, she could never trust me again. I tried the commitment thing one more time before I got married, and it didn't work, again, because of my infidelity; so I just gave up on ever being committed or ever getting married, until I turned thirty-five and met my wife.

When I met my wife, I knew immediately she was the one for me. Just like the old folks used to say, when you meet the right one, you'll know. They were right. I knew. She was totally different from any woman I'd ever met, and she made me feel something no other woman had ever been able to make me feel before her. I knew she was the one, I knew we were going to get married, and I knew she was going to have my kids; however, the one thing I didn't know was whether I would be able to be faithful to her. I realized I was older, saved, and a much different person than I was when I was thirteen and my father gave me that piece of advice. Not only that, but now I realized what my father told me back then was totally wrong.

With all this realization, you would think I wouldn't have a problem at all being faithful to my beautiful, loving, caring, God-sent wife. Wrong again. Some thirty years later, I'm still constantly reminding myself, *Craig, that's not the godly way. One woman's breasts shall satisfy thee.* The power of the father's words through verbal initiation—whether it's right or wrong, good or bad, spiritual or satanic, it's definitely life altering.

• • • • • • • • • • • • •

Visual initiation

The second way we as Western men initiate our boys is through visual initiation.

It was Saturday afternoon in the middle of July, and I was on my way home from the barbershop. I pulled up beside this car with the music blasting. Now normally, when I pull up to a car with loud music, I don't look over to see who's disturbing my peace; but for some reason, on this particular day, I looked, and what I saw shocked me enough to mention it in this book. There was a man and his son sitting in the car at the light. The man had on a baseball cap tilted to the side, and so did his son. The man had a cigar in his mouth, and his son had a straw in his mouth. The man was nodding his head to the beat of the expletive lyrics, and so was the son. Here's my problem with that: If you're a grown man and you've pretty much lived your life exactly the way you wanted to live it and this is where you've ended up, fine; but give your son a chance at something different in life if he so desires.

Visual initiation can be summed up as this: "Monkey see, monkey do." Remember that saying from back in the day, when we do something and our friends would copy us, we would say, "Monkey see, monkey do!" I'll never forget my best friend's dad would always come up to us with a cigarette hanging out of his mouth and say, "Don't smoke, boys. It'll give you cancer." Then he'll take a puff of his cigarette and walk off.

Back then it was "Do as I say, and not as I do"; but in reality, it's always been monkey see, monkey do. Truth is, we can teach our sons more in one day by what they see us do then we can tell them in one month by what they hear us say. I have a six year old son, and I am amazed at just how much he imitates his father. I can't do anything without him copying me. He copies the way I walk, the way I talk, the way I brush my teeth, the way I shave, and even my facial expression. It's really scary, because when I think about it, for the rest of his life he's going to be imitating his father.

Abe Lincoln, the man of steel and velvet, once said, "There is just one way to bring up a child in the way he should go, and that is to travel that way yourself."

Jesus puts it like this in the book of Matthew 5:19, "I tell you the truth, the Son can do nothing by himself; he can only do what he sees his Father doing, because whatever the Father does the Son also does."

I'm reminded of an episode of the number one hit sitcom *The Cosby Show*, when Dr. Cliff Huxtable (played by Bill Cosby) was teaching his son Theo (played by Malcolm-Jamal Warner) how to carve the Thanksgiving turkey. This was a huge deal for the men of the Huxtable family. It was a kind of coming-into-manhood tradition for the men, and they took this initiation very, very seriously!

When the day came for the carving knife to be passed down to Theo, Dr. Huxtable not only took his time explaining the process of carving the turkey, but he literally took Theo by the hand and walked him step by step through the process. Even though Theo didn't quite get it, the explanation of the process of the initiation was excellent!

As fathers, we need to ask ourselves, "How well are we training ours sons to be men based on the lifestyle we live?" I've always said, you can't expect no more out of your son than you put in him.

Look, if you go to the bank and you have insufficient funds, don't expect to withdraw a thousand dollars from your account, because it ain't going to happen. Now, most of us wouldn't do that at a bank, but we do it all the time with our sons. We spend years investing junk into them, and when they turn eighteen, we tell them, "Now go out and make your daddy proud!"

As I said before, monkey see, monkey do. If you want your son to be a success, it all starts with *you*.

• • • • • • • • • • • • • •

I know you're probably wondering about me as the author of this book, knowing there's no known traditional rite of passage in our society today, how will I take on the responsibility of initiating my sons when the time comes? Well, believe it or not, I think I'll use the" monkey see, monkey do" method of initiation—meaning I will initiate by example. Truth is, our sons can learn more in one day of walking with us than they can in a whole month of talking to us! As I said before, my father gave me two very valuable pieces of advice: One was "Don't do drugs, they'll make you crazy." And the other was "Always have at least two women—one to marry and one to do everything with but marry." One piece of advice was positive, and it helped me to stay drug free for over four decades; while the other piece of advice was negative, and it's something I still have to be conscious of even until this day. Both were life altering and eventually would shape and mold me into the man that I am today.

However, it wasn't just what my father told me that shaped and molded me for manhood, it was also what he showed me that was equally important. There were three things my father showed me growing up, and I was able to see the devastating effects of his actions, which makes me say I'll never do those things as an adult.

• • • • • • • • • • • • • •

The first was gambling. I was always my father's favorite son, and he would take me everywhere with him even when he went on all-night gambling binges. We would leave the house at about nine or ten o'clock at night and go to the local liquor house to gamble. My father would always start out good, winning up a storm; but sometime during the night, he would end up losing every penny he'd won, and then some. He would start the night with a couple of hundred dollars, which happened to be the rent money; and he would end up owing someone before we would leave the next morning. See, my father never had a problem with winning money. His problem was leaving with it. I remember some of the worst physical abuse from my father would come on the heels of one of these all-night-long losing gambling binges. Not only that, but time after time, our family was evicted from apartments—and even from our one and only house—because of my father's gambling addiction. His desire to go out and party and gamble all night long heavily outweighed his desire to be a responsible adult and pay his rent and keep a roof over his family's head. As a result of me being so close and so involved in this lifestyle growing up, I made a vow to never gamble; and for over four decades, I've been able to keep that vow. I don't do scratch offs, I don't bet on ballgames, I don't run numbers—*nothing*. Now that I am an adult with a job, the way I see it, I work way too hard for my money to throw it away on gambling! My father was initiating me without even realizing it.

The second was adultery. As I said before, my father and I were like two peas in a pod. Everywhere he went, I was sure to follow, even to his mistress's houses. I was about nine or ten years old when my father first took me to his mistress house to meet my sister. Not only did I meet my sister, but I also met his mistress, and I'll never forget how they looked at one another and how they acted around one another.

I remember thinking to myself. They acted a lot like my dad and my mom used to act. This affair would go on for years, until finally, my mother would find out about it in the most unusual way. My mother was a homebody, due mostly to the fact my father was physically abusive, and he didn't allow her to have any friends; so the outside world to her was pretty much non existent. So even though my sister was only six miles away, and everyone in our hometown knew about the affair and about her. It never did get back to Mom—until one day the sheriff knocked on our door and all heck broke loose! I remember the day as if it were yesterday. It was one of those school days my mother had kept us out of school to keep her company because she was always lonely during the day, with no friends or anyone to talk to. It was about lunchtime when we heard a knock on the door. My mom got up and looked out the window, and to her surprise, she saw a sheriff standing there. She went to the door opened it and said,

"Sir, may I help you?" he said. "Ma'am, good evening. Is James Stafford home?"

My mom said, "No, he's at work at the moment. What's the problem?" He said. "Could you give him this? It was some papers. My mother said, "What is this?"

The sheriff said, "This is a warrant for failure to pay child support."

My mother said, "Oh no, Mr. Sheriff, you have the wrong man. My husband has only three children, and they all live here with me, and I've never made him pay child support."

The sheriff responded, "Are you Mrs. Betty?"

My mother said, "Who?"

He said, "Betty. That's who filed the warrant against your husband."

I will never forget the look on my mother's face. At that moment, it was a look I'd never seen before, and neither have I seen since. I didn't know then, but now that I'm an adult, I realize the look I saw on my mother's face that day was that of total betrayal, hurt, shame, and embarrassment. She had no idea my father was being unfaithful, let alone, had a child out of wedlock, who was at least eight or nine years old. Not only will I never forget the look on my mother's face that day, I also will never forget the devastating effects my father's infidelity would have on my mother and our family as a whole. The affair would cause my mother to become a heavy drinker, which would lead to her becoming an alcoholic, which would in turn be the reason she would end up in the hospital in a comma due to a nervous breakdown.

Even as a child, I was old enough to realize this whole devastating current of events involving my mother all started with my dad's affair! I made up my mind as a child that if I ever did get married, I would not cheat on my wife. The way I see it, if I ever feel the need to be unfaithful to my wife, I will simply ask for a divorce and move on. I would never put my wife, my best friend, my soul mate, through what my father put my mother through Never! My father was initiating me without even realizing it.

The third was spousal abuse. My father was a wife beater, and that was the thing I hated most about him. Despite everything bad he did in his life, the physical abuse he inflicted upon my mother was by far the thing I despised the most about him. My dad was such a coward. I never saw him fight a man, but I often saw the results of him fighting my mother.

My mother is a beautiful woman, both inside and out. She's a bright-skinned lady with a beautiful smile, and one of the nicest people you would ever meet. Even though my father hardly ever hit my mother in front of us, we always knew when she had been abused. Not only could we hear the blows through the door, but oftentimes, after a beating from my father, my mother would stay in her bedroom for two or three days, trying to recover physically and emotionally before she would face her children. She would usually be abused on Friday nights, after my dad had been out drinking all night long, gotten drunk, lost all his money, and came home wanting to take it out on somebody. And unfortunately, my mother was his favorite target. I literally saw my mother go from this beautiful, strong, confident woman to this bruised, scarred, broken, weak lady with very low self-esteem. After seeing the devastating, destructive crumbling of my beautiful mother caused by my father's physical abuse, I vowed that I would *never* strike a woman for as long as I live!

Once again, my father was initiating me without even realizing it.

• • • • • • • • • • • • • •

At this time, I would like to talk to the single moms and grandmoms who are reading this book, totally frustrated trying to raise boys without a male influence at home. I know you're probably saying to yourself, *Okay, I get the fact that it takes a man to raise a man, and not only that, but it takes a man to initiate man. However, what if there is just not a man around at this time to take on that responsibility? What can I do to help my son as a single mom or grandmom to make the crucial transition from boyhood to manhood?*

Well, I'm glad you asked. Even though I'm a firm believer in the presence of a male influence in a boy's life, I do believe there are four things a single mom or grandmom can do to help her son or grandson become the man they desire for him to be.

• • • • • • • • • • • • • •

Nurture

The first thing you can do is to be a nurturer. To be a nurturer simply means this: It's your job as moms or grandmoms to nurture your sons or grandsons. The word *nurture* means "support and encourage." Moms and grandmoms, you must support and encourage your sons or grandsons in whatever they decide to do, as long as it's accepted by your standards of life. In other words, if it's something you condemn, then I'm certainly not telling you to support or encourage it. But if it's something acceptable to you and your family, then by all means, you must support and encourage them.

I was sitting in my office one Saturday afternoon when a woman called and asked if she could bring her troubled son to one of our meetings to get him straightened out. I asked her, "How old is your son?" She said he was fourteen. I asked, "What seems to be the problem with him?"

She said, "I think he may be doing drugs, and he's very disrespectful to me."

I thought, *Sounds like it's too late for me to help.* But of course, I told her to bring him over. The following Saturday, she brought him to our meeting; and of course, that day, he had very little to say to anyone. For the next three months, she brought him to our meetings, and each time we saw him, he loosened up more and more—until one day, we mentioned a flag football tournament we were hosting, and he just lit up! We could not shut him up after that, he had asked so many questions about the tournament and mentioned on more than one occasion that football was by far his favorite sport.

I remember thinking, *We've finally found something that this young man is passionate about. Now let's use it to our advantage and try to get him saved.* So as the tournament neared, we began to talk more and more with this young man and got to know him quite well. And then finally, after he'd been coming to our meetings for a little over four months, one Saturday morning, when salvation was offered to the group, he stood up and said he wanted to be saved. We led him into the salvation prayer, and he received Jesus on that day.

His mother came to pick him up later that day, and I told her about his confession of faith, and she said, "Well, I just hope it's real because he's so fake and full of crap that I don't believe nothing he says!"

I was totally thrown for a loop. I did not expect her to respond that way at all! I thought she might say something like, "Wow, that's great! Now I don't have to worry about him anymore, thank God!" Not "I hope it's real, he's a piece of crap, and I don't believe anything he says." I remember thinking, I can see where half his problem stems from—his mom. And of course, the other half was the fact he never met his father and did not have a male influence in his life. The day of the tournament finally came, and our new friend was totally fired up. He had gone out and bought new shoes, gloves, and a water bottle for this epic event.

As the team lined up for the kickoff, our new friend went way back deep to receive it. They kicked it to him, and he ran about eighty yards, untouched, for the touchdown. We all looked at one another with our jaws dropped, and said, "Wow! No wonder this cat likes football. He's awesome!"

He went on to totally amaze us. He was by far the fastest player on the field, and the most athletic. His mom finally arrived to see him score his fourth touchdown of the day; and after he scored, he ran over to her with a big old smile on his face, as excited as he could be, and said, "Look, Mom, I scored a touchdown! It's my fourth of the day!"

She looked him dead in the eyes and said, "You worthless piece of crap. You're a failure in school, you're a criminal, and you're a failure in life. I'm glad you can do something right!" Then she turned around and walked off.

I will remember that day for as long as I live. Earlier in this book, I mentioned how you can't literally talk someone to death, but you can talk the life completely out of them. This was a prime example of that. I will never forget the look on that young man's face when his mother burst his bubble. It was as though I watched the life get sucked right out of this child's body before my very own eyes. Life and death are in the power of the tongue. Moms and grandmoms, you must be careful about the words you're speaking over your sons and grandsons.

Well, needless to say, that young man is now serving a fifteen-year sentence for rape and sodomy. Moms and grandmoms, I said all that to say this: in a perfectly functioning family, I believe it's the father's responsibility to support and encourage his son in everything he does, as long as it's spiritually and morally acceptable. However, when Dad is not around, this is one of those times when moms and grandmoms have to step up to the plate and fill in. The importance of your son feeling the support and encouragement coming from you in this very crucial time of their lives is so very important. Now most mothers have this support and encouragement thing down pat.

Have you ever noticed the mom at the basketball game watching her son play basketball? Her son is not the best player on the team—he may even be the worst player in the entire league, and everybody in the gym knows this except for his mom. When the coach finally has to put him in the game, Dad leaves the gym, but Mom stands up and claps her hands and says, "That's my baby going in the game. He's my son, and he's the best player on the court."

The statement is so untrue it even embarrasses the son, but in Mom's eyes, he is the best player on the court, and she's going to support him as though he was the best player in the world. Why? Because that's her baby!

Or how about the mother of one of the most notorious killers in American history, who goes on television pleading for her son's life? Explaining to the judge that no one understands her son but her. "He's not that monster you're trying to portray him to be. He's just a little lost boy that needs his mother." We as men look at her, like, "Lady, are you crazy? Do you know what your son has done? Do you really understand the severity of what just happened here?" Even his father might say, "Hey, he deserves whatever he gets. I don't know what he was thinking about, and he definitely was not raised that way. Again whatever he gets, he deserves."

But not Mom. She still pleads for her son's life, because to her, he's still that little boy that she encouraged and supported all his life, and she's not going to stop now when he needs her the most.

· · · · · · · · · · · · · ·

Cheering on

The second thing you can do as moms and grandmoms to help your sons and grandsons make the crucial transition from boyhood to manhood is to be their biggest cheerleader. I'm not saying you literally put on a skirt and grab some pompoms and start cheering at their ball games. However, I am saying observe your sons, see what they like to do, and if it's spiritually and morally accepted in your household, cheer them on and support them 110 percent in whatever they decide they want to do! Again, for most women, this is not a problem at all; but for some, it can be, because some single moms think their sons can only play or participate in manly activities.

For example, most single moms think that their sons have to play football, basketball, or baseball in order to be a real man. If they see them take an interest in playing music, the arts, dancing, or anything else that may not be considered to be masculine, they may completely ignore the gift and try to explain to them that "no man on our side of the family has ever played the flute, and neither will you. Only females play the flute!"

Here's the problem with that: If his passion is playing the flute, and God has given him the ability to do so, this could very well be his God-given purpose here on earth. And who are you to deny your son his God-given purpose just because you don't think it's manly enough? So you deny him his passion for playing the flute, and you try to give him a purpose—playing football— and he fails terribly at it, and you begin to call him names such as a loser, a wimp, a wuss, and a failure. And to be honest with you, he is a failure at what you called him to be, but he's a success at what God has called him to be! Plainly put, you made him miss out on his dream trying to fulfill your own. Let him be who God has called him to be, and watch him make you proud!

• • • • • • • • • • • • • •

Discipline

The third thing you can do as moms and grandmoms to help your sons and grandsons make the crucial transition from boyhood to manhood is to be a disciplinarian. Moms, I know what you are thinking: *It's hard to discipline boys because they're so hardheaded, and they're going to do what they want to do anyway, regardless of what you tell them. Let's face it, they're bigger than us, stronger than us, and if they wanted to, they could physically dominate us, so how in the world can we honestly get them to do what we tell them to?*

It's quite simple. Who pays the bills in your house? I mean, who pays for the Xbox, the computer, the cell phone, and the electricity? Here is how it works: You come home from work one day, and you tell little Jonnie you want him to start doing chores. He says, "Mom, I'm way too cool for chores."

The next day, when he comes home from school, make his Xbox disappear. When he asks what happened to it, tell him he'll get it back as soon as he finishes his chores. If that doesn't work, the next day, take his computer from him. If that doesn't work, the next day, take his cell phone from him. And so on and so forth.

My point is this: If you pay the bills in the house, and if everything he has belongs to you, then you have more power over him than you think to make him do want you want him to do! You must learn how to say no and stick to it! What I see way too often in dealing with young men with no fatherly influence in their lives is the guilty yes mom. This is the mom who feels guilty because she failed to give her son a father, for whatever the situation may have been, whether it was a one-night stand, a failed relationship, or even the father passing away. The mother feels guilty that her son doesn't have the father he deserves to go to the games with him. Throw the ball with him, and to take him under his wing and shape, and mold him into the man she would like for him to be.

For whatever reason, this guilty mom often turns into a yes mom. What is a yes mom? Just what it says—she's a mom who finds it very difficult to tell her son no because she does not want to upset him. She figures, *If I just go along with him and give him what he wants, say what he wants me to say, and do what he wants me to do, and not rock the boat, I'll be fine.* She'll never have to hear him say the four words that would be like a sword stuck in the middle of her heart. "Mom, I hate you!"

This is a killer for the guilty yes mom, and the last thing she wants to hear coming out of her son's mouth, because she already feels that she's failed him as a mother; and now she feels as though she has failed him as a friend as well. A word for the guilty mom: you don't owe your son anything other than to be the best mother you can be to him. If the situation causes you to say no, and to do what's best for your son at that time, make the right decision and say no. He may say he hates you at the time, but in the long run, he'll love you for it, trust me.

The truth of the matter is that the heart of every boy yearns to be disciplined—it's just part of the young man's makeup.

• • • • • • • • • • • • • •

Find them a male mentor

And last, but certainly not least, moms and grandmoms, you should find your sons or grandsons a male mentor. Now when I say find him a male mentor, I'm not talking about someone you see in the neighborhood who seems like a great guy to take your son or grandson under his wing and teach him the ropes. Instead, you should go through the yellow pages, find a respectable male mentoring program, check them out thoroughly, and enroll your son or grandson into their program.

I would enroll them as early as five, but no later than eight. I know you're probably thinking, *What in the world does an eight-year-old need with a mentor? He's too young to be a troubled child at that age.* Exactly! And that's why this age is the perfect age.

Here's how I see it: From the ages eight, nine, ten, and eleven, these are the forming years. Your son is being formed. From the ages of twelve, thirteen, and fourteen, these are the shaping years. Your son is being shaped. From the ages of fifteen, sixteen, and seventeen, these are the molding years. Your son is being molded. And from the ages of eighteen, nineteen, twenty, and twenty-one, these are the becoming years. Your son is becoming the man he shall be.

So pretty much what you see from a boy at the age of seventeen and eighteen is more than likely what you'll see from that same young man from the age of nineteen onward. Unless the Lord Jesus gets a hold of his heart and changes him for eternity. So this is why I say your sons or grandsons should get with their mentor by the age of eight, so the mentor can have three-six years during the most formative years of the boy's life to form and shape him.

By the time the boy hits the molding years and needs someone to help him with becoming a man, he will no longer be confiding in a male mentor. Rather, after six years of true friendship and growing close to one another, he'll be confiding in a friend. Big difference! I tell strangers very little about myself, I tell friends a little more about myself, but my closest friends (like my wife and my accountability partner) know me inside out. Why is that, you ask? Because I've spent years confiding in them and learning to trust them, and now I feel as though I can trust them with my life.

You remember my friend's story in the last chapter, about the son in the gang who lost his life two days before his eighteenth birthday. She actually did bring him to one of our meetings. She introduced us and said to him, "Baby, now you go into Mr. Jonathan's office and tell him what's going on with you!"

I remember the young man walked back to my office and sat down directly across from me. I said, "Hey there, buddy, my name is Jonathan. What seems to be the problem?"

The young man lifted his head up and said to me: "Nigga, I don't know you. I aint telling you jack! It shocked me at the time, and I was even somewhat offended. But now, years later, knowing what I know, he was absolutely right. He didn't know me, and he should not have been asked to confide in me about anything, especially about matters of the heart. I often wonder what that young's man life would have been like had I known him from the ages of eight, nine, ten, or eleven. Moms and grandmoms, get your sons and grandsons a male mentor early—as early as five but no later than eight. It could possibly save their lives.

The Search for a Hero

It's a boy! Wow, I was finally having a little boy of my own, and I was so excited. It seemed as though I'd been waiting a lifetime for this day to come. I remember sitting in the doctor's office Thursday, November 29, 2007, watching the nurse perform an ultrasound on my wife to determine the sex of our child. The ultrasound itself was one of the most amazing experiences I'd ever witnessed in my life—sitting there watching a part of me in my wife's womb moving, turning, yawning, alive!

Then the nurse asked the question, "Are you guys ready to find out the sex of your baby?" I looked at my wife, she looked at me, and we both said, "Yes." Now for about twenty-one weeks, I just knew my wife and I were having a boy. I was absolutely sure of it. However, on the morning of November 29, 2007, I woke up with the thought of a little girl heavy on my mind. It was the first time since I found out my wife was pregnant that I thought for a moment that it could possibly be a girl, which would have been perfectly fine with me, don't get me wrong. But for twenty-one weeks, I was 99.9 percent positive we were having a little boy.

Now all of a sudden, the thought of me and my wife having a little girl was so heavy on my mind I went to work the same day telling all my friends I could've been wrong about the sex of my firstborn. I said, "Hey guys, I know I've been screaming boy, boy, boy for twenty-one weeks now. However, this morning, I got the feeling my wife and I just might be having a little girl." Honestly, we didn't care if we had a boy or a girl as long as it's healthy. That was our prayer from day one.

Okay, back to the doctor's office. "Are you guys ready to find out the sex of your baby?" asked the nurse. And we said, "Sure!" Here's the package: She said, "It's a boy!"

I remember sitting in the doctor's office in a complete daze, not knowing what to feel or what to think. I just kind of stared at the blank wall in front of me. On the one hand, this was the day I had waited for my entire adult life, to have a son of my own; but on the other hand, I was somewhat afraid because I knew that in about four mouths, I would automatically become someone's *hero*, whether or not I was ready for it!

Fathers, do you realize that as a dad, you are your child's first choice for a hero, whether you like or not, regardless of yourself? Meaning, it does not matter if you're good or bad, big or small, rich or poor, or black or white—you are your child's first choice for a hero. Why do I believe this? Well, I'll tell you why. In an average American home where Dad is present, the man is the primary provider, protector, and visionary for the family. I remember, as a child, seeing my father get up at five o'clock each morning and leave the house at five thirty, walking on his way to work because he had to be there at six thirty.

There were two things about my father concerning work that never occurred to the best of my knowledge. The first was that my father was never late for work. He taught all of us to always arrive at work fifteen or twenty minutes before you had to be there. Just in case you came up on an accident or got caught in traffic, you could still get to work on time. This is advice I have personally kept until this very day. The second thing is that my father never missed a day of work. This one really amazed me, because there was a time when I lived with my father, and I would see him stay up all night long drinking well into the wee hours of the morning, take a three-hour nap, and get up and go to work cutting steel for eleven or twelve hours a day like it was nothing.

Yeah, you heard me right. My father cut steel for a living. At the time, cutting steel was a very dangerous occupation for a sober man, let alone one under the influence of alcohol; but my father managed to do it for seventeen years, safely. Not only was my father the sole provider for our family. He was also our protector. My father was a big rabbit hunter, and because of that, he owned a 12-gauge shotgun, which he kept loaded at all times, just in case someone felt lucky to choose our house to break into.

Everyone in the hood knew my father. They knew he had a shotgun, they knew he drank, and they knew he was crazy—not a house you would want to break into, not even for the most hardened criminal. I guess that explains why I always felt safe when my father was home, because he was our protector day and night, and I never felt fear of anybody or anything when he was around. Isn't that how a real hero is supposed to make you feel? I remember that even as a youngster getting into arguments with other kids, I would always threaten them with going and getting my daddy. The argument would go something like this:

"You better leave me alone."

You leave him alone. I'm gonna go get my daddy."

"I'm gonna get my daddy."

"My daddy's bigger than your daddy."

"No, he ain't. My daddy, bigger than your daddy. My daddy can whip your daddy."

"No, he can't. My daddy can whip your daddy.

"Well, go to get your daddy! You go get your daddy!"

What we were really saying to one another is this: You go get your hero, and I'll go get my hero, and we'll see whose hero is the baddest of the two. The truth of the matter is, I believe all kids, little boys as well as little girls, see their fathers as their hero, whether or not they realize it. Sometimes it takes until they're grown before it hits them: "Wow, my father was, and still is, my hero."

Lastly, when dads are around, they usually provide provision for their families. Well, my father was two for three; but in this area, he failed, badly. My father did not provide a healthy vision for his family due to the fact that he was the most selfish person I think I ever met; therefore, any vision or goals my father set for the future didn't involve no one but himself!

• • • • • • • • • • • • • •

I recently conducted a survey with a group of males between the ages of twelve and eighteen, and I asked them this question: "Who is your hero?" And to be honest with you, I was not at all shocked with the response I received.

About 60 percent of the guys said LeBron James, about 30 percent said Kobe Bryant, and about 10 percent said Michael Vick (pre–dogfighting). As I said before, I was not shocked at all with the response; however, I was somewhat surprised that not even one of the young men responded with a dad, a mom, a grandparent, or even an older brother or sister. But then again, in our society today unless you shoot a basketball, run a football, throw a baseball, hit a golf ball, star in a block buster movie, or perform in front of a sellout crowd, you're not worthy to be considered someone's hero. It's a shame when our kids have to look outside their own homes to find a hero. For some reason, they look right past the person who puts food on the table, clothes on their backs, and a roof over their heads, to someone they've never met before, someone who has never made any sacrifices for them, and to someone who doesn't even know they exist, to be their hero. For the rest of this chapter, I would like to share with you my top six heroes of all time, starting with my father coming in at number six. I know you're probably thinking your father, at number six. Yes, my father at number six. I placed my father at number six on my list simply because he was my first choice for a hero.

• • • • • • • • • • • • • •

Although the year 1968 offered quite a few heroes for one to chose from, such as the great Jackie Robinson, Wilt Chamberlain, Bill Russell, Babe Ruth, and Mr. Jim Brown. I chose my first hero from within my very own home—my father. At the time, I considered my father to be a great choice for a hero. He was tall, about six feet. He was good-looking, very charming. My father could charm anyone out of anything, and such a socialite that people loved to be around him. I remember, as a kid, saying to myself, *I want to be just like my daddy when I grow up. I want to walk like him, talk like him, and act like him.*

My father was a smoker, and I was totally mesmerized with the way he would smoke a cigarette. I remember watching him take these long puffs of his cigarette and then flick his ashes in the ashtray with such coolness it blew my little mind. So much so that it's no wonder I became a straw smoker and, later on, a smoker myself. Even though my father was a heavy drinker, smoker, and womanizer, in my eyes he could do no wrong, and I would tell my mother all the time I was going to "be just like daddy when I grow up." She would always say, "Baby, please don't." I guess looking back on it, I could see my mother knew something I didn't, but I would eventually find out.

My father had it all—a beautiful family, nice cars, and a great job. Honestly, what else could you ask for in a hero? Not to mention he was an excellent athlete, excelling in both basketball and baseball. You could often hear some of the locals sitting around talking about my father, saying how he was one of the best basketball players they'd ever seen in the state of Georgia. He definitely had a career in the NBA, but he gave it all up to get married and start a family. My father was my one and only hero all the way up until the day he began to physically abuse my mother. I could deal with the drinking, the smoking, the womanizing, and even the gambling, but wife beating—that did it for me!

Although, I never actually saw my father hit my mother, we often saw the evidence of a woman battered. When I look at my mother today, I can't help but smile and think to myself, what a beautiful, strong, courageous, and awesome woman she is! My mother went through hell and high water (as the old folks would say) with my father, and my father did his best to break her. Yet, still she is standing strong at sixty-nine years of age—with no hatred of any kind in her heart toward my father. As I said before, what an amazing woman she is.

Okay, back to my father as my hero. The physical abuse pretty much did it for me. He was no longer someone I looked up to, someone I imitated, nor was he someone I wanted to be like when I grew up. Now it was just the opposite. I truly despised the man! Because I believe the heart of every young man longs for a hero (someone to identify with, to associate with, and to connect with), my search for an authentic hero began.

I would meet Hero Number 5 at the most usual place for me—a gym. By the time I made it to middle school, I ate, slept, and drank basketball. I'm telling you, if I could have grown that extra eight inches I was praying for all throughout high school, I could have been the next Michael Jordan. I loved the sport called basketball! I remember we played basketball literally all day long. We would start at eight in the morning at one person's house, play for a couple of hours, then go to the next person's house to play for another couple hours, then the next, so on, and so on, until night fell.

I inherited the love of basketball from both my parents. My mother played basketball, but my father was a basketball player. They say he was one of the best in town, and the man knew just about everything there is to know about the game of basketball, and he always had my brother and me outside playing basketball, sometimes with him, but most of the time against one another.

The worst fight I ever had with my brother was over a stupid basketball game—at least that's what he called it. I called it the best game of my life because it was the first time I had ever beaten my brother in a game of one-on-one. When it came to athletic skills, I was a step ahead of my brother; and when I finally got good enough to beat him in a game of one-on-one, he couldn't handle it. After all, he was the older brother, and in his mind, I was never supposed to ever beat him at anything! I'll never forget it. The game was very close. I'm talking maybe two points decided it. I remember going in for a lay-up and my brother fouled me. I called the foul, but of course, he protested the call; so we began to argue with one another.

Finally, he chunked the ball at me, hitting me in the mouth, and said, "There, you can have it. I quit!" Now I knew on my best day, I could not whip my brother. He was way too strong for me; but I also knew my mouth was hurting pretty bad, and this was probably the most upset I had ever been with him. Something came over me, I picked up the basketball, and as he was walking around the corner of the house to go inside, I reared back my hand with the ball in it and threw it as hard as I could, striking him in the back of the head.

My brother turned around and looked at me; he was angrier than I had ever seen him before in my lifetime. He was fuming; at that very moment, I knew if I wanted to live I'd better get gone, so that was exactly what I did. I got gone! As I said before, I was a slightly better athlete than my brother, which also meant I could run just a tad bit faster than he could, which probably saved my life that day! I ran to my best friend's house, a guy who went by the name of Big Herbert.

Big Herbert was one of the baddest dudes in the entire neighborhood, and he also just happened to be one of my very best friends. Every time I needed protection, even from my own brother, I would run to his house, and he would protect me. As I was saying, basketball was my life back then. I ate, drank, and slept basketball! And now my brother finally had to come to grips with the fact that I was a tad bit better than him in the sport even though that would be the last game of one-on-one we would ever play.

• • • • • • • • • • • • • • •

As I said before, when I was younger, we would travel by foot from court to court in the neighborhood all day long, playing basketball until the sun went down; but when I became a teenager and hit middle school, there was only one place for a true baller to be on Tuesday and Thursday nights and Sunday evening, and that was at the local gym. Every true baller from all over the metro area would come to our town, to our gym, to compete on a level I had never seen before in my life.

Back then, every guy on the court seemed to me as though he could have played professional basketball somewhere; but the sad reality of it was that these guys, most of whom had dropped out of high school, would never show their stuff to anyone but to the people who showed up on Tuesday, Thursday, and Sunday evenings at open gym. The age limit to play was supposed to be fifteen and up, but after about a year or so of me coming and shooting around on the side goals the entire two hours, eagerly wanting to get on the court, the director saw how much I loved the game, and he began to let me play with the big boys.

Needless to say, I was very happy! By the time I hit ninth grade, basketball had become my God (I'm ashamed to admit that now but it was). The director would always get to the gym about an hour early to set up and to take about two hundred shots to warm up. I remember I used to think, *Now that's a good idea.* So I would walk about two to three miles to the gym every Tuesday, Thursday, and Sunday evening so I could get there an hour or so before open gym started, so I could also work on my game before everyone else got there. The people I sometimes rode with weren't about to get to the gym an hour early. They just weren't that serious about their game. Now they might arrive an hour late to the gym and wonder why they couldn't play, but never an hour early.

So I had to put on my walking shoes and hit the road by myself. I remember the first time I arrived an hour early for open gym, the director was hesitant to let me in at first. Then he opened the door and said, "What are you doing here?"

I said, "I want to work on my game like you do every time before we play."

He said, "Son, you really do love basketball, don't you?"

I said, "Yes, sir!"

He said, "Come on in."

I went in, and I watched him warm up. He must have taken a thousand shoots and made nine hundred and ninety nine of them. He was awesome! I would find out sometime later that he had played basketball for the University of Georgia and was their all-time leading scorer until a man by the name of Dominique Wilkins came there.

I thought, I wanted to shoot the basketball just like this man. I wanted to dribble the ball just like this man. I wanted to pass the ball just like this man. In essence, what I was saying was this: not only did I want this man's love, desire, and passion for the game of basketball, but I wanted his skills to go along with it.

It wouldn't take long for the director to take me under his wing and teach me all the tricks of the trade—well, maybe not all of them, but he taught me an awful lot. And before long, I was getting there an hour before open gym started and staying an hour after it closed. I had gotten to a point where I was shooting one hundred free throws, one hundred layups, fifty right-handed, and fifty left-handed, and taking fifty three-point shots each Tuesday, Thursday, and Sunday before open gym started. I had gotten very serious about this game called basketball! You would probably think the director of open gym would be a perfect candidate for my Hero Number 5, since it seemed as though he had done everything I wanted to with the game I loved so much. I mean, he went to college on a basketball scholarship, set records in the sport, and got a college education along the way. Now he was doing exactly what he wanted to do, which was to coach high school basketball. Maybe he should have been Hero Number 5, but he wasn't.

However, I did meet Hero Number 5 while at open gym one Sunday.

• • • • • • • • • • • • • •

It was a scorching hot Sunday at open gym the summer of my ninth grade year when I met Hero Number 5. I'll never forget the day. This new guy drove up in a brand-new BMW 5 Series; I think it was a 535. Anyway, it was very clean, and no one else was rolling like that back in the day. My team had just played, so we were outside getting some fresh air, when he drove up. He got out of his car, and the first thing I noticed was this guy was pretty tall, probably about six feet four or six feet five. He asked, "Is this where you guys play ball at?" We said yeah, and he said, "All right, cool."

He walked into the gym and took off his slippers and put on his Nike Air Jordan. Now at the time, I didn't know that real ballers wore slippers to and from the gym. I know now, and to this day, if I see someone walk into the gym with their shoes in their hand and slippers on their feet, I say to myself, *That guy right there can ball!* But like I said, back in the day, I didn't know that. As a matter of fact, my best friend and I started cracking on him, until he got on the court. Because of his size, he was a quick pick; and because of his ability to play basketball, he stayed on the court the entire time. His team won every game they played, and he turned out to be a *beast!*

The first time he touched the ball, he drove baseline and reverse-dunked over two people. And after I saw that, there was no laughing at him. He clearly wasn't a joke. And all of a sudden, I had found myself a hero! This guy's game was exactly where I wanted mine to be, so I automatically took to him. After my new friend finished putting on a show for us country folks, I went to him and began to befriend him.

I told him, "Hey man, I love your game. You are awesome! What's your name?" He said, "My name is Carter,"

I said, "Okay, Carter, I'll be honest with you. I want to play basketball like you, and maybe even drive a car like yours."

He smiled. "Okay, little bro, ya'll play again Tuesday, right?"

"Yeah."

"I'll see you then."

"Cool!"

Tuesday rolled around, and just like he promised, he showed up; and because he was so good, the director chose him as a captain. He got to choose his own team, and to my complete amazement, Carter chose me to play on his team. I was beside myself! Throughout the summer, for the next three months, Carter would choose his own team, which would include me; and of course, we would win just about every time we stepped onto the court. Also, over this same period of time, I began to hang out with my new best friend. Often, after we would play basketball on Sundays, he would take me out to eat at some very nice and expensive restaurants. Now you have to understand, me and the fellas used to scrap up a few dollars and grab some McDonald's to eat on the way home on Sundays; but my new friend always had plenty of money, and we always went to nice places to eat.

I remember one particular time, we went out to eat at a very nice restaurant, and when the waitress brought the bill, Carter opened up his wallet and said, "Little bro, look."

I looked in his wallet and saw what looked like to be at least thirty $100 bills. My eyes almost popped right out of my head. I had never seen a $100 bill before, let alone thirty, in one wallet belonging to the same person. It was at this time I asked my friend, "Man, where are you from, and what do you do?"

He said, "I'm from Miami, and I play basketball for the University of Miami Hurricanes."

I said, "Where did you get all that money from?"

"They pay me to play. This year coming up will be my junior year. I'll have one more after this one. Then I should be a first-round pick in the NBA draft."

Now this did not surprise me at all. I mean, as well as he played, I could totally see him playing for the University of Miami; and I could totally see him getting paid for it. And even though I didn't know exactly what a first-round draft pick was, I could see him doing that as well. He was just that good to me! Okay, it was settled. This guy was my new hero. I wanted to be just like him when I grew up. I wanted to play for the University of Miami, I wanted to drive a BMW, and I wanted to be a first-round draft pick, whatever that was, just like Carter. I had finally found someone who was real!

My new hero and I would continue to hang out and play basketball, and of course, we got to know each other better. I remember one Sunday in particular, after open gym, we went to one of his favorite restaurants for a nice, expensive lunch. His beeper went off, and he said, "Excuse me little bro." He got up and left the table for about thirty minutes, and when he returned, he said, "Little bro, we got to go right now!"

I was like, "Okay, cool."

We left the restaurant, jumped into the Beemer, and he took me home. The entire ride home, he didn't say a word, and neither did I. I wouldn't see Hero Number 5 for about a month or so; and since I never got his telephone number, I had no way to get in touch with him to see what was going on. He would eventually surface—not on the basketball court but face down on the ground, with about twenty armed police officers standing over him!

• • • • • • • • • • • • • • •

As I said before, I didn't see my buddy for quite some time, until one Thursday evening, I was walking on my way to open gym with a good friend of mine, and we walked by a car that looked an awful lot like my hero's 535 BMW. My friend looked over and saw the car stopped in the middle of the road by the police. It had every door open, every window down, and the trunk was wide open. It was obvious the officers were looking for something of value in this automobile.

My friend said, "Craig, ain't that your boy's car?"

My first thought was, *Absolutely not! What would Carter be doing facedown with police officers over him with weapons drawn. He's not even from here. He's a University of Miami starting shooting guard getting ready to go pro.* But then I took a closer look at the scene, and now that he had mentioned it, it did look like my friend's 535. As we got closer to the car, I could see the officers had someone of African American descent, about six feet four or six feet five, facedown on the ground. They were going through his pockets.

I peered around the corner onto the ground and saw Hero Number 5 looking up at me. And the look he gave me said it all. *Hey, little bro, I'm sorry I wasn't who you thought I was. I really didn't mean to disappoint you.*

The next day, my hero made the front page of our local newspaper, and the headline read, "Miami drug lord captured in local town." The article went on to say my hero was caught red-handed with fifty kilos of cocaine on him yesterday, which would guarantee him a life sentence without the possibility of parole.

Well, he was honest about one thing: He was from Miami, but he wasn't a big-time basketball player—he was a big-time drug dealer. A part of me died that day, because let the truth be told, a part of me was living through him! So now I was back to where I started—looking for a hero.

• • • • • • • • • • • • •

I met Hero Number 4 the summer of my senior year of high school through a mutual friend of mine. By the time I hit seventeen or eighteen, my dreams of becoming a professional basketball player had taken a backseat. Not only because of the terrible disappointment I had felt from Hero Number 5, but also because of the fact that I never did grow that extra six to seven inches I needed to make it in the NBA. I mean, I had crazy skills, and a heart and desire for the game that was incredible; but I was just too short—at least that was what everyone kept telling me!

So by the time I hit my senior year, I had changed my career plans. I wanted to be an entrepreneur—that's right, whatever that was! I remember my great-uncle and aunt owned houses that they would rent out to people; and even though I never heard them talk about the money they were making off those houses, people in the neighborhood were. They would say stuff like, "Man, your uncle is making a killing off of those houses he rents out. He's a real entrepreneur!"

That would be the first time I would hear that word, and even though I didn't quite understand it, I liked the sound of it. As I started my senior year of high school, I became very interested in the idea of buying and selling houses. Unlike my great-uncle and aunt, I didn't really want the hassle of renting houses out. Mainly because I would sometimes go with Uncle to collect rent money, and it was a nightmare. Literally, nobody seemed to ever have the rent money due on rent day. They always needed more time, always! So as a result of my experience in the collection business, I was totally turned off from the whole landlord deal.

Now I will be honest with you: Even though it was definitely against my better judgment, I did try the landlord deal one time, and it was just as I thought—a nightmare! See, you have to have a hard heart and a thick skin to be a landlord. I was just too nice. It was always hard for me to collect money from people who said they just didn't have it! For some reason, I always thought that was the truth, until one day I went to collect rent money from a young man who said he didn't have it because he had just gotten out of jail, but he had a brand-new 52" flat screen television. I would eventually put him out with the help of the sheriff's department and sell my rental property.

Now back to high school. As I said before, I met Hero Number 4 the summer of my senior year of high school. This guy, who was called Romeo, was a real entrepreneur. He owned somewhere in the area of forty to fifty homes, most of which he had purchased with cash money with the intent to flip them. Now, of course, I had no idea what flipping a house meant back then, so he had to explain to me. It simply meant buying a house, fixing it up, and then selling it for a profit. Now that's what I'm talking about, I thought.

I met Romeo on a Monday at a friend's house, and by Friday of the same week, we were the best of friends. We started to hang out, and he slowly let me in on what he did for a living. As far as the buying, the fixing, and the selling of the houses, he would later turn around and sell them for a profit. I thought, *This is one very intelligent young brother.* This was the first time I had ever seen a young black man with a mind-set like his.

He was very business oriented. He knew where he wanted to be in the next five, ten, and twenty years from now. I thought that was pretty impressive, because I had no idea where I wanted to be in the next five, ten, and twenty years from now. Romeo had slowly, but surely, become my new hero! Over the next year or so, he and I would spend more and more time together. He had begun to take me to purchase homes with him, I got to watch his crew fix them up, and even went to closing on several occasions. It was almost like we were a team. On one occasion, he even said that his entire empire could be mine one day if I continued to keep a good head on my shoulders and stayed out of trouble. Now I was positive with what I wanted to do with the rest of my life: I wanted to be an entrepreneur like my hero, Romeo.

Now you're probably wondering why I call Hero Number 4 Romeo, because of course, that's not his real name. Well, just when I thought it couldn't get any better with my new best friend, he finally invited me to his main home one night. He owned several homes, outside of the ones he bought and sold for his business. Each home had at least five bedrooms and four baths. Now you have to understand this was back in the late eighties. Not just anybody could afford a home of that size, unless they had some serious cash flow. Romeo had several. His main home, however, was in one of the most sought out subdivisions in the entire county. It had six bedrooms, six baths, and was huge!

I remember pulling up to the house and thinking, *So this is what a mansion looks like.* The house was absolutely gorgeous inside and outside. Now growing up in the hood, I had never, ever seen anything quiet like this house, so I was totally impressed; but it was what I saw upon entering that made me start calling Romeo Hero Number 4. We entered the house, and there must have been twenty-five to thirty beautiful and scantily dressed women of all nationalities running up to him and calling him Daddy. He looked at me and said, "See anything you like, just pick. She's all yours."

I thought, *I see a lot that I like.* But thank God I didn't sleep with any of them. In retrospect, it seems as though God has always had his hand on me and would not let me go too far, because as bad as I wanted to grow up that night and become a real man, the Lord wouldn't let me. I guess what I'm trying to say is this: Even with all those beautiful, fine women available to me, not just that night but every night, I still felt that there was more to this thing called life than that! So I chose not to indulge in that lifestyle of sin that night.

Another thing that I realized that night was that my new best friend was doing more than just buying and selling houses, I didn't know what, but it was something more than just that. My mother raised me well; she would tell us, "If it looks like a rat and smells like a rat, then it's probably a rat." And she was always right. There was definitely something smelly about my new hero, and it would take about a year for me to find out what it was.

After that night, I stopped hanging out with my new best friend. He would often ask, "What happened? What's wrong? What's going on?" And I would always say, "Oh, nothing. I'm just busy now. I'm not in high school anymore. I'm working full-time now. I don't have much time to hang out. Of course, that wasn't the real reason. I knew something big was about to go down with him, and if I kept hanging out with him, I was going down too! Sure enough, a little over a year after the last time I saw him at one of his homes, I would read about my hero in the local newspaper. It was a Saturday morning, and I was sitting on my front porch playing with my dog when my dad walked up.

He said, "Did you hear about the bust last night?"

I said, "No, what are you talking about?"

There was a smirk on his face. "Your buddy got busted last night with weed, cocaine, and heroin. He's going to be gone for a very long time." I was devastated.

A part of me died that day, because a part of me, let the truth be told, was living through him. At first, I wanted to get upset with my father for bringing the bad news. For a moment, I thought maybe it wasn't true. But then again, if my father knew anything, it was gossip. He knew where to get the story, and where to get it right. I think what made me mad with him on this particular day was that I felt as though it was all his fault that I was out here trying to find a hero for myself because he never was one, and now the hero I thought I had found—someone to look up to, to admire, and to want to be like when I grew up—turned out to be like all the rest: a fake, not at all what or who I thought he was!

I would go on for another four or five years searching for an authentic hero, the same one I'd been searching for my entire life, until I turned twenty-six. Something amazing happened to me when I turned twenty-six years old, I got saved and gave my heart to Jesus! Praise God, what a glorious day; and not only did my life change for the better, but the way I searched for a hero changed as well. Before I got saved I chose my hero's based solely on people who were doing what I wanted to do. Once I got saved, and became wiser, I began to choose my heroes based solely on people who had done what I didn't have to. See, before it was me wanting to do what my heroes were doing, and now it was me not having to do because my heroes had already done! Which led me to three characteristics any authentic hero must have.

1. An authentic hero must be willing to sacrifice.

2. An authentic hero must be persistence.

3. An authentic hero must be able to put others before themselves. So with that being said, I will proudly present to you my top three heroes of all time!

• • • • • • • • • • • • • •

Coming in at number 3 is a man who needs no introduction, but I feel the need to introduce him anyhow. So here goes. My number 3 hero of all time is a man I feel is one of the greatest human beings to ever walk on the face of the earth. His name is Martin Luther King Jr.

Dr. King was born on January 15, 1929, in Atlanta, Georgia. King, both a Baptist minister and civil rights activist, had a seismic impact on race relations in the United States beginning in the mid-1950s. Among many efforts, King headed the SCLC. Through his activism, he played a pivotal role in ending the legal segregation of African American citizens in the South and other areas of the nation, as well as the creation of the Civil Rights Acts of 1964, and the voting right of 1965. King received the Nobel Peace Prize in 1964, at the age of thirty-five, making him the youngest person to ever receive the award. In 1963, he graced the cover of *Time* magazine as their Man of the Year. He would be given many other awards over his short life span before he was assassinated in April 1968. King is still remembered as one of the most lauded African American leaders in history, often referenced by his 1963 speech, "I Have a Dream."

Born Michael King Jr. on January, 15, 1929, Martin Luther King Jr. was the middle child of Michael King Sr. and Alberta Williamson King. The Kings and the Williamsons were rooted in rural Georgia. Martin Jr.'s grandfather A.D.Williams the small struggling Ebenezer Baptist Church with around thirteen members and made it into a forceful congregation. Michael King Sr. stepped in as pastor of Ebenezer Baptist Church upon the death of his father-in-law in 1931. He too became a successful minister and adopted the name *Martin Luther King Sr.* in honor of the German Protestant religious leader Martin Luther. In due time, Michael Junior would follow his father's lead and adopt the name himself. Young Martin had an older sister, Willie Christine, and a younger brother, Alfred Daniel Williams King. The King family grew up in a secure and loving environment. Martin Senior was more the disciplinarian, while his wife's gentleness easily balanced out the father's more strict hand. Though they undoubtedly tried with Martin Junior they couldn't shield him completely from racism. Martin Senior fought against racial prejudice, not just because his race suffered but because he considered racism and segregation to be an affront to God's will. He strongly discouraged any sense of class superiority in his children, which left a lasting impression on Martin Junior.

Growing up in Atlanta, Georgia, Martin Luther King Jr. entered public school at the age of five. In May 1936, he was baptized; but the event made little impression on him. In May 1941, Martin was twelve years old when his grandmother Jennie died of a heart attack. The event was traumatic for Martin, more so because he was watching a parade against his parents' wishes when she died. Distraught at the news, young Martin jumped from a second-story window at the family home, allegedly attempting suicide.

King would attend Booker T. Washington High School, where he was said to be a precocious student. He would graduate at the age of fifteen; and after high school, he would attend

Morehouse College in Atlanta. After graduating Morehouse, he would travel to Boston University to attend Crozer Theological Seminary. Somewhere between Morehouse and Crozer, Martin would meet his beautiful wife Coretta Scott King, settle down in Alabama, and start a family. At the age of twenty-six years old, Martin Luther King Jr. was thrust into the national spotlight when he became the leader of the SCLS. One of their first order of business was a 381-day bus boycott, which was lead by him. After the boycott ended, and the law was passed to segregate the buses, Martin Luther King Jr. became the official face of equality in America.

From 1957 to April 4, 1968, the time of his death, Martin Luther Jr. traveled over 600 million miles, delivered 2,500 speeches, wrote five books, and had dozens of articles written on him in the name of racial equality. These statistics here are mind-boggling. Six hundred million miles traveled over an eleven-year span, and you better believe that most of those miles were walking. It kills me to see this stat, and then to go to a King Day celebration and hear folks complaining about marching two miles in honor of this great man, because what you've got to understand is that the marches that he led in protest and the birthday celebration marches are two totally different marches. The birthday celebration marches held in honor of him are quiet and peaceful, with little to no resistance.

At times, people my age even come out on their porches or place of business and actually cheer you on as you walk down the street. A lot of support for the peaceful birthday celebration march. Of course, this was not the case back in the mid-fifties and the mid-sixties. Not only were the marchers not met with a city full of supporters, but they were oftentimes met with forceful, and sometimes even deadly, resistance! For example, the marchers were met with attack dogs that were let loose on them by the good old police—the very people who made a vow to protect and serve their community. They were also treated like animals when the good old police would take out their water hoses and use the force of the water to contain and stop the marchers, but of course, nothing could stop them. They just kept going, and going, and going. I believe that's where the Energizer bunny got its slogan from. By the time they got to where they were going, not only were they totally exhausted from the march, but they were also soaking wet from the water hoses or nursing flesh wounds left by the attack dogs!

Marching back in those times wasn't a joke. It involved long hours. It was physically demanding, it was degrading, it was humiliating, it was embarrassing, it was painful, and sometimes even deadly; but according to Martin Luther King Jr., marching back in those days was very necessary. I mean, let's face it—we were never going to get our equal rights by simply asking for them! Without every single step taken by every single person in protest of injustice for our people, there's no telling where we would be today! That's why I make it my business to take my six-year-old son out to the local marches every year, and I dare him to say anything about the distance we may be walking; and if he does, I give the whole hour-and-a-half rundown of why we're there in the first place, and it usually stops the complaining.

There's one more part of those amazing statistics that I would like to elaborate on—the over 2,500 speeches delivered by Martin Luther King Jr. in his lifetime. I can't lie. I am a huge fan of his speeches. I love to watch him speak, even though I've heard maybe only twenty to twenty-five of his speeches, which means there are 2,475 speeches of his that I've yet to hear. Wow! At this time, I would like to share parts of my two favorite speeches by Martin Luther King Jr. with you, along with some of my favorite quotes from the man himself.

First, let's take a look at "I Have a Dream," his most famous speech, and certainly one of my all-time favorites. I absolutely love this speech, but there are certain parts of the speech that even until this day, every time I read them, chills run up and down my spine.

These parts are as follows:

I say to you today, my friends that in spite of the difficulties and frustrations of the moment, I still have a dream. It is a dream deeply rooted in the American dream.

I have a dream that one day this nation will rise up and live out the true meaning of its creed: We hold these truth to be self-evident: that all men are created equal.

I have a dream that one day on the red hills of Georgia the sons of former slaves and the sons of former slave owners will be able to sit down together at a table of brotherhood.

I have a dream that my four children will one day live in a nation where they will not be judge by the color of their skin but by the content of their character.

I have a dream that one day every valley shall be exalted, every hill and mountain shall be made low, the rough places will be made plain, and the crooked places will be made straight, and the glory of the Lord shall be revealed, and all flesh shall see it together

This is our hope. This is the faith with which I return to the South.

And if America is to be a great nation this must become true. So let freedom ring from the prodigious hilltop of New Hampshire. Let freedom ring from the mighty mountains of New York. Let freedom ring from the heightening Alleghenies of Pennsylvania!

Let freedom ring from the snowcapped Rockies of Colorado!

Let freedom ring from the curvaceous peaks of California!

But not only that; let freedom ring from Stone Mountain of Georgia!

Let freedom ring from Lookout Mountain of Tennessee!

Let freedom ring from every hill and every molehill of Mississippi. From every mountainside let freedom ring.

When we let freedom ring, when we let it ring from every village and every hamlet, from every state and every city, we will be able to speed up that day when all God's children, black men and white men, Jews and Gentiles, Protestants and Catholics, will be able to join hands and sing in the words of the old Negro spiritual, Free at last! Free at last! Thank God Almighty, we are free at last!

The next speech is actually my favorite Martin Luther King Jr. speech of all time because of one paragraph in the entire eight-page speech that really summed up what type of man he was, and how devoted he was to the cause of equality. The name of this speech is "I've Been to the Mountaintop." This was Dr. King's last and final speech delivered on April 3, 1968. The following is my favorite part in the entire speech, which happens to be the last paragraph:

Like anybody, I would like to live a long life. Longevity has its place. But I'm not concerned about that now. I just want to do God's will. And He's allowed me to go up to the mountain. And I've looked over. And I've seen the Promised Land. I may not get there with you. But I want you to know tonight, that we, as a people, will get to the promised land!

I believe two things to be true the night Martin Luther King Jr. gave his last and final speech.

First of all, I believe that because he was a man of God, he knew in his spirit that he would be assassinated and would not get to the promised land with his people. Meaning, he would not live to see the day when all of God's children are treated fairly and judged not by the color of their skin but, rather, by the content of their character. Just when we thought, as a people, that day was right around the corner, the Trayvon Martin case happens, and we take five huge steps backward!

127

Second, again, because Martin Luther King Jr. was a man of God, I believe God allowed him to not only go to the mountaintop, but also to take a peek over into it and see that it was good; and just like Moses, Martin Luther King Jr. was able to come down from the mountaintop and tell his people that what he saw on the other side of the struggle was good: It's a lot better than where we are now, and I promise you that we as a people, we will get there!

Okay, here are my top ten favorite quotes of all time, starting at number 10:

10. If physical death is the price that I must pay to free my white brothers and sisters from a permanent death of the spirit, then nothing can be more redemptive.

9. Everything that we see is a shadow cast by that which we do not see.

8. At the center of nonviolence stands the principle of love.

7. A riot is the language of the unheard.

6. Our scientific power has outrun our spiritual power. We have guided missiles and misguided men.

5. The ultimate measure of a man is not where he stands in moments of comforts and convenience, but where he stands at times of challenge and controversy.

4. Our lives begin to end the day we become silent about things that matter.

3. The time is always right to do what is right.

2. Injustice anywhere is a threat to justice everywhere.

1. If a man hasn't discovered something that he will die for, he isn't fit to live.

There you have it, ten of my favorite quotes of all time, from my favorite speaker of all time, Dr. Martin Luther King Jr.

• • • • • • • • • • • • •

As I said earlier, an authentic hero must be someone who is willing to sacrifice, persistent, and willing to put others before themselves. So let's see how Hero Number 3 measures up to the three must-haves.

1. Willing to sacrifice

   Well, let's look back at quote number 10, when Martin Luther King Jr. said, "If physical death is the price I must pay to free my white brothers and sisters from a permanent death of the spirit, then nothing can be more redemptive." Not only that, he was jailed over twenty times, stabbed in the chest, and he and his family lived under constant death threats! Willing to sacrifice? Check

2. Persistent

   Over 600 millions miles traveled in an eleven-year span! Enough said. Persistent? Check.

3. Willing to put others before themselves

4. Let's go back to the "I've Been to the Mountaintop" speech, and let's look at the last paragraph when Dr. King talks about looking over the mountaintop and seeing the promised land, and goes on to say, "I might not get there with you, but we as a people will get to the promised land!" Willing to put others before themselves? Check.

   I think I've found an authentic hero in Dr. Martin Luther King Jr.

• • • • • • • • • • • • •

I remember back when I was a kid, my mother would come to an open window in front of our house, stick her head out, and call out to us when it was suppertime. Sometimes I would be right up under the windowsill, just far enough out of sight so she couldn't see me; and after she yelled, I would jump up and say, "Here I am!" She would always say, "Boy, if you were a snake, you would have bit me!"

I often think of that saying when I think about my number 2 hero of all time, because he was truly right there with me the whole time. As a matter of fact, he was there the day I was born, and has been in my corner ever since. The person who comes in at number 2 on my all-time favorite hero list is none other than my big brother, James Darrin Stafford, better known to us as Darrell.

I chose my big brother as one of my all-time favorite heroes because he is! My big brother was born December 28, 1964, in a small town about twenty-eight miles north of Atlanta, Georgia. He was the oldest of three siblings, making him the obvious choice to take over as head of the household when my dad left home. Growing up, my brother was quiet and somewhat shy; however, he had lots of friends. He was more of the introvert kind, who kept to himself, whereas I was more of an extrovert, more of a people's person. Now once my brother got to know you, you were a friend for life.

Even though my brother wasn't that outgoing, he did, however, excel in sports, particularly basketball and football, which he played all throughout recreation, and even some high school, before he was forced to quit school and take care of the family. At that point and time, I believe my brother begin to live his life of sports vicariously through me. Bette Midler sings a song called "Wind Beneath My Wings." My brother doesn't know it, but every time I hear that song, I think of him.

The first verse in the song says it all:

> It must have been cold there in my shadow
> to never have sunlight on your face,
> You were content to let me shine, that's your way,
> You always walked a step behind.

And of course, the song goes on to say,

Did you ever know that you're my hero,
you're everything I would like to be?
I can fly higher than an eagle;
'Cause you are the wind beneath my wings

That verse and chorus of this song describes to a tee the relationship between my brother and me growing up. I always felt as though my brother lived in my shadow, walking behind me, and content with it. When my dad left, it was either me or him to drop out of school and step up to the plate and take over the fatherly duties. My brother looked at my situation with sports and school and probably thought, *He may get a little farther than I would at this time, so I guess it will be me who quits school and take care of him and the rest of the family, and support him the best I can with what I have.* And that's exactly what he did.

About the ninth or tenth grade, my big brother quit school to take care of our family. My brother always kept a job and had his spending money, but now that spending money would become bill-paying money. The entire time my brother supported us, I never saw him miss a day of work, never saw him running late, and I never heard him complain, and we're talking about a teenager here raising another man's family. I never heard him once say, "Why me? Why don't I have a life of my own? Why am I here stuck raising my daddy's family?" Nope.

For the most part, my big brother is very laid back and easygoing; however, if you take the time to upset him, may the lord be with you! I've seen my big brother blow his lid twice in my lifetime. The first was the day he forcefully evicted my dad from our home, which I mentioned earlier in the book; and the second time was the day he went toe to toe with a county sheriff.

Now the second time I saw my brother blow his lid was just as scary as the first, almost. On this particular day, my brother and I were going to the local Laundromat to wash our clothes.

As we proceeded to go up this one-way road that led there, we came face-to-face with this automobile coming down the same way. Now, you have to understand, in the hood, there are no one-way arrows or signs on the road, you just have to figure it out as you go. So we're driving up this road that, according to the county sheriff, was a one-way, in which he was coming down; and eventually, the cars stopped.

Hand motions and words were exchanged by both my brother and the sheriff, and then my brother got out of the car, the sheriff got out of his car, and all heck broke loose! Then they began to go at each other's necks, and after about fifteen minutes of going at it right to the brink of throwing blows, the officer whipped out his badge. I thought, *Oh Lord*—even though I wasn't yet saved back then, I knew whom to call on when I got in trouble—*my big brother is about to go to jail!*

As I said, the officer showed my brother his badge. My brother stopped for a second, looked at the badge, and continued to explain to the officer that he was wrong, and that there wasn't anybody going anywhere until he backed his car up because we had the right of way! The officer turned around, got back into his vehicle, and backed up so we could pass through. When we got to the Laundromat, I asked my brother, "Man, didn't you see that badge?" he said.

"Yeah, I saw it! But right is right, and wrong is wrong, and that man, regardless of who he was, was wrong, and he knew it!" Then he told me something I'll never forget: "Craig, always stand up for what's right!"

Now let's see how Hero Number 2 measures up to the three must-haves for any authentic hero:

1. Willing to sacrifice
    My brother became head of the household when he was fifteen or sixteen years old. This meant all the responsibility

of running a house that now belonged to him, which included being the provider, protector, and visionary. My brother was an excellent provider. He worked all the time, and every penny he made went toward taking care of us. He was a great protector. When he wasn't at work, he was home with his family. As far as a visionary, I believe at that time in our lives, our only vision was to someday make a better life for our children than we had for ourselves. My brother always sacrificed—he sacrificed his teenage years to raise a family that wasn't his; he sacrificed his friends, and girlfriends, for us. Everything he wanted to do had to be scheduled around what needed to be done in the house first. For example, if I had basketball practice or a game on Friday night, my brother couldn't go out with the fellows or on a date until after my practice or game was over. Any girl whom he dated back then understood that his family came first, which is probably not how it should've been, but because of my brother's dedication to his family, that was the way it was.

I always knew my big brother would make a great husband and father because of the way he took care of us. As I sit here and think about all the many sacrifices my brother made for me and our family, I'm reminded of the biggest sacrifice he ever made for me in 1984. I was in the eighth grade. As I have said, growing up in a small town, hood basketball was about all we had to do with our spare time, and we would literally go from house to house playing basketball; and eventually, I would fall in love with the sport. So of course, when it came time for the eighth grade basketball tryouts, I tried out, and of course, I made the team. Now I'm not bragging or anything, but back in those days, if you could make a left-handed layup, you were on the team. I remember coming home and telling my brother, "I made the team man!"

He looked at me and said, "Little bro, that's awesome!"
I said, "There's only one little problem."
"What is it?"
I told him the team shoes they required us to wear that year was the brand Air Jordans. He said, "Man, that's great. I love those shoes!"

Then I went on to explain to him that I was responsible for buying them, and all of a sudden, it hit him, and he had this look on his face that simply said, *Little bro, you know we cannot afford an $80 pair of basketball shoes.* I looked at him and said, "I know. I'll just wear what I got. I'm sure you don't have to have those particular shoes to play. They probably just said that to make us go and buy them and make Michael Jordan rich. I'll be alright. Shoes ain't never made a player anyway. The player makes the shoes!"

Now you have to understand that back in those days, we didn't live from check to check— we lived two checks behind. My grandmother would say it like this: "Hun, it's gone before I can even get it." As a child, of course I didn't quite understand exactly what she meant by that statement. I mean, how could a check be gone before you even cashed it? But my brother, as the new head of the household, knew exactly what she meant. Our house was paid for, which kept it from going into foreclosure; but every service we had stayed at least two months behind. The light bill, the water bill, the gas bill, the telephone bill, etc. So to have any extra money for anything other than food was impossible. I remember going to my room that night, grabbing my old torn-up dirty basketball shoes, getting a warm washcloth, and wiping them off to get them ready for the season opener. After I got them all shiny and looking brand new, I looked up and saw my brother standing in the doorway.

He said, "When do you need the shoes?"

"Next Tuesday," I said.

He said, "Let me see what I can do. I can't make any promises, but let me see what I can do."

"Okay," I said.

• • • • • • • • • • • • • • •

I went to practice the rest of the week in my torn-up basketball shoes. And then came game day. I had worn a pair of dress shoes that I borrowed from my brother because we had to dress up on game day. This was cool with me, because no one knew whether I had the new Air Jordans, which was perfectly fine with me because the longer I could go without revealing the truth about me not having the team shoes, the better off I would be.

Finally school was over, and we all loaded up on the bus to travel to our first game of the season about fifteen or twenty miles away. Now back then, if you were on the boys' team, you had to watch the first half of the girls' game, which was about another thirty minutes I could hold off the moment of truth. Halftime of the girls game would come and the moment of truth would be upon me. We went into the locker room, sat down and went over our pregame warm-ups, and then came time to get dressed. I remember looking around the locker room at everyone, watching them pull out their brand-new Air Jordans; and it hit me: This was going to be tougher than I thought, because everyone had them except for me! I changed my clothes, reached into my gym bag, and pulled out my old, torn-up basketball shoes and put them on. I remember feeling so inadequate, somewhat embarrassed, and not even feeling that I belonged on the same court with the rest of the guys, not because of my basketball game— because I had earned starting position—but because I couldn't afford the game shoes that everyone else had on.

Oddly enough, no one said a word as we lined up and ran out of the locker room into the gym. We ran out onto the court and started warming up. Then all of a sudden, I heard someone calling, "Craig, over here?" I looked around, and there was my big brother, standing in the doorway with a red-and-black box in his hand. He looked at me and said, "I have something for you. Come and get 'em!"

I looked at my coach and motioned to him that I'd be right back, and then I went and got my game shoes. A brand-new pair of Air Jordans size 9.5. I grabbed the box, sat down, took the old ones off, and put on the new. I'll never forget it. I was, as the old folks would say, grinning from ear to ear! That night I played the best basketball of my career. It was the best game ever! I don't know if it was because of the shoes or because I knew my big brother had made a way out of no way for me to have them. When I got home that night, my brother met me at the door and asked, "Did ya'll win?"

I said, "Shoot, yeah!"

He said, "Did you play well?"

"Shoot, yeah. Now I have a question for you."

"What is it?"

"Where in the world did you get the money for these shoes?"

He said, "Don't worry. I got 'em, didn't I."

I said, "Yes, you did, but you didn't do anything illegal, did you?"

He said, "No, fool!"

"Just checking," I said.

The next day, when I got home from school, I sat down to watch a little television, but the television didn't come on. I got up and turned on the lights, and they didn't come on either, and it became clear to me where my brother got the money for my brand-new shoes. I got up to go to his room to see what the problem was—as if I didn't already know, but my little sister had already beat me there, because by now, she too knew something was going on with the power.

We arrived at his room at the same time with the same question: "Why is the power off?"

My brother looked over my sister's head at me and said, "Yesterday a decision had to be made. Because of the decision that was made, we will be without lights for at least two weeks."

My sister stomped her feet and stormed out the room. I told my brother, "Man, you really didn't have to do that. I would have been just fine!"

He said, "Do you like the shoes?"

I said, "Of course!"

He said, "Well, some sacrifices are worth making, and I felt this was one of them. Don't worry, Mama and our sister will be all right." He smiled and shut his door.

Willing to sacrifice. Check!

2. Persistent

Well, let's see, as I said before, my big brother dropped out of high school when he was about fifteen or sixteen years old and didn't get his GED until he was in his late twenty or early thirties. During the time when he was waiting to get his own GED, he worked to put his wife through college and made sure that both of his girls would be able to graduate college themselves, before he pursued his goal to further his own education. Just like the old saying goes, "Good things come to those that wait."

Not only does my brother have his GED, but he also has plans of taking even more classes to further his education in the near future. To talk to him, you would think you were talking to a Harvard graduate. He has really educated himself very well. I almost have to get a dictionary out when he comes over because I know he's going to use at least one word that I'm going to have no idea what it means. Overall, my brother's persistence has really paid off. He's doing very well. He has a daughter who just graduated with her PHD, and another daughter who just graduated with her Bachelor's Degree, and is preparing to pursue her Master's this summer.

He has a beautiful, well-educated family. I'm very proud of my big brother. When I grow up, I want to be just like him! I even ask the Lord sometimes, "Lord, why have you chosen me to do the things you've called me to do? I mean, if I were you, and I had to choose one of my dad's boys to do something great, or small, for my kingdom of God, it would definitely be my brother. And time and time again, the Lord keeps telling me, "I don't choose the qualified. I qualify the chosen.

The fact that it took my brother almost fifteen years to get his GED is inspiring to me. He never gave up hope, and he hung in there until he achieved that which he set out to achieve. Persistent. Check!

3. Willing to put others before themselves

Well, let's see. I think we've already seen that my big brother had no problem doing just that. However, there is a story I would like to share with you. Growing up in our house, there was only one car—my brother's—so when we needed to go somewhere, he had to take us, or if he was in a good mood, he would sometimes let me drive. Such was supposed to be the case this particular weekend.

For about six months, I worked at KFC alongside my brother, and often, I would check his work schedule out to see what Saturday nights he worked, because if he worked on a Saturday night and I offered to wash his car, he would usually let me borrow it to go out that night. I went into work on Wednesday, checked the schedule for the week, and found out my brother was working on Saturday night. Then I put my plan in motion. I got up early Saturday morning, cut the grass, and, by noon, took the car to the carwash to vacuum it out and wash it up. I would take it to the carwash to put water on it, but the real work wouldn't take place until I got it back home. That's where I would detail it and make it look pretty.

After I finished washing the car around three or four, it was time for my brother to go to work. He walked up and said, "Man, the car looks good." I just knew I was going to get the car for tonight, so much so I had already called my girlfriend to let her know I would be over around six o'clock. My brother got into his freshly cleaned car and went to work. I was totally shocked, because usually, when he would let me borrow his car, he would let me take him to work and drop him off, and then I would get the car for the night. But not this time.

So I gave him about twenty minutes to call me and tell me to come and get the car. When he didn't, I called him. "Hey bro, what's up with the car? Can I get it tonight?"

He said, "Nope, I got a date tonight."

I was totally upset—not only because I had spent my entire Saturday afternoon washing his car, which he, not I, was now going to use on a date, but because I had to call my girlfriend and cancel our plans. Most of the time, my brother was willing to put others before himself, but not this time. I remember thinking, *This girl he's going out with tonight must be pretty dog gone special.* And she was. My brother married her, and they've been married for twenty-seven years and have two beautiful daughters.

• • • • • • • • • • • • • •

The following Monday, when I arrived at school, my girlfriend came up to me and said, "You've got to make up for Saturday night. Ride the bus home with me." Now, this was not a good idea. First of all, it was a school night, and I couldn't go out on school nights. Second, she lived on the other side of town, and if I rode home with her, I wouldn't have a way to get home myself. My girlfriend lived with her father, and he didn't have a car, so if I went home with her, I would be totally stranded. I thought about it for about thirty seconds and said, ""Okay, what bus line are you in?" She told me what bus line, and I said, "Okay, I'll meet you there at 2:10 p.m." I went home with her, we hung out all day long, and had a great time; and before we knew it, it was nighttime.

Now I had a problem: how in the world was I going to get home? Her father had made it perfectly clear I could come and hang out for as long I wanted to, but I could not spend the night! My first thought was one of my best friends. At the time, his parents had several cars, and he usually could use one whenever he wanted to. I called him up at about eight o'clock and said, "Hey man, I'm at my girlfriend's house, and I need a ride home. Can you get one of your folks' cars and come and get me?"

He said, "Man, I got in trouble today at school. My parents put me on lockdown." My heart sank, because I was really depending on my boy to save the day, or should I say save the night, because by now, it was good and dark, and my girlfriend wasn't going to let me walk home by myself.

In retrospect, this is when I should have called my brother and asked him to come and pick me up, but I didn't I waited for another five hours before I called him. See, the longer I waited, the harder it became to pick up the phone and call. I think I called everybody I knew to come and get me that night. I called people I didn't even like, because I really did not want to hear my brother's mouth about me over at my girlfriend's house on a school night in the first place. Not only that, but now it was one in the morning, and he had to be at work at five. If I called him now, waking him up, talking about some come-and-get-me when my butt should be at home, oh, he was going to be very, very upset!

So I sat there for another ten minutes or so until my girlfriend's dad finally came into the room and said, "Son, you're going to have to call your brother to come and get you. It's one in the morning."

"Yes, sir." I picked up the phone and called my brother. It was the hardest thing I'd ever had to do in my entire fifteen years of living, but I had to do it. I called, He answered the phone, I said, "Bro, I'm over at my girlfriend's house, and I need a ride home."

He didn't say a word; he just hung up the phone. Within about twenty minutes, he was there. I remember telling my girlfriend, "If you don't see me tomorrow, it's because my brother is going to kill me tonight!" I got in the car, and he didn't say a word the entire twenty-minute ride home. I remember thinking, *He's going to really let me have it when we get home.* We pulled into the driveway, he got out the car, walked into the house, and went straight to his room and went to bed. He got up the next morning, after about two and a half hours of sleep, and he went to work; and to this day, he's never said a word about that night.

Willing to put others before themselves. Check!

• • • • • • • • • • • • • •

Finally, we have arrived at number 1 on my list of all-time favorite heroes. My introduction for this guy would go something like this: When I was lost, he saved me;

when I was down, he raised me; when I was abandoned, he claimed me; and when I was nameless, he named me. Not only that, but I hear he's a father to the fatherless, he's healer to the sick, he's peace to the restless, he's deliverance to those who are bound, and he's life to those who are dead. His name is Jesus.

I was twenty-six years old when I met Hero Number 1. I met him in an apartment at about two o'clock in the morning. I was face down on the floor feeling like I was dying from a heart attack. I'll never forget that night for as long I live. It was a Saturday night, and my best friend and I had hooked up early that day to go out and start drinking. I think we got together about eleven o'clock that morning.

Now that morning, like any other Saturday morning for me, would start out with my usual Saturday breakfast, which consisted of a forty-ounce of malt liquor. We rode around and drank from eleven in the morning, till midnight. At about twelve thirty, my buddy dropped me off at my apartment. I stumbled up the steps, opened the door, and fell to the floor. *Plop!* And I pretty much stayed right there on that floor till about two o'clock in the morning. I remember just lying there for what seemed like forever. Suddenly my chest started tightening, and sharp pains soon followed.

Now, I had never had a heart attack before, but I remembered what comedian Richard Pryor said about having one in one of his stand-up performances. And from what he described, and from what I felt, I knew I was having a heart attack. So I did what anyone, whether saved or not, would do: I began to pray, and hoped I was praying to a real God, because I needed some real help! I said, "God, if you save me tonight, I'll serve you for the rest of my life."

And it was as if God himself said, "Finally, I have your attention!" God saved me that night from a physical death, and a couple months later, he would save me from a spiritual death.

But let me show you how Satan works. I had a friend who was always trying to get me to come to church with him. It had gotten so bad that every time he would call and ask me to come over, I would come up with an excuse, because I didn't want to hear about how drinking was bad, and how I was going to hell if I didnt repent for my sins and get baptized. Basically, his message to me every time he saw me was, "Brother, you need Jesus!" And for some reason, that night, as I lay on the floor in my one-bedroom apartment, my friend was the first person, and the only person, I thought of.

It's funny how God works things out. This just happened to be on a Saturday night, which meant church was the following day, so I called my friend at about two thirty in the morning to let him know I was going to church with him tomorrow. He said. "Okay, I'll be at your house around eleven o'clock."

I said, "Eleven o'clock!"

He said, "Yeah, church doesn't start till twelve."

I remember thinking, *Who goes to church at noon?* Now, this is how Satan works: The next day, I woke up about ten forty-five. I, sat in my La-Z-Boy chair, and thought to myself since I was feeling much better I'll just stay at home today, I don't need to go to church. I got up and was headed towards the refrigerator to get my breakfast for the day, an ice cold Keystone Light. As soon as I grabbed the can I heard a knock at the door, I went to the door and said, "Who is it?" The voice on the other side responded, "It's Jeremiah."

I said, "Oh yeah, I meant to call you this morning. I changed my mind about that church thing. I feel much better today!" I mean, after all, I had prayed that same prayer hundreds of times before; but God knew there was something different about this time. He knew I was ready, and that's why he made sure my friend got to my apartment before I popped the top on breakfast. God knew, as well as I did, if I had popped the top on that beer and started drinking it, I wouldn't have gone to church that day, and I would have probably never gotten saved! My friend knocked again, and I said to myself, *Man, I'm going to have to open this door.* I opened the door, and he walked in and said, "Put the beer down. We're going to church,"

I said, "Man, I told you I'm good,"

He said, "That's not what you told me last night. Last night you said you were dying, and if God saved you through the night, you wanted to come to church today."

I said, "Yeah, I was drunk last night, but I'm telling you, I'm fine now!"

He said, "Craig, I'm going to give you five minutes to get dressed, and we're leaving."

I thank God to this day that my friend happened to be a Georgia Tech football star who stood about six feet two and weighed about 280 pounds, so when he says "Get your clothes on" and "Let's go," if you have any sense, you better get your clothes and get moving. I had one more trick up my sleeve: I told him I didn't have anything to wear to church. He went through my closet, picked out some dress pants that didn't even fit anymore, and told me to put them on. Then he found a shirt, which I didn't know was in the closet, and tossed it to me and told me to put it on and button it up.

"Yes, sir," I said, and off we went to church. I'm so grateful to my friend Jeremiah for doing what the Lord told him to do, in spite of me. My friend had already told me what time church started, but, what he failed to tell me was what time it ended, so I asked. He told me they usually got out around three o'clock, but sometimes they went on longer if the spirit was moving.

I said, "Three o'clock! You gotta be out of your mind!" Now I didn't know what the spirit was, nor did I know what it looked like when it was moving, but I did know this much: I wasn't fixing to sit in nobody's church for no three hours! So upon arriving at the church, I already had a chip on my shoulder. But that chip would quickly disappear as soon as I walked through those doors.

The first thing I noticed was that the people were very friendly. They all spoke to me and made me feel that they were glad I was there. Then I sat down on the back row, and after a couple of songs and a few testimonies, the pastor began to preach, and it seemed as though he had an audience of one—me. He preached my life story, and without knowing me, he told me everything I had done and everything I was doing; but before he sat down, he said four words that sounded like sweet music to my ears. He said, "Whatever you're going through, God can fix it. Just bring it to him!"

God can fix it! To this day, those four words are like sweet music to my ears. See, now that I've been saved for almost twenty years, I understand that those words are not just words. They are power, and food for the believer to live by. I would like to pass those words on to my young male readers who may feel like all hope is gone, and there is nothing more to life than what they are experiencing. I'd like to tell you that God can fix it—not only can he, but he wants to. Just bring it to him in prayer, and he will do the rest.

As I said, I've been saved now for almost twenty years, and God has used me to minister through a lot of different ministries, but none more so than the one he called me to start myself, which is appropriately named God's Posse Ministries. GPM is a ministry for young men between the ages of twelve and eighteen. The purpose of this ministry is to lead the young off the streets and into the kingdom of God. We do this through the bond of brotherhood. I started God's Posse Ministries on September 20, 2004, and from then until now, we have had the opportunity to minister to hundreds of young men through various outreach events, none more so than our annual 3-on-3 basketball tournaments.

We've been doing our 3-on-3 basketball tournament for almost ten years now, and we've had over 150 teams in attendance, and almost ninety young men come to know Jesus Christ for the first time. Not bad. I thank God every day that he had seen something in me that was worth saving, and worth using! It's good to know that when people write you off, God can still write you in—your name in the Book of Life, that is!

Now let's see how Hero Number 1 measures up to the three must-haves for any authentic hero.

1. Willing to sacrifice

Well, let's see, The Bible tells us in John 3:16, "For God so loved the world, that he gave his only begotten Son, that whosoever believeth in him, should not perish, but have everlasting life."

I tell people all the time, "You better be glad I'm not God, because it would be extremely difficult for me to give up either of my son's lives for someone whom I don't even know, but God did! Not only that, but the Bible says in Romans 5:8, "But God commendeth his love towards us, in that, while we were yet sinners, Christ died for us."

Not only did Jesus die for us, but he did it while we were still jacked up! What an awesome God. He didn't wait for us to get our stuff together before he sacrificed his son to die on the cross for our sin. No he made the ultimate sacrifice while we were aliens, and he himself was a stranger to us. Sacrifice. Check!

2. Persistent

The best example of Jesus's persistence with me is found in Luke 22:40–44.

> And when he was at the place, he said unto them, Pray that ye enter not into temptation. And he was withdrawn from them about a stone's cast, and kneeled down, and prayed, Saying, Father, if thou be willing, remove this cup from me; nevertheless not my will, but thine, be done. And there appeared an angel unto him from heaven strengthening him. And being in agony he prayed more earnestly; and his sweat was as if great drops of blood falling down to the ground.

Persistence. Check!

3. Willing to put others before themselves

Hebrews 12:2 reads,

> Looking unto Jesus the author and finisher of our faith; who for the joy that was set before him endured the cross, despising the shame, and is set down at the right hand of the throne of God.

Every time I see this passage of scripture in the Bible I can't help but to think that the joy that was set before Jesus while he was nailed to the cross, was us. It was you, it was me, it was all of mankind. In other words, we can say that for mankind Jesus endured the death of the cross.

Willing to put others before himself. Check!

• • • • • • • • • • • • •

Now I cannot tell you who your hero should be—that's for you to decide, and for you only. But I can tell you who your hero could be. It could be the person, male or female, who has made the biggest sacrifice of his or her own life so that you could make the best out of yours. Or the person, male or female, who has shown great persistence in helping you pursue your dream while theirs remains on hold. How about the male or female who has put you first in their life from day one? Their one and only priority in life is to make sure you are well taken care of. All I ask is this: As you evaluate what an authentic hero is, you do it with a different mind-set.

Think not about the person who can dunk a basketball, run a football, or hit a baseball; instead, think about the person in your life who has been willing to sacrifice for you, persistent for you, and the person who is willing to put you before themselves. I think it was Charles Barkley who once said, "I'm not paid to be a role model. Parents should be role models." In my opinion, it's okay for an athlete to be heroic without that person being considered a hero. Now there is a lot of stuff that Mr. Barkley said that I don't agree with, but this is not one of them. I totally agree with him in that. Professional athletes, entertainers, and movie stars should not be our kids' choice for an authentic hero, especially if they have food on their table, clothes on their back, and a roof over their head. They shouldn't have to look any farther than their own home, because as I've said before, an authentic hero is someone who is willing to sacrifice, is persistent, and is willing to put others before themselves.

We're living in a bad day and time when our children, especially our young men, have to find role models and heroes from a group of murderers, rapists, and adulterers. I challenge my young readers: take a good look around your own home. Can't you find someone worthy to be called a hero? To sum it all up, an authentic hero is someone who has done something heroic on your behalf. What do I mean by this? I'm glad you asked.

Can you think back to a time in your life where either Mom, Dad, Grandmother, Grandfather, your brother or your sister did something heroic on your behalf? Meaning if they didn't do whatever it was they did, you wouldn't have been able to do whatever it was you were able to do. Now think back to a time in your life where LeBron James, Kobe Bryant, or Michael Vick did the same thing for you. My point exactly: an authentic hero is someone who does something heroic on your behalf.

The Eight Responsibilities of a Father

And ye shall teach them your children, speaking of them
when thou sittest in thine house, and when thou walkest
by the way, when thou liest down, and when thou risest up.
[Deuteronomy 11:19]

He rises up early in the morning before the rooster crows, grabs
a cup of coffee, a bagel, and out the door he goes.

He arrives home late after the sun has already set, and before
I can tell him about my day, he replies, "Son, not now. I really
need the rest."

He enters the house, kicks off his shoes, and leaves them at
the door.

He grabs the remote control, turns on the television (to
SportsCenter, of course) to check out all the latest scores.

On the weekend, I often ask my father, "Can we go to the
park and play?"

His response always seems to be the same. "With all this
work, son, I'm sorry, there's just no way!"

Oh, how I always wanted my father and me to be the best
of friends.

Instead, I often feel like I never met the man!

Fathers, is this you? Statistics have shown the average father
spends about seven and a half minutes a week talking to his son.
That's right, a week! With most of the conversation between the

two resulting in small talk about topics such as sports, cars, and, of course, girls. Seven and a half minutes a week!

The first time I heard this stat, it really blew my mind; and to be honest, I didn't believe it—so much so that I thought, *How in the world could that be?* However, now that I'm married and have a teenage son of my own, it has become clear to me how something like this could be possible. If you are a parent of a teenage boy, then you already know that holding a conversation with him for more than two minutes is like setting a new Guinness record—unless, of course, you are talking about something that interests them, like sports, cars, or girls. If you think about it, the average conversation between the average father and the average son will probably go something like this:

"Hey son."

"Hi, Dad."

"How was your day?"

"It was fine."

"How was school?"

"Good."

Then the son might ask, "Are the Hawks playing tonight?"

Dad responds, "Yes."

The son might ask, " Who are they playing?"

Dad responds, "The Bulls."

"All right, talk to you later, Dad."

"Okay, son."

Lets take a look at this average conversation between an average father and an average son. The conversation itself took about fifteen seconds. Multiply that by seven, and you have 1:45 seconds a week. For the average father that's not a lot of time conversating with his son. On the contrary, the average teenage boy spends somewhere between three to five hours a day Monday to Friday, and on the weekends somewhere between eight to eleven hours watching television. This consists of watching television programs, watching movies, or playing video games.

And we as parents wonder where we're losing our sons, and how in the world they could turn out the way they have.

The answer is quite simple. We're not parenting our kids anymore; the television is. Or if it's not the television, it's the computer. If it's not the computer, it's the iPod, and if it's not the iPod, it's the iPad. Let's face it, we as parents, with our measly 1:45 seconds a week cannot compete with hours upon hours of BET, MTV, SPIKE TV, Xbox, Xbox Live, Nintendo, Game Boy, Wii, Lil Wayne, TI, 50 Cent, and so on and so forth. No competition! We are losing the battle for our young men's hearts, minds, and their souls!

In this chapter, I would like to address the fathers who are in their sons' homes but not in their lives. Do you know it's possible to live in the same house, eat from the same table, share the same family with your sons, and still be aliens to one another? For the rest of this chapter, I would like to share with you my top eight responsibilities of a father. Notice I said a father, not a baby daddy. A baby daddy's job is over at the point of conception; however, a father's job is just beginning. Baby daddy's look for ways to get out of their responsibilities, and fathers look for ways to fulfill their responsibilities. It doesn't take much to be a baby daddy, just being in the wrong place at the wrong time; but it takes a lot to be a father. Being a father means you have to be at the right place at the right time. You have to be where your son needs for you to be when he needs you to be there. So with that being said, here are my top eight responsibilities of a father, starting at number eight.

• • • • • • • • • • • • •

Cheerleader/Supporter

Now when I say cheerleader, I don't mean the ones you see on the sidelines singing two bits, four bits, six bits, a dollar all for the Black Knights stand up and holla. No, I'm not talking about that, but what I am saying is this: we as fathers must be our sons' biggest supporters. You must observe them early on and see what it is that they are passionate about, and then if it's morally and spiritually acceptable in your household, you must get behind them 110 percent. For example, I'm an athlete, so obviously, when my first son was born, my initial thought was, *Lord, please let him be taller than me so he can fulfill my dream of becoming a professional basketball player.*

And just as I prayed, the Lord did bless my son with the tall gene, but something unexpected happened when he was about two years old: he began to show an interest in music. Now I have never played an instrument before in my life and can't hold a note of any kind; however, when I saw the passion my son had developed for the guitar and the drums, I went out and bought him a brand-new guitar; and for Christmas that same year, we bought him a brand-new set of drums. Next stop for him was lessons, because the truth of the matter was, it was not my dream anymore.

I have faced the fact that I will never be another Spud Webb. I'll never play in the NBA, and I'm cool with that. It's all about my son now, and what God has called him to do with his life, and whatever that may be, guess what, if it's spiritually and morally acceptable in my household, then I am behind my son 110 percent!

The biggest mistakes that we make as fathers with our sons is when we try to make our dreams their dreams. Our sons may be little versions of us, but they are not an extension of us. God gave us dreams to fulfill, and he gave them their own dreams to fulfill. The problem with most dads occurs when the dream they've been dreaming for years fail to be realized in their lifetime, or in their sons.

I'm reminded of one of my good friends growing up. His father was an All-County baseball player. And he would often tell anyone who would listen that the only reason he was All-County and not an All-American was that he was too short and too slow. So naturally, when his first son was born, he began to research food that he could feed him to make him grow tall. And he also would physically stretch his son's body, determined to make him taller than he was. Not only that, but from the time his son was old enough to run, he would make him run ten forty-yard dashes a day; and each year he had to run it faster than he did the year before. By the time he reached high school, it seemed as though all the hard work had paid off. His son was taller than him, faster than him, and a much better athlete than he was.

Now with all that being said, his son, just like his father, was an All-County baseball player—nothing more, nothing less. And when he was offered a scholarship from a small college out in the middle of nowhere. He turned it down. Not because the school was small and he always dreamed of playing at a Division 1 school, but because he hated baseball and he didn't want to spend the next four years of his life doing something he hated doing. After all, he had spent the last fifteen years of his life playing baseball, a sport he despised for a man he despised; and he decided he just could not do it any longer, especially on the college level, where it would be very demanding.

It's funny because when he confronted his father, I was actually with him. We walked into his parents' room, and his dad asked him, "Why did you turn down that baseball scholarship?" My friend looked at his dad with resentment in his eyes and said, "Dad, I've never liked baseball! Never! The only reason I've been playing for the last fifteen years is you made me play—because it's always been your dream to play in the Major Leagues. It never was mine, and I was always too scared to tell you how I really felt about the sport. But not anymore! The truth is, I can't stand baseball, and I can't stand you! I've always wanted to play football, and you never would let me, instead, making me waste my entire youth years on a sport that I cannot stand! Dad, you know how you would always say you felt like I wasn't giving the sport my all? Well, you were exactly right. I never gave it my all, because I never wanted to be in it in the first place!"

His dad's response to him not only was shocking, but it was something I'll never forget for as long as I live. He said, "You are a terrible excuse for a son and the biggest failure I've ever seen in my entire life. Now get out of my room before I whip your little butt!"

I remember leaving the room with my friend, thinking, *You are absolutely right. He is a terrible you, but he is an awesome him! He may have failed at your dreams, but he's going to do great with his own.*

As I said before, our sons are not extensions of us. God has made them fearfully and wonderfully individual, with the key word being *individual*. Even though they may walk like you, talk like you, and even act like you, they are not you, and they could, or could not, share the same passion, and have the same desire in life as you do. If your son happens to have the same passions and desires for the same things in life as you do, then glory be to God. You guys will always have something to talk about; but if he doesn't, it's your job as a father to figure out what he's passionate about and have a great desire for, and if it's morally and spiritually acceptable in your home, then you need to get behind your son 110 percent and become his biggest cheerleader. Because, as you can see, with the story of my friend, oftentimes, when we try to fulfill our dreams through our sons, not only could it lead to them missing out on their God-given purpose here on earth, but it could also cause your son to despise and resent you, when it's all said and done.

I talk to fathers all the time who are heartbroken because their sons despise them and don't want to have anything to do with them. After a short counseling session, I'll begin to ask questions about their son's upbringing. For example, "What was your son's childhood like? After about five or ten minutes of talking with the father about the upbringing of his son, I usually can see exactly where the problem occurred. The father would say something to this effect, "I was probably a little hard on him, but I just wanted him to make something out of himself, and to be somebody."

Fathers, we've got to be careful. It's not our job to make our sons somebody. God has already done that, it's our job to sit back and watch them become somebody! Often, we as fathers are trying to turn our sons into the person we would love to see them be, instead of sitting back and watching them become the person God has already made them to be. To this day, I still find it hard to believe that my friend would spend that much time of his life trying to please his father when it was tearing him up on the inside; but then again, maybe it's not, because little boys love to impress their mommies, but that they live to please their daddies. This is evident to me every time I take my six-year-old into the backyard to play football.

As I said before, my six-year-old loves music, but now he's also acquired this passion and desire to play football. He eats football, he drinks football, and he sleeps football. Literally, he sleeps with the football in his bed. Anyhow, every time we go out into the backyard to play football before we start the game, he'll run over to his mother and say, "Mommy, which team do you like?" She'll say, "Yours, sweetie!" Then when he catches a pass or runs a touchdown, he'll come to me and say, "Daddy, did I do good?" And I'll say, "Sure, son, you did awesome!"

Little boys love to impress their mommies, but they live to please their daddies. Fathers, don't be afraid to tell your sons that you are proud of them, because you have no idea how important those four words will become to your sons as they make the transition from boyhood to manhood.

Fathers, when was the last time you told your sons you were proud of them? Just because they're your son, not because they broke the homerun-scoring record, or rushing record at their school. Not because they're the class president and was recently voted most likely to succeed, and not because they have maintained a 4.0 grade point average and are on their way to

Harvard. Now all these things are great, don't get me wrong; but you should tell your sons on a regular basis that you are proud of him just because he's your son. I tell my sons all the time that I'm proud of them. I tell my six-year-old so often he looked at me the other day and said, "Dad, you tell me that every day. I get it!"

I said, "Good, because you need to get it, and you need to get it good!"

Fathers, what I mean when I say we should be our sons biggest cheerleader/supporter is this: We should never try to fit our sons into our mold, so that we can fulfill our dreams through them, because in the end, they just might resent and despise us for it. On the other hand, when they find something they do well and are passionate about, as long as it is spiritually and morally acceptable in your home, don't be afraid to tell your sons that you're proud of them, and support them 110 percent.

• • • • • • • • • • • • • •

Counselor

Isaiah 9:6 reads, "For unto us a child is born, unto us a son is given: and the government shall be upon his shoulders: and his name shall be called Wonderful, Counselor, The Mighty God, The everlasting Father, The prince of Peace."

In this passage of scripture, the Bible refers to God as a wonderful Counselor, the father of the universe, and our Heavenly Father is known as a wonderful counselor. Which leads me to believe that we as earthly fathers should also be our sons' counselors. Maybe not wonderful, because we are not perfect, but definitely their counselors. I looked up the word counselor, and it is defined: a person who counsels, or an adviser. An adviser—I found that interesting and thought, as fathers we are responsible for advising our sons, or better yet, for giving them advice pertaining to life.

I personally believe there are six stages of life when we fathers are responsible for giving our sons advice that will shape and mold them into the men that God has called them to be.

. . . .

Stage 1: Boundaries (0–2)

From our sons' birth until the age of two, we should advise or counsel our sons in the area of setting boundaries. Setting boundaries for our sons is one of the important responsibilities of a father, if not the most important. However, it is also the most difficult. Why, I am not quite sure, but it might have something to do with the fact that most fathers don't know exactly when or how to set them. When it's simple, you set boundaries for your sons as soon as they understand the difference between right and wrong. I set boundaries with my six year old when he was about six months old. Since every child is different, we are still working with my nineteen-month-old. He hasn't quite gotten it yet. The deal is, you know your son better than anyone else, and you will know when it's time to set boundaries for him.

The reason we have terrible twos is that we have disobedient six-month-olds who turn into defiant one-year-olds, who turn into rebellious eighteen-month-olds, which produce terrible two-year-olds. The reason this happens is that often, when they're that young, everything they do seems to be cute to us; and by the time they reach two or three, it's not cute anymore. But by now, they've been doing it for so long they're pretty much set in their ways, and we don't do anything to disturb them. Okay, that takes care of the *when*. Not let's look at the *how*. Well, the how is simple as well—with discipline.

What is discipline? I'm glad you asked. Discipline is whatever form of punishment that works on your child. Growing up, discipline meant one word—a spanking. Every time I messed up, no matter what I did; the punishment was always a spanking. Now that's fine and dandy if it works, and to be honest with you it didn't always work, but for my father it was the only form of discipline he used. With that being said I'll say this, "A spanking is the correct form of discipline only if it works. If it doesn't, it's just exercise, and a way for us to get out our frustration with our child." Every child is different, as a result, what worked for one may not work for the other. For example, when my six year was about two or three we tried the spanking with him and it didn't work. We would spank him for something he did wrong and within hours he was right back at it. Then one day my wife said, "Why don't we try time-out with him?" We did, and we found he hates confinement. Guess what, time-out is our form of discipline when it comes to our six year old. For my nineteen month, now that's a whole other story. The beauty of discipline is trial and error, you keep trying different forms of discipline until you find something that works, and then you apply it as the correct form of discipline for your kids.

Fathers, I do believe that one of the main purposes for setting boundaries is to teach our sons how to come under authority, and respect it. As we know, the reason this is so important is that throughout life, we all have to come under someone's authority, and respect it. And to be honest with you, it's a lot easier to set boundaries for a toddler than it is for a teenager. Look at it like this: have you ever wondered how life would be on our highways if there wasn't a speed limit. I mean, you could drive as fast as your car would go, for as long as you wanted to, every single day. I know some of you guys are saying, "Wow, that would be great!"

And it would be for a short time, but eventually, a major accident would occur, because driving without a speed limit is a major train wreck just waiting to happen. Same could be said about the young men who are in our society living a life without boundaries. We see it all the time—young men having no respect for their parents, for themselves, for authority, and even for life itself, doing exactly what they want to do, when they want to do it, how they want to do it, and as often as they want to do it;

and nobody can tell them anything. Fathers, all I am saying is this: if we don't set boundaries for our boys, someone else will set boundaries for our young men!

• • • • • • • • • • • • • •

Stage 2: Responsibility (3–5)

From about three to five years of age, I think it's the father's responsibility to teach his son how to be responsible. I know you guys are probably thinking, *What can my son do at three, four, and five years old that I can hold him responsible for?*

Actually, there is a lot that he can do at those ages that he should be held responsible for. For example, my five-year-old has chores, and have had them since he was four. Of course, his chores are consistent with his age, but still, he has them and is required to do them every week. He cleans his own room. He doesn't do his own laundry yet, but he does bring all his dirty clothes to the laundry room to be washed. He doesn't mow the lawn yet, but he does pick up the yard so that I can mow it. He doesn't wash the car by himself yet, but he does rinse it off after I wash it.

My wife used to cut up his food for him, but since we discovered that he was capable of doing that himself, he is now responsible for it. I know you guys are probably thinking, *Cutting up his food—what's the big deal with that? That's harmless. And it is, if he didn't know how to do it; but since he does, it's hurtful.* See, the problem we have as parents raising boys is that we do too much for them for too long. If we continue to do for our boys the things they can do for themselves, we paralyze them and make them useless to themselves and to others.

Once you see that they are capable of doing something themselves, you should make it their responsibility from that point on.

Fathers, give your sons responsibilities as a child, and they'll take responsibility as an adult.

. . . .

Stage 3: Sex (8–12)

From about the age of eight till about eleven or twelve, fathers, it is our responsibility to counsel or advise our sons on the topic of sex. That's right—the first sex education class our sons should attend should be the one taught by us at home; and by the time they teach them at school, he should know everything he needs to know about sex. The reason the age margin is three to four years here is that, in my opinion, it should be based on your son's level of maturity. Knowing our sons like we do, we should be able to determine at what age it would be appropriate for them to learn about such an important and profound topic.

When I got home yesterday, my five-year-old ran up to me and said, "Daddy, I got Bethany Ann's telephone number today!"

I said, "No, you didn't."

He said, "Yes, I did."

By this time, my wife was backing him up, nodding her head yes. I asked, "Did he call her?"

"Yes."

"What did they talk about?"

She said, absolutely nothing. "Jonathan called her and said hello about three times, and good-bye once, and the conversation was over."

I thought, *How funny. I wish it would stay like this, and then I wouldn't ever have to talk to him about the birds and the bees.* But of course, it won't. And one day, I am going to have to talk to my son about sex! Me, personally, I'm going to wait until my son turns about nine or ten, and then I'm going to ask him, what does he know about sex? His reaction better be "Sex! What is that?" Then I'm going to ask him again the following year, and again the following year, and again the following year, until he finally says, "Sex. Eww!" Now it's time to have the talk, because

162

at this point and time, he's heard enough about sex to think that it's gross and discussing. Here's the deal: I never want my sons to misunderstand sex. I never want them to think that sex is gross, nasty, disgusting, and terribly bad for you. As we Christians know, this could be no farther from the truth. How could something God created for good be all those negative things? God created sex as a privilege for husbands and wives, not as a curse for them. As fathers, I believe it's very important that we warn our sons on the dangers of having sex out of wedlock (and most of us do a good job of that), I also believe it is equally important that we inform our sons on the beauty of sex within a marriage.

I heard a pastor once say that sex is like a fire. When it's contained in the confinement of a fireplace, it is a beautiful thing to watch, but to see that same fire burning out of control in the forest, it could be very destructive. To sum it all up, I definitely want my sons to know that sex was created by God for a husband and a wife, and that in its proper place, it is a beautiful thing. Outside of its proper confinement, it is very destructive, and even somewhat dangerous! Not only is sex a beautiful thing in the confinement of marriage, but it is also necessary for us as men to fulfill one of the most important responsibilities as a man, which is to be fruitful and multiply (Genesis 1:22). Then I'll look my sons straight in the eye and ask them, "How do you think you got here?" Talk about priceless. Check out the look on their face while they ponder that question for a minute.

• • • • • • • • • • • • • •

Stage 4: Job Responsibility (13–15)

Somewhere between the ages of thirteen and fifteen, we should teach our sons how to work and how to receive a paycheck for it. Often, we as fathers think our sons should work for free. Now don't get me wrong, they should have chores around the house where that they are responsible for, but anything over and above their chores, I believe they should be paid for it. For example, if you take your son along with you to Grandma's house to chop down an old dead tree that's about to fall on the house at any day; and they spend the entire day chopping down this tree and cutting it up, they should get paid for that. I would even tell them something like, "Hey son, we're going over to Grandma's house to work, and I'm going to pay you $5 an hour as your salary for the day."

At the end of the day, you take his number of hours worked, times $5 an hour, and pay him what he earned (see 1Timothy 5:18). 1 mean we don't work for free, do we? Not only will it inspire them to work harder, but it will teach them a valuable lesson—which is that they will be rewarded for the work they do in the real world, and that will motivate them, just as it does us?.

Not only should we teach our sons how to work for a paycheck, but we should also teach them how to make their paycheck work for them. For example, we should teach them how to open their own checking and savings accounts. We should teach them how to save money, how to invest money, and last but not least, the most important message we can ever teach our sons about money would have to be this one: If you don't have it, then you don't spend it. That lesson, and how to stay out of credit card debt, in my opinion, are the two most important messages we can teach our sons about being responsible with money.

• • • • • • • • • • • • • •

Stage 5: Driving and Operating an Automobile (16–19)

Somewhere between the ages of sixteen and nineteen, we should advise or counsel our sons on the automobile. Not only should we teach them how to operate an automobile but we should teach them how the automobile operates. Fathers, when was the last time you took your son outside to look under the hood of the car and explained to him what job each component performs and how to operate the vehicle? I know you're probably saying to yourself, *I have no idea what my engine looks like. I've never seen it myself.* Well then, take your car to a mechanic, and the both of you can learn about it at the same time. By doing this, you will be able to see how each component works to power such a powerful and deadly machine. The most important lesson that you will learn will be this: the automobile is not a toy. It's nothing to play with; and in the wrong hands, it can easily become a very deadly weapon.

· · · · · · · · · · · · · ·

Stage Life Lessons (18–20)

Somewhere between the ages of eighteen and twenty, we as fathers should advise or counsel sons on life. Preparing them to live outside the confinements of our home. How do we do that? Great question, and I'm not sure I have the correct answer for you; however, I will share with you how I plan to prepare my sons for life outside of my home. To be quite honest with you, if we've done our jobs as fathers from stage 1 up until stage 6, then they should be pretty well prepared for life outside of Mom and Dad's home. There are a couple of things I didn't mention, but definitely would make sure my sons have a good understanding about, before I turn them loose on the world. One is being chivalrous: Regardless of what you see, and what you may have heard, chivalry is not dead, not even sick. It is very much alive!

Fathers, we must teach our sons how to treat women with respect and honor, because if we don't, who will? MTV? If we're waiting for the television, or even society itself, to teach our boys how to respect women, then we're in a world of trouble, because television, music, the Internet, and society itself tells us that women are no more than garden utensils and female dogs. I was at the doctor's office one day with my six -year-old, and the doctor asked him a question, and he answered her with "Yes, ma'am."

She said, "Wow, you don't hear that any more. How do you get him to say that on his own like that?"

I said, "Ma'am, ever since he was old enough to talk, he's been saying 'Yes, ma'am,' and 'No, ma'am,' 'Yes, sir,' and 'No, sir.'" I went on to say, "And it's not optional in my house—it's mandatory! The way I see it, if we teach our sons how to respect their moms when they're still kids, then we won't have to worry about them respecting their wives as adults." Along the same line, fathers, teach your sons how to open doors for women, how to pull out chairs for them, and, most importantly, how to flatter them with roses. A lot of fathers use the old roses charm to get themselves out of the doghouse, but the best time to send roses to your special someone is for no particular reason other than to say, "Honey, I love you!"

I remember when my wife and I first got married. I would either send her roses or bring them home to her at least once a month, for no other reason than to tell her I love her. One of the clerks at Publix, where I would buy roses for my wife, asked me one time, "You must be the unluckiest man we've ever seen in here. You seem to be always buying roses trying to get out the doghouse, at least once a month."

I said, "Ma'am, I've actually never been in the doghouse with my wife. I buy her roses as often as I do to show her I appreciate her, and that I love her."

She looked at me and said, "Well, I guess we were wrong about you. You're not the unluckiest guy we've ever seen in here. You are the sweetest and most romantic guy we've ever seen in here. I wish my husband did that!" Chivalry's not dead, it's very much alive.

• • • • • • • • • • • • •

Confidant

It's five o'clock Friday afternoon, I call my wife to let her know what time to expect me home, and she puts my six-year-old son on the phone. He says, "Dad, I hope you get off at a decent hour because I've got the cars all set up for cars on the

map? I said, "Okay, son, Daddy will get home as soon as I can."
Now, you have to understand, in my line of work, a decent hour
is about seven o'clock, and I really have to bust my chops to make
that happen every day. Cars on the map—those are not my most
favorite words to hear; however, I love to hear them coming out
of my son's mouth. They're not my most favorite words to hear
because I don't really like playing cars on the map. I love to hear
those words come out of my son's mouth because I love time
spent playing with him.

What is cars on the map? I'm glad you asked. My oldest son
bought my six-year-old a map of a city made out of cloth for
Christmas one year. My six-year-old spreads this map out on his
floor and sets his matchbox cars up on the map at certain places
he liked to go. When I arrive at home I sit down on the floor
and we begin to move our cars from place to place, all around the
map. Now the game itself is not so bad, except for the fact that
it's played on the floor.

I have a very physical job that totally wears me out for ten,
eleven, and even sometimes twelve hours a day; and by the time
I get home at the end of the day, the last thing I want to do is sit
down on the floor for an hour playing with matchbox cars. The
game makes no sense to me, but my son understands it perfectly.
To me it's boring; to him it's exciting. To me it's a waste of time;
to him it's quality time.

Fathers, most of us have no idea what quality time with our
sons consist of. We think that spending quality time with them is
allowing them to enter our world by taking them along with us
to spend the day doing something we love to do. For example, if
you're a golfer, spending quality time with your son may be taking
your son along with you to play a round of golf. Or if you like to
hunt, spending quality time with your son might be to take him
hunting on the weekends. Or maybe you love sports, so spending
quality time with your son may mean bringing him along with
you to watch your favorite team play.

I know you're asking yourself, what's wrong with everything I just mentioned? Well, nothing at all, if we're talking about you. However, we're not. We're talking about your son, and to him, quality time is this. Not taking him along with you to do something you love to do, but going along with him to spend a day doing something he loves to do. Big difference. Spending a day doing what you love to do is all about you; spending a day doing what he loves to do is all about him.

One of my fondest memories of my father when I was growing up was when I was about four or five years old. My father built me and my two siblings a tree house in our backyard. My brother and I would go up into the tree house at least twice a day every day. We had so much fun in that tree house, we absolutely loved it. I remember one day my brother and I were in the tree house playing, and he left to go get some water. After about five minutes or so, I heard someone climbing up the tree house steps. Of course, I automatically thought it was just my brother returning from the house, so I didn't think anything of it. The steps got closer, and closer, and closer, until finally, they made it to the top. I turned around and looked toward the door, and up popped my father's head. I said, "Daddy, what are you doing up here?"

He said, "I just wanted to see what you were doing up here." My father, all six foot one inch of him, came into the tree house and sat with me for what seemed like forever; and I absolutely loved every moment of that visit. Why? Because it was the first and the last time my father made an intentional effort to get on my level and spend quality time with me doing something I love to do. I had never before, or after, felt as close to my father as I did during those twenty minutes or so he spent with me in that tree house on that particular day.

Reflecting back on this day with my dad made me think of another very special time I spent with my own son. He was two years old at the time, and we were in the backyard playing football.

He was the running back, and I was the middle linebacker. He grabbed the football, made his move, and I tackled him, bringing him to the ground. As he lay on the ground, face up, laughing his little head off, I went over and lay beside him.

He looked over at me and said, "Daddy, are you happy?"

I looked at him and said, "Of course, son. Why do you ask?"

"Because I'm happy."

For as long as I live, I will never forget that day. Because, the truth of the matter is, I wasn't very happy at the time. I had so much on my mind with everything going on from work, to how I was going to pay the bills. I was totally not happy—until he said he was. Then all of a sudden, everything was alright; and I thought, *This is life, and I have a great one!* The fact that he was happy made me feel that I was doing something right. Because here's the deal: Kids spell love *T-I-M-E!* They don't spell it *money*, they don't spell it *stuff*, they don't spell it *private school*, they don't spell it *big house*, and they don't spell it *nice cars*. No, they simply spell it *time*.

I'm reminded of a friend of mine who used to have a husband who worked for a very popular grocery store. They have two kids, a six-year-old boy and a four-year-old girl. The husband would work five-to-twelve shifts each week, leaving very little time for his family. I remember this one particular time she shared with me concerning her then-two-year-old son. She told me about how one day she was doing laundry down the hall when she heard her son in the room next door crying uncontrollably. She walked out of the laundry room and into his room, where he was sitting with his back toward her, holding a picture. She called him by his name and said, "Baby, what's wrong?"

The little boy turned around, gripping a picture of his father. She looked at him and said, "You miss him, don't you?" And the little boy nodded his head yes. She said, "Yeah, I know, I do too."

Fathers, they know as early as two years old, when you're more absent than present. I know you're probably wondering, What does all this have to do with being a confidant? Well, I'll tell you what it has to do with being a confidant. True confidentiality comes out of true intimacy. I once heard a pastor give his definition of intimacy, and it was something like this: Open up and allow someone to look into you.

I've said this once, and I'll say it a thousand times: the more you feel you know a person, the more you'll let that person know you. Of course, when I say true intimacy between a father and his son, I'm not talking about an unhealthy intimate relationship. I'm talking about the healthy relationship between a father and his son, which is honest, transparent, and true.

Fathers, it is our responsibility to be our sons' confidant. I know you might be thinking, *What is the difference between a counselor and a confidant?* I'm glad you asked, as we've already learned a counselor is an adviser, or someone who counsels; and on the contrary, a confidant is a person to whom secrets are confided, or with whom private matters are discussed. The difference between the two is like that between a one guard and a two guard in the game of basketball. The one guard is normally the point guard, and his job is to distribute the basketball and run the offense; and the two guard is normally the shooting guard, and his job is to shoot the ball.

Now can a shooting guard be a point guard? "Yes" and can a point a guard be a shooting guard? Yes again. But the job of the one guard and the job of the two guard are totally different. Such is the case with a counselor and a confidant. Can a counselor be a confidant? Yes. Can a confidant be a counselor? Yes again. But they are two totally different people, with the biggest difference being this: in order for someone to be a confidant, they must have an intimate relationship with the person who's confiding in them, whereas to being a counselor, all you have to do is give good advice.

I truly believe that in order to be a confidant to someone, or to confide in someone yourself, you must spend quality time with that person, getting to know them and seeing what makes them who they are. For those of us who are married, can you remember back when you first started dating your wife? Do you remember all the time you spent with her, doing stuff you didn't want to do, going places you didn't want to go, but doing it all in the name of love. We went to all these crazy places and did all these crazy things, trying to get to a place of intimacy with our love interest for the main purpose of getting to know them better.

Now can you remember after you got to that place, whether it was before or after marriage, how your guard fell down and you became completely open with this person, and how they became completely open with you? Look, there is no one who should know you better than your spouse. My wife and I did not start our marriage as best friends and confidants to one another; but we are now. My wife seemed to think that just because we were married, we would automatically become best friends and each other's confidant; but as we would soon find out, that's not always the case. I dated my wife for a year, and we were engaged for four months; so by the time we got married, we had one year and one month of knowing each other under our belts, which to me wasn't enough time to let her into me and for me to open up completely to her about who I really am.

But now, since we've been together for almost ten years, and been through what we've been through, I feel that I can talk to my wife about anything. Now that doesn't mean I do, but I know I can. Fathers, my point is this: with the same kind of intentionality and passion we pursued our wives with to form an intimate relationship with them to get to know them better should be the same intentionality and passion we pursue our sons with to form an intimate relationship with them, to get to know them better. Have the same desire to want to get to know your son better, as you did your wife, because real confidentiality comes from real intimacy.

Not only do I get on the floor with my son to play cars on the map, but every time we play a game, I always get down on his level, because I remember how important I felt the time my father came down to my level and visited me. There's something very important about the eye-to-eye contact when trying to form an intimate relationship with your son. However, to me, the most important thing I do to form intimacy with my son is every single night, after I read him a bedtime story and tuck him in, I ask him the same question: "Son, what do you want to talk about today?" This simply means, did anything happen today that you would like to tell Daddy about?

As a matter of fact, I say it so often my son now says, "Dad, you ask me the same question every single night." And my response to him is, "I know, I do it because I want to make sure you know on any given day you can talk to me about anything at all!" And the funny thing about it is, I've been doing this before he was even able to talk. And the reason I am consistent with it, and been doing it so long, is that I'm trying to establish and intimate relationship with my son for later on in life.

Not so much for the ninety-nine times he doesn't need to talk, but for the one time he does. See, right now, he doesn't have much to talk about. Sometimes he talks for a couple of minutes, and sometimes he doesn't have anything to say at all. But one day he will. One day he will have a lot to say about something very important to him, and he's going to need his father's advice. My prayer is, by that time, we will be so close from years of me making myself available to him every single night, that he will be able to talk to me about anything, and everything.

Fathers, find the time to spend time, because your son doesn't care what you know until he knows that you care. Don't get me wrong, there is nothing wrong with a boy talking and confiding in his mother with certain issues, but when it comes to matters of the heart and life-changing decisions, no one is better equipped to counsel their sons than their fathers. It's kind of like owning a Mercedes Benz and having a problem with it, and taking it to a Honda dealership and telling the people there what the car is doing wrong. They may say something like, "Well, it sounds like this, that, or the other, but you would really have to take it to the Mercedes Benz shop to find out exactly what's wrong with the car because they designed and built it. They know more about this particular car than anyone else.

One of the biggest mistakes we make as fathers is we don't think we need to communicate with our sons, nor do they need to communicate with us, until they are teenagers. Truth of the matter is, if you don't have a relationship with your son by the time he has reached puberty, you won't have one with him once he goes through it. I said all that to say this: Communicate with your sons early on if you want them to communicate with you later on, because true confidentiality comes from true intimacy!

• • • • • • • • • • • • • •

Decision Maker

We read in Genesis 2:19, "And out of the ground the Lord God formed every beast of the field, and every fowl of the air; and brought them unto Adam to see what he would call them; and whatsoever Adam called every living creature, that was the name thereof."

What an incredible assignment for the first man to ever set foot on earth, for God to bring all of mankind to him, and for him to decide on what to call them. Fathers, it is our responsibility to make decisions in our home concerning our families. Growing up when my father was in our house, he made all the decisions, whether they were bad or good, right or wrong—he made them all. Every time I would go to my mother and ask to go somewhere, or to do something, she would say, "Go ask your daddy." And every time I would ask my dad, he would usually say no.

Very seldom did my father grant me permission to do anything I wanted to do. Before long, I stopped asking to go anywhere or do anything, because I knew my mother was going to direct me to my dad, and I knew he was going to say no, because he always had the last say-so. Now don't get me wrong. I'm not saying do not discuss each and every decision that needs to be made in the house with your spouse, but I'm saying after you've discussed it, and got her take on the situation, ultimately, the last say-so belongs to you.

I will never forget a forty-eight-hour mystery television program I watched with my wife one Saturday night about this couple whose young daughter was kidnapped some twenty-five years prior and was presumed to be dead. This couple had three daughters, whose ages I believe ranged from about eight to twelve. One night the couple went three houses down to visit friends and hang out for a while, leaving the three young girls home alone. After a short while, the oldest girl called the mom to ask her if she and her sisters could walk about a block to the store to get some candy, and the mom put the dad on the phone. The dad would later admit that he really didn't want them to be out at night by themselves; but since it was all three of them, and it wasn't quite dark yet, and since the store was less than a block away, he gave in and told the oldest yes, but that they should go straight to the store and then go straight home.

The girls did just as their father had told them, they went straight to the store, and were on their way straight home when a man came out of nowhere and abducted one of the young girls. The other two, terrified, racing home. Even though the other two sisters were able to give a good description of the kidnapper, they never did find him, or the young girl. The parents of the little girl went on this television show, before the American audience, being asked the question everyone wanted to know: "Who gave the girls permission to go to the store?"

The dad boldly said, "I did."

I thought that was pretty amazing, considering the decision he made, all by himself, had cost him and his wife their little girl's life. It was amazing to me because he could've been like most men, including the first man to ever walk the earth, Adam, and put the blame on his wife. Like Adam did when God confronted him for eating of the fruit from the tree of good and evil. God said, "Have thou eaten of the tree, whereof I commanded thee that thou shouldest not eat?" Now check out what Adam said in Genesis 3:12: "And the man said, The woman whom thou gavest to be with me, she gave me of the tree, and I did eat." In other words, Adam was saying, "Look, God, yes, I ate of the fruit, but it wasn't my fault. It was the fault of the woman you gave me. Or better yet, "Since you gave her to me, it was your fault. In no way is it my fault!"

The girl's father could have very easily said, "Well, the girls asked my wife first, and since she didn't say anything, I told them yeah, I guess." Or he could have said, "I wanted to tell them no, but every time I tell them no, my wife always gets upset and tells me I should have told them yes, so I just went ahead and said yes so I wouldn't have to hear her mouth." However, he stood up like a man and took full responsibility for the decision he made that caused his family the most unthinkable pain they had ever experienced. I believe the reason we have so many men who are passive and pass all the decision-making responsibility on to their wives is that they are afraid to man up and accept the consequences for the decisions they make. Fathers, man up and stand up and make the call.

· · · · · · · · · · · · · ·

Disciplinarian

Fathers, it is our responsibility to discipline our sons. The book of Proverbs talks about sparing the rod and spoiling the child. My father never spared the rod, so I guess none of us should be spoiled. Growing up, I saw the rod plenty of times; and most of the time, the rod in my father's hand got the job done;

especially during this one particular time I'll never forget when I was about nine or ten.

As I said before, when I was about nine or ten, my parents separated, and I went to live with my father for a couple of years. During that time, I was very rebellious, mainly because I didn't want to go and live with my father and be separated from my siblings, so I began to act out a lot. One of the things I started doing, simply because I knew my father would have a fit if he knew I was doing it, was smoking.

My best friend at the time was a guy named Al, and his parents owned a convenience store. We could get anything in the store free of charge, anytime we wanted to get it; and of course, our choice of freebies was cigarettes. He was a little older than I was, and had been smoking for years when I met him; but when we met, it was an instant friendship, and we became best friends right away. Now I had always been curious about smoking because my father smoked, and he used to make smoking a cigarette look so cool. So when I started hanging out with my new best friend, and because we had access to cigarettes and permission to get them whenever we wanted to, it was just a matter of time before I started smoking.

I remember the day I started smoking. Al and I were at the pool swimming. We took a break and sat down against the fence, and he whipped out a cigarette. He lit it up and said, "Man, you wanna hit it?" I said yeah, and just like that, I became a smoker. Every time we got together, we would smoke cigarettes; and before long, even when I wasn't with him, I was smoking.

My father would put his cigarettes out in the ashtray, and when he would go to sleep, I would go through the ashtray and get all the cigarette butts that were long enough to smoke, grab my father's lighter, go to the bathroom, turn on the vent, and smoke what was left of the cigarettes. This would go on for about a year or so, until one Fourth of July morning, my father caught me smoking, and what he did to me would change my life forever.

As I said, it was the Fourth of July, and my best friend and I had snuck out of our apartments and jumped over the pool fence at about two in the morning to go swimming. Everything was going very well for about thirty minutes, and then our morning out took a drastic turn for the worse. I was sitting outside the pool with my back to the fence, smoking a cigarette, watching my friend swim. As Al swam toward me, he lifted his head, and the look on his face scared the living daylight out of me. "What!" I shouted.

He pointed behind me, and when I turned around to see what was so frightening, I saw my dad's old, worn-out work boots just on the other side of the fence. I quickly turned back around so I could put my cigarette out, because I knew I was going to get killed for sneaking out of the house at two o'clock in the morning, and I didn't want to get a double punishment for being out there smoking as well.

My dad said, "You don't have to put it out. You can go ahead and smoke that one. I promise you, that will be the last cigarette you ever smoke." "When you finish it, I'll be waiting for you in the apartment."

"Okay," I said." Man, what did he say that for? I put out the cigarette, jumped onto my mini bike, and rode across town to my grandmother's house where my mom lived. I was riding as fast as that mini bike would carry me, hitting every back road I knew, trying to get to my grandmother's house as fast as I possibly could. And wouldn't you know it—by the time I pulled up in the driveway, my dad was already there, waiting for me. As soon as I parked the mini bike, I jumped off and ran to my big moma and said, "Big Moma, please don't let Daddy take me back home tonight. He's going to kill me!"

Now you have to understand my big moma was my heart. She was everything to me, and she used to always tell me, "Baby I'll never let anyone harm you, never." She asked me, "Baby, what happened?"

I said, "Nothing."

"What are you doing over here at three in the morning if everything is okay?"

I said, "Big Moma, I promise I didn't do anything wrong!"

She said, "Your daddy said you were over there at the pool with your little buddy smoking cigarettes."

"No, I wasn't!"

My dad said, "Yes, you were."

My grandmother looked at me and then she looked at my dad, and then back at me; and said, "Baby, you're going have to go home tonight." And she turned around and walked off.

That really tore my heart apart, and this was by far the worst night of my young life—not because I knew my dad was going to kill me for smoking but because my grandmother, the most important person in my life, betrayed me. I was crushed that my grandmother was going to let my daddy take me back home and do whatever he wanted to do with me, and she wasn't going to say a word about it.

I got in the car with my dad, and we drove off. By the time we got home, he had about an hour before he had to get up and go to work, and if I remember right, he spent that hour spanking on my butt. I truly believe that on more than one occasion that night, my dad was going to kill me.

It was really a severe beating.

That night I hated my dad, and I didn't care much for my beloved grandmother either. However, today I thank my father for that severe beating every time I see someone smoking a cigarette; and my grandmother still holds a special place in my heart. My father was right, I have never smoked another cigarette, or even held one, ever since that night. As a matter of fact, for years, every time I would see someone smoking a cigarette, I would start shaking, and thoughts of that night would begin to play over and over and over again in my head. What I didn't understand at the time, but is perfectly clear to me now, is that both my dad and my grandmother were working together for my good; and because of their teamwork on that particular night, I'm a better person today. You know, it's funny, but when I look back over my life at situations such as that one, it becomes clear that God uses a lot of people and a lot of situations to put me in the place I'm in today. And for that, I say thank you, Lord!

Now in this particular situation, at this particular time, a severe spanking was sufficient discipline for me; but that was not always the case growing up. Here's the deal: a spanking is a correct form of discipline only when it works! If it doesn't work, then it's merely a stress reliever, an exercise, for the person administering it. Whether it's a spanking, a time out, or both, fathers, it's your responsibility to administer it.

• • • • • • • • • • • • • •

Leader

Fathers it is our responsibility to lead our families. Believe it or not, as fathers, we are natural leaders of our families, especially our young boys. One time I was sitting in our living room with my beautiful wife, having a conversation about our nineteen-month-old, when my six–year-old walked into the room and said, "Here's the deal." And before he could say anything else, my wife and I looked at each other and burst out laughing. Why, you ask? I'll tell you why: Because that's one my favorite lines, and not only did he imitate me with his body language, but he said it just like I would say it. It was like looking at and listening to a little me. Scary.

I asked him, "Jonathan, where did you get that from?"

He looked at me and started laughing and said, "You, Daddy, you!" Now this was cool to us because it was something funny, but what if I would have come home and found him in his room smoking a joint, and when asked "Who taught you how to smoke a joint?" he would look up at me, higher than a kite, and say, "You,

Daddy, you!" Not so funny, huh? We must be careful how we lead by example in front of our sons.

However, when I think of a great leader, I think of someone who has the power to influence others. In other words, a great leader is a great influencer. The Bible is full of men who were great leaders, but the one who stands out to me the most is a man named Elijah. He was a great prophet who was used mightily by the Lord God. He performed at least eight miracles by the power of the Holy Spirit, and when it was time for him to return home to be with the Lord, God told him to go and find this young prophet by the name of Elisha and place his mantle upon him, that he might be the next great prophet used by the Lord God. The Lord even told Elijah where to find this next great prophet. He told him Elisha would be plowing with twelve yokes of oxen before him.

Elijah found Elisha and took him under his wing for several years to train him to be the next great prophet; and through Elijah's influence, Elisha, overtime, became just that. At the end of Elijah's life, when he was on his way home to be with the Lord, he asked Elisha, what did Elisha want him to do for him before he was taken away?"

Elisha said, "That I may have a double portion of what you have."

What an amazing thing for a trainee to ask of his trainer—a double portion of what they have. Now that's influence. I intentionally named my first son Elisha, after the prophet in the Bible, because my prayer is that my influence on him throughout my life will be so great that when I'm old and on my deathbed, he will look at me and say, "Dad, I don't care about money, fame, or fortune. All I want is a double portion of whatever it is that you have."

Fathers, that's my prayer; and it should also be each one of yours. We should strive to live a life that should be so impactful and influential, that our sons want nothing more than a double portion of what we have. Fathers, it's our responsibilities to lead our families.

. . . .

Protector

Fathers, it is our responsibility to protect our families. Most fathers I know have this one mastered—or so they think. However, when it comes to protecting our families, there's more to it than you may be aware of. In Mark 3:27, Jesus puts it like this: "No man can enter into a strong man's house, and spoil his goods, except he will first bind the strong man; and then he will spoil his house."

What I get from that passage of scripture is that no man can break into your home and take control of it, unless they first bind you. When most of us think about being bound, we think about being tied up by the hands and feet, and with something stuck in our mouths; but that's not the only way the enemy can bind you and take control of your home. You're bound and the enemy has control of your home if you're an alcoholic, a drug addict, addicted to pornography, if there's division between you and your wife, and lastly, if you don't Jesus.

So as you can see, there are several ways the enemy can enter into your house, bind you up, and take control of your home. Now let's talk about protecting our family from physical harm. Every night before I got to bed, I go through my house when everyone else is asleep, and I check each door to make sure they're all locked and secured; twice. Why? Because I realize that if anyone ever does break into my home and harm my family, the blame will be all mine, since God has appointed me not only as head of the house but also as the protector of the home.

Fathers, we are responsible for protecting our homes not only from physical invasion but also from spiritual invasion. What do I mean by that? I'm glad you asked. It is our responsibility as fathers to protect our family from spiritual break-ins. What I'm trying to say is this: it's our responsibility to protect our family from any and everything that comes into our home that is contrary to the Word of God (if you are a believer).

Now, fathers, in order to get this one right, it's going take some work on your part. The reason I say that is you're going to have to know what kind of music your kids are listening to. That means you're going to have to know what's on their iPod, what kind of music they have downloaded on their phones, what kinds of CDs they're listening to, and so on. This means that every now and then, you're going to have to do a random check of all these things. I know what you're thinking: *I can't do that. That would be too much like invading their privacy. Well* you can look at it as an invasion of privacy, or you can look at it as a father who cares about what's entering his home and ministering to his kids. Fathers, get off your La-Z-Boys and parent your children. Second, you're going to have know what sights they frequent on their computers. Again, you're going to have to get up out of your La-Z-Boy and go to their rooms to check the sites they visit on their computers, and see what kind of activity is going on. I know you're thinking, *I just can't up and go in their room without warning. Again, that's like disturbing their peace and invading their privacy. And not only that, they probably won't let me see their computer anyway. Then what do I do?*

That's simple: take it away. What if they bought it? Tell them thank you! Look, here's the deal: it really doesn't matter who bought what. You pay the bills, don't you? And if you ask them to do something and they refuse, then start taking stuff away until you get what want.

Lastly, we need to do a random check of their CD collections and see whose ministering to our kids. I say ministering because whoever they spend most of their time listening to on their CDs will have way more influence in their lives than we will. Again, just go to their rooms, open the door, and go through their CDs. I know you're probably saying to yourself, you don't understand.

My son has this big sign on his door that says, DO NOT ENTER, and if he catches me in his room, he'll have a fit! Again, who pays the bills in the house? That sign should mean absolutely nothing to you! You're the head of the house. You can go into any room, at any time, on any given day. Exercise your authority!

Another way the enemy will bind you and take control of your home is through the television programs we allow our kids to watch. I love what a pastor once said about the way he chooses what he allows his family to watch. He asks himself, *Would I watch this program if my pastor was sitting here between me and my wife?* I actually go a step farther with my question, and I ask myself, *Would I watch this program if Jesus was sitting in the room with me and my wife?* Fathers, we need to know what our kids are watching when they're not in the room with us. Get up out of your La-Z-Boy and go check it out.

A funny thing happened to me in April 2013. I got a deal with my cable company—a promotional deal, they called it. And what they did was gave me a deal on my cable services—more stations for less money. Great deal, huh? Yeah, that's what I thought too. I received all the stations I wanted and a couple that I didn't want, like the two movie channels they included. I know most of you guys are saying, What's wrong with the free movie channels? Well, some of the movie channels aren't that bad; however, I can do without the soft porn stations they offer along with them. Being a former porn addict, I wasn't that excited when they told me that along with the extra channels I wanted, they were going to throw in a couple of premium movie channels that I didn't ask for, which would include the soft porn stations. I even told the woman, "Ma'am, that's okay about the premium movies channels. We hardly ever watch movies anyway in our house."

She said, "You don't want the movie channel?"

"No, ma'am, not at all!"

"Wow, never heard of anyone turning down free movie channels for three months at no charge to them."

She called it a free promotional gift, and it was free. I called it a curse straight from the pit of hell, and it came with a price. I just could not see myself allowing those spirits to enter my home and loom over my sons' beds every night. Fathers, we have to be careful not to allow those spirits of sex, drugs, and cursing to enter our homes, whether it be through music, the Internet, or television. We must block them and do what we're called to do as men and as fathers. Protect and serve. Protect our home, and serve notice on the devil that he's not going to bind us and take control of our home.

• • • • • • • • • • • • • •

Provider

And finally, fathers, it is our responsibility to provide for our families. Again, this one comes naturally to most men, because most men were raised with the knowledge that it's a man's responsibility to provide financially for his family. Every morning, I get up at six forty-five, wash my face, brush my teeth, get dressed, and hit the door on my way to the workhouse. Rain, sleet, or snow, I have to go and make the doughnuts for my family.

Now I don't really work at a doughnut shop; however, I do make the dough for our home. I learned early on in life that real men worked and supported their families. My wife and I have a great understanding: I make the dough, and she cooks it. I don't ask her to go to work and help pay the bills, and she doesn't ask me to help out with supper, and we love it like that. I've always said I would never stop a woman from working, and I would never make a woman work. What I mean with this statement is simply this: if I should marry a woman who has a great career and wants to continue to work after we're married, I would never try to stop her from doing so. On the other hand, if I should marry a woman who wants to stay home and raise our kids, I will never force her to work.

Anyone who knows me has heard me say on numerous occasions that I don't care if a man's wife is the top brain surgeon in the world, and he's a pizza maker. It's still his responsibility to financially support his family. Now don't get me wrong. If you guys worked something out where she worked and you stayed at home with the kids, and she was fine with that, then more power to you. But just because she has a better job than you, making way more money than you do does not automatically make her the financial supporter for your family. You're the man, and that will always be your responsibility. With that being said, I would like to warn some of you guys who are workaholics, who say you do it in the name of providing for your family, please be careful, or you'll lose the very thing you're working to keep.

My pastor preached an awesome message on this very topic. He spoke on the way that we as men put our jobs before our families, and the devastating effects they may have on our children. He mentioned something to the effect that the more time we spend away from our kids, the less excited they are to see us when we do get home. The message really hit home with me, so the next day, I went to work to see if there was any way I could shave some time off my workday and spend more time with my family. I found out there are two ways to do this.

One was to ask for a lighter workday, and I did. And they gave it to me. Sometimes you'll be amazed at what you can get just by asking. The other thing was to skip half my lunch each day, and I started doing that as well, and because of these two things, I have secured an extra two hours at home with my family. The first thing I did was easy; the second was a little more difficult. The company I work for took an hour out on us each day for lunch, whether we take it or not, so to skip half my lunch for the next year would have me actually giving back to this huge company— who needs no money, especially not from me—about $7,600. That sounds like a lot of money to some, but to me, it's nothing compared to what I gained—an extra two hours with my family.

As I said before, my son spells *love T-I-M-E;* so for me to gain an extra two hours of love to give to him is priceless! Now, fathers, here's my question to you: "What is it worth to you to be the father your family needs for you to be? What is it worth to you to be at your son's season opener, or to be at the first father-daughter dance? What is it worth to you, to be able to tuck your kids in at night, or to be there when they wake up in the morning to go to school? And finally, what is it worth to you to dress your son for his first prom, or to watch your daughter graduate from high school? Whatever it's worth, I recommend you do it right away, because your family needs you! This may mean cutting your overtime out, so do it. It may mean you have to stop taking the optional weeklong trips for extra money, so do it. It may mean downsizing, so do it. It may mean driving used cars that are paid for rather than the brand-new ones right off the showroom floor that you are accustomed to, so do it. Whatever it is, I suggest you make it happen for your family's sake. I've got this friend at work who says his son understands that Daddy has to work all the time to pay the bills and to keep up the lifestyle they're accustomed to.

Well, I beg to differ, and I told him, "Your son doesn't understand why you guys live in a six-bedroom home, and it's just the three of you. He doesn't understand that. He doesn't understand why he rides in a brand-new Mercedes Benz 500 series to school each day, and his friends ride the school bus. He doesn't understand that. He doesn't understand why his father became a member of the country club and plays golf every week instead of spending time with him. He doesn't understand that. He doesn't understand why his mother goes to tea parties once a week and fellowship with women she doesn't even like. He doesn't understand that. But I'll tell you what he does understand. He understands he loves you, he misses you, he needs you, and you are absent!

Fathers, our sons need us now more than ever before. Let's stop what we're doing, and drop what we're doing, and rush to be with our sons. Men, let's be honest. When we chase after the almighty dollar, are we trying to make a better life for our kids, or for ourselves? Being a financial provider is an obvious one, but what other ways has God called us to provide for our families? I believe there is at least one other way in which God has called us to provide for our families, spiritually Fathers I believe we are our family's spiritual providers. I believe it's our responsibility to lead our families in the way of the Lord. What does that mean? I'm glad you asked. I applaud the dads who drop their kids off at church, but as fathers, we should not only drive them to church, we should get out the car and lead them into church. "I have no greater joy than to hear that my children walk in truth" (3 John1:4).

When it's all said and done, and the rubber hits the road, this should be every father's prayer for their children—to become men and women of truth. My six-year-old is such a smart and intelligent young boy; and from time to time, we will hear someone either at the school or at church tell us how smart he is, or how well he reads scriptures; and it really blesses our hearts to hear such awesome things about our son. I'll give my dad credit for one thing: Every Sunday morning, he had us in church, early. We were always the first ones to get there, and the last ones to leave. Whether my dad lived a life that was consistent with that of a Christian or not, he still made sure that I, my brother, and my sister were in church every other Sunday morning. And you know what, a funny thing happened: all three of us are in church today, and living for the Lord Jesus!

There must be some truth to the scripture that talks about training a child the way he should go, and when he is old, he will not depart from it. I was the last one of my dad's children to get saved. I think he really worried about me. I personally believed God allowed my dad to live long enough to see me saved, baptized, and on fire for the Lord Jesus. I say that because shortly after I got saved, my father passed away. Fathers, it is our responsibility to provide spirituality for our families, which would make us their spiritual provider, as well as financial providers. God has called us to provide for our family.

I would like to share one more thing with you guys in closing: Statistics have shown that kids whose fathers are more hands-on are smarter, have more self-confidence, have more self-control, and have greater social skills than those kids whose fathers are absent from their lives. With that being said, fathers, get involved, stay involved, and be involved. Your child's well-being depends on it.

The P-Word

If the Son therefore shall make you free, ye shall be free indeed"

—John 8:36

It was a cool and rainy Saturday morning as I sat patiently at the barbershop, waiting for my biweekly cut. I glanced to the right of me, and there was this young boy who looked to be no older than six years old, sneaking a peak at the latest edition of *GQ*. You could tell the youngster was really struggling with whether he should look at the magazine or not. He would look at the magazine and then turn away, and then look again, and then turn away again. It almost looked like a cat playing with a mouse, debating on whether he should go ahead and kill the mouse or play with it a little while longer. They say the third time is always the charm, and it was for him. The next time he looked at the magazine, he reached over, and picked it up. The little boy looked at the cover of the magazine and then looked at his grandmother, who had brought him to the barbershop, and said, "Look, Granny, a naked woman."

His granny replied, "What are you talking about?" as she jerked the magazine out of the boy's hand. She looked at the very popular male-targeted magazine and saw one of the hottest female actors of our time gracing the cover, dressed in nothing

189

but a necktie, and gave the magazine back to the youngster. "That's not *Playboy*, that's just a *GQ* magazine." Was it merely an innocent *GQ* cover, or was it that young man's introduction to *porniea* (the Greek word for pornography)? Well, I'm sure by now you've figured out what the *P* stands for. You're absolutely right—*pornography*.

When we look at this word *pornography*, and the way it has been defined over the years; we define it as two types, or two different forms. First type is the hardcore XXX-rated movies, the second type is hard core XXX-rated magazines; and this sums it up for most people. However, according to the definition of the word, there's a lot more to it than just those two examples. The word *pornography* is defined as follows: writing, pictures, etc., intended to arouse sexual desire. Any picture or writing whose main purpose is to sexuality arouse a person. By the end of this chapter hopefully we will have a better understanding of what is, and what is not considered to be pornography.

There is so much I could write about on this topic. I have been studying it for the better part of the last decade. However, I'm going to try to stick to the three stages of pornography that I often teach about. Which is my introduction, my struggle, and my victory. That's right, I said victory. Because there is victory for those who are struggling with porn addiction; and my prayer is that by the end of this chapter, you will have learned how you yourself can be free from all bondage, especially that which is caused by the spirit of pornography.

Stage 1: My Introduction

Everything has an introduction. There is an introduction to life, walking, talking, school, sports, girls, and for some, there's an introduction to alcohol, drugs, gangs, and, yes, even pornography. Statistics have shown that in America, the average age of a boy when he is introduced to pornography is somewhere around seven years old; and it usually involves him finding his father's stash of porn. This is first, and only, stat that was right on target with me. I was about seven years old when I found my dad's stash of dirty magazines between the mattress of my parents' bed. Growing up, we were very poor and didn't have a lot of money, so when an opportunity came to make a few dollars, we literally fought for the chance.

My dad was an alcoholic, and there were times when he would get drunk and hide money in the house and sober up and couldn't find it. This was one of those times. He had lost $200 somewhere in the house. He told me and my little sister that if we found it, he would give us $20, so we took off tearing the house apart looking for this money. She went toward the kitchen and the den, and I went straight to the bedroom. I first started looking in the closet, thinking maybe he left the money in a coat pocket that he wore out that weekend. No luck. Then I looked through all the drawers. No luck. Then I had a brilliant idea. I thought, *If it was me, where would I hide it?*

You guessed it—between the mattress. I went over to my father's side of the bed and yanked up his side of the mattress, and out fell a dirty magazine. I looked around to make sure no one saw it hit the floor. Then I knelt down to pick it up. On the cover was this brick house of a woman (36-24-36) cupping her breasts. I opened the magazine, turned the page, and saw my first completely naked woman; and from that moment on, I was hooked. It was like I totally forgot all about the money I was looking for, because I had found gold in that dirty magazine.

Every evening, I would find my way back into my parents, room for a glance at my new girlfriend, and every evening, the glances got longer and longer, until I found myself staring at the woman in the magazine. And even though I didn't know why it was wrong, I knew it was wrong. And even though I wasn't quite sure what it was I felt, I knew I liked it. I would continue to sneak into my parents' room to see my new girlfriend for years, until my dad left the house. When he left, he took his magazines with him I had no way of getting any dirty magazines for myself, so my fascination with porn would have to wait for some sixteen years before I would pick it up again; and this time, it would become an all-out pornography addiction.

When I was twenty-three years old, our house burned down. We lost everything. I lost all my clothes, all my valuables, all my money. I had $500, my life savings in the pocket of my favorite sports coat that was burned in the fire, but most of all, we lost our house. My mother and I were the only two people living there, and thank God, we both were gone the night it burned down. After the fire my mother went to stay with my sister, and I went to stay with one my best friends at the time. I hated losing my house, but I loved being out on my own. Staying with my friend was cool, because he was never there. He spent most of his time at his girlfriend's house, so it was like I had my own place, except without the responsibilities. For me, it didn't get any better than that.

Shortly after I moved in, I noticed my friend's very large movie collection. He had this huge wooden cabinet full of movies. It must have been over a hundred or so, and after about three weeks of me sitting around the house by myself, doing nothing, I began to go through them. Most of the movies were legit and had names on them, but then there were the ones without any kind of identification on them at all. And just like Curious George, those were the ones I popped into the VCR. It wouldn't take long for me to realize why these movies were not identified or properly marked. They were porn movies!

I remember I popped the first one in and for the first time in my life, I saw two people having sex. I had seen women naked before, even two women naked with each other before, but never in a movie. This was like bringing the pages of the dirty magazine to life, and I loved it. That night, I stayed up until three in the morning going through every porn movie my friend had. His collection of porn was just as good as the porn store. He had it all. He had women on women, he had black porn, he had white porn, and he had black and white together porn. Whatever you were looking for, he had it; and for me, I became like a kid in the candy store. Every night, I could pick and choose what and who, I wanted for that night.

Over the next three years, I would indulge in pornography, finding myself experiencing forms of pornography that I didn't even know existed. The funny thing about being addicted to pornography is that you can never get enough of it. I could sit at my friend's house all weekend long by myself watching pornography, and wake up Monday morning, getting ready to go to work, finding myself watching it while I brushed my teeth. The thing with the flesh, the more you give it, the more it wants. That's why pornography addiction is one of the toughest addictions for men to break free from; because once it has you, it seems to have you for good; and whenever you try to break free from it, the flesh tells you it wants more, and more, and more.

When I turned twenty-six, the greatest thing that could ever happened to me happened. I got saved! Salvation is by far the best thing that could have ever happen to anyone. It doesn't get any better than that. My life was a mess, and I was very depressed from time, to time. My favorite prayer before I got saved was this: "Father, if I knew without a doubt I was going to heaven tonight, if I died, you could take me right now."

That was my prayer every night, until I met Jesus, because I knew there was more to life than what I was experiencing, and I also knew I would never be able to enjoy it because I stayed high all the time. Although death looked better at that time to me than life, I wasn't brave enough to take my own, so I prayed that God would. Thank God once again that his plan was not my plan! Anyway, I got saved when I was twenty-six, and I would love to tell you that my pornography addiction stopped that day, and I've never laid eyes on porn again.

But I cannot tell you that and be telling the truth. The truth is I was still addicted to porn the day I was saved, and it would take years for me to throw away my stash of porn for good. I remember I tried to get rid of my stash of pornography and come clean from it. I had been saved for about a year and a half, and God had convicted me of the sin. I came home from church that Sunday, went straight to my room, grabbed the movies, and tossed them in the trash, and went to bed. The next day, I got up, went to the trash can, and retrieved the movies and popped one in the VCR and watched it before I went to work that morning. That freedom lasted every bit of seven hours and thirty-seven minutes. The second time was about a year later, and again, the Lord convicted me of this ongoing sin I was hiding. Again, I came home from church that Sunday with being free from pornography on my mind. However, this time I would wait until Monday morning to toss my videos into the trash can because I knew the trash man would come early Tuesday morning and pick up the trash from our complex. My mind-set this time was *I have to get these movies out of my house.* So I did. I dropped them off Monday morning in the dumpster, and Monday night, I picked them up right where I dropped them off from the dumpster. This had to be the lowest point of my life, to literally go through a trash dumpster full of other people's dirty trash, looking for porn movies. It was right then and there that I realized I had a terrible addiction; and I couldn't even imagine myself free from it!

Can you remember the first time you were introduced to pornography? Do you remember the rush, the thrill, and the high you got from seeing a naked woman for the first time? Can you remember where you were? How old were you? Who was it you saw? Can you remember the magazine she was in? Can you remember the rush, the thrill, and the high you got from seeing a naked body for the first time in a magazine? Or better yet, how about a naked booby in person? I was about eight years old the first time I saw a naked vagina in person. My friend and I were outside of our apartment one rainy day, sitting on the steps watching the rain fall down, when out of the blue, a young lady came out of her apartment and sat down on the steps above us. We lived on the first floor, she lived on the second, so we came out to sit on our doorstep. She was behind us and up a flight of steps. We had our backs to her and couldn't see her unless we literally turned our bodies around and looked up, which we decided to do after she had been outside for about ten minutes. My friend looked first, and then quickly turned around. He looked at me and said, "Man, look at her!" I turned to look, and the woman who looked to have been in her thirties, was sitting in front of her door, on the second floor, with a skirt on and no underwear. I also quickly turned around. My friend looked at me and said, "Wow can you believe her sitting like that?" I mean, with no panties on and all.

I said, "Not really. But I'm going to try to get me another quick peek."

I turned around, and she was looking right at me, smiling. I quickly turned back around. I told my friend, "Hey man, she likes us. She was looking at me smiling." He said, "No, she's not!" I said, "Yes, she is!" So he turned around and looked for himself, and there she was, staring right at him with this big old smile on her face. We would later find out that this young lady had mental issues, which would totally explain why she was outside with no underwear on, and more importantly, why she sat above us, with her legs spread wide open letting us look between them. Nevertheless, this was the first time I'd ever seen a real live vagina. It got to the point where the more we looked, the more she smiled, until we stopped turning back around because we were ashamed to be looking, and we just looked. We got a good long look at this woman's vagina, so much so that I thought about it, and even visualized it, for the next two weeks. I talked earlier about the rush, the thrill, and the high of seeing a naked woman for the first time, remember that.

Good. Because the reason so many men have spent their entire adult life addicted to pornography is that they are chasing that feeling they felt the first very time they were exposed to pornography—better known as the first-time thrill. Now it's foolish to chase after this first time thrill because you'll never feel it agai!. That's why it's called a first-time thrill. It's just like anything else (walking, talking, riding a bike, driving a car, or even having sex), you can do it a thousand times, and you'll never capture that first-time feeling again. I do believe that part of the problem with men and sexual addictions, is that we always believe that we can revisit the thrill of the first time—in the newest porn magazine with the newest model, in the newest sex tape with the newest porn star, or in a new relationship with a new woman. But let the truth be told. It's not possible, just like it's not possible to capture the feeling that you had the very first time you walked, talked, rode a bike by yourself, drove a car, or had sex.

• • • • • • • • • • • • •

Stage 2: My Struggle

My little niece always says, "Uncle Craig the struggle is real!" Bless her heart, she's only seventeen years old, so I have no idea what she could be talking about; however, I do know that when it comes to struggling with pornography, that struggle is very real, and this addiction does not care who it goes to battle with. It has defeated men all the way from the crack house to the White House. It has blindsided men all the way from the football field to the golf course, and it has caused men to fall by multitudes all the way from the movie industry to the pulpit. Some of the greatest, most powerful men of our time have fallen victim to porn addiction of one form or another.

For quite some time, it seemed as though every other month some power figure with great influence was having a news conference with his wife by his side to confess his infidelity. After a while, it begins to sound like a broken record, the same song, but by a different artist. So here's my question to you: If it wasn't a struggle, then how in the world could porn addiction bring so many powerful men of great influence down to their knees weeping like a baby? There is a television show called *To Catch a Predator*. This TV show is about older men soliciting young girls for sex on the Internet, and when they go to have sex with the young girls, the police and the TV crew will be at the house waiting for them.

The predator arrives and rings the doorbell or knocks on the door, the decoy, posing as the young lady, opens the door and leads him in. Inside, the camera crew pops out to bust the guy. They let him go outside, where he is then arrested and taken to jail and charged with a felony. I'm not saying this is one of my favorite shows or anything like that, but I did use to watch it quite a bit to see what kind of man would commit this type of crime. And what I found was astonishing: All types of men commit these types of crimes. I saw pastors, ministers, reverends, bishops; I saw doctors, lawyers, congressmen; I saw military personnel, school bus drivers, and even schoolteachers; and so on and so forth. I kid you not. I've seen all types of men from all kinds of different backgrounds, races, and religions featured on this television show. They all have one thing in common—the struggle with pornography. One of the main reasons I believe the struggle with pornography is greater now than it has ever been in the history of mankind is its accessibility. These days you can access pornography from anywhere at any time, making it stock, and popularity rise at an alarming rate. Here are a few stats I would like to share with you in regard to the incredible success of the porn business over the last decade.

- A total of $11 billion will be spent on sex tapes this year alone. Compared to the 750 million spent in 1998.

- The porn industry will release 470 porn movies this year alone.

- The porn industry will produce nine movies a week.

- A total of 40 million people will log on to some type of sex-oriented website this year alone.

- A total of $5 billion will be made in prostitution this year alone.

- A total of $3 billion will be made on sex slaves this year alone.

- Porn magazine and movies continue to sell and rent by the millions.

According to the American Family Association, the rental of XXX-rated videos jumped from 5 percent of all video rental in 1995 to 13 percent of all video rental in 1998.

Hugh Hefner continues to be one of the wealthiest men in America, thanks to his *Playboy* Empire. He's estimated to be worth more than a half billion dollars.

Last but not least, the porn industry made more money than ABC, NBC, and CBS combined, and also more than NBA, MLB, and NFL all put together. Now that's some serious dough!

It's a fact that the porn industry is one of the most profitable businesses in America, and it seems to be here to stay. But why is this so? I'll tell you why: Men are visual creatures, and we react to what we see, and have been this way since the beginning of time. Don't believe me? Take a look at Genesis 3:6. "And when the woman saw that tree was good for food, and that it was pleasant to the eyes, and a tree to be desired to make one wise, she took of the fruit thereof, and did eat, and gave also unto her husband with her, and he did eat."

If you know the story, then you know God forbid Adam to eat of the tree of good and evil. Not Eve. And the devil knew that he didn't have a chance with going straight to Adam to try to manipulate him to go against God's command, so he went through his wife, Eve. See, the devil is smart, and he knew that Eve, like most women today, are more likely to react to what they hear rather than what they see. He also understood that

Adam, like most men today, are more likely to react to what they see rather than what they hear. So Satan whispered to Eve and persuaded her to sin against God, because he knew she would react to what she heard rather than what she saw, knowing that if Adam saw her eat of the fruit, he too would eat the of fruit since he was a man, and men react to what we see rather than what we hear.

Have you ever been in a mall and seen this very attractive young lady with this dog-ugly dude and thought to yourself, *How in the world did that happen?* And as you passed by her, you could see on her face she was asking herself the same exact question. *Yeah, how in the world did this happen?* I'll tell how it happened: he told her exactly what she wanted to here. One of my best friends growing up had this uncanny ability to get some of the finest women God ever created and placed on earth, and he must have been the ugliest dude in the whole neighborhood. For years, I wondered, how in the world could this dude, who was nowhere near as attractive as I was, get these fine women? I mean, what was he doing that I wasn't? What did he know that I didn't know?

Then finally, one day, we were in his bedroom when his girlfriend called. He answered the phone, and I'll never forget the words he spoke to her. They started with small talk, and then she must have asked, "How much do you love me?" Because he responded with, "Girl, I love you so much I'll take a trip to the moon tonight, steal every shining star out of the sky on the way back home, and give them to you, because that's how beautiful you are to me!" Then he put the phone to my ear so I could hear her response.

She said, "Baby that is so sweet! I love you so much. You are the greatest!"

I was totally tripping out. I thought to myself, *Dude, you can go to the moon tonight. You can't even go to the gas station 'cause you ain't got no car.* And then I thought about how stupid she was for believing it. Once he got off the phone with her, I told him,

"She may be fine, but she is as stupid as a doorknob to believe that mess."

It would take me years to understand that the young lady didn't really believe that my friend could got to the moon and steal all the stars from the sky on the way back and give them to her; however, she did believe that if he could, he would, and that's what made her fall in love with him. Women react to what they hear; men react to what they see. This is why the *Playboy* magazine has made Mr. Hefner a very wealthy man known all over the world, and why no one can tell you who the publisher of *Playgirl* is, which is supposed to be the women's version of *Playboy*. That's because the *Playgirl* hasn't been anywhere near as successful as *Playboy*.

Why is that? I'm glad you asked. Because women react to what they hear, and men react to what we see. And this is the reason why pornography is destroying the men in this country at an alarming rate. Ted Bundy once said in an interview that he was introduced to pornography at the age of eleven, and of course, we know what he went on to do. Not only him, but Jeffrey Dahmer also confessed to being addicted to pornography, and again, we know his story. This list goes on and on; as a matter of fact, I would go out on a limb and say that every serial rapist, killer, and child molester struggles with some form of porn addiction. The struggle is real!

• • • • • • • • • • • • • •

I heard an alarming statistic the other day that said, "Somewhere between 65 and 75 percent of all churchgoing men visit a pornographic website weekly. At first, I thought to myself this has to be a typo, there is no way that many church going men are viewing pornography on a regular basics. But then I thought to myself, just because a person goes to church does not make them a Christian, so this could very well be true.

And even if they are striving to be like Christ, they could still have issues with pornography. I'm reminded of some of the biggest and most powerful names in the Christian arena to fall victim to this spirit of pornography. Before anyone even thought about television ministry, this man had the biggest one in the country. Of course, I'm talking about Jim Baker. His huge television ministry, was seen by millions each week around the world was destroyed by sexual immorality, caused by porn addiction.

And what about Jimmy Swaggart? Again a huge ministry with thousands of faithful followers. Destroyed by sexual immorality caused by porn addiction. Ted Haggard, the head of the Baptist denomination in America, fell due to sexual immorality caused by porn addiction. And then there is Bishop Eddie Long, the leader of the largest African American church in America fell due to sexual misconduct.

So if you think for one moment that it's not real, and there is no such thing called porn addiction, you better think again. I mean, why else would these godly men, who seemed to have had it all, risk it all for something that wasn't real? Men, don't fool yourselves. This struggle is very real and could lead you down the road to destruction—quickly! Not every person whose life has been destroyed by sexual immorality, caused by porn addiction, is famous. Which reminds me of a friend of mine who, at one time, was one of the most sought after youth pastors in the state of Georgia. I met this guy about fifteen years ago at a church we both attended. I arrived at the church about six months before he did. The pastor of the church was new and looking to plant a church in the area. He brought me on as the outreach minister and my friend as the youth pastor.

I remember the first Sunday at the church: He walked in with his family, as clean and as confident as I had ever seen a pastor. Although he kind of put me in the mind of a politician because he shook hands and spoke to everyone in the church. He had the perfect charismatic personality for the job. And right from the start, everyone fell in love with him. My friend came in with a lot of energy and a lot of great ideas, and really took the children's ministry at the church to another level. He was great with the kids and with their parents. He fed off of them, and they definitely fed off of him. Everything was perfect for about five years, until my friend felt it was time for him and his family to move on.

I would occasionally hear from my friend from time to time, for the first couple of years after he left the church. And then there was nothing. Until one night I got a call from the county jail saying they had a collect call for me. Would I accept? I said yes, and it was my friend. He said, "Man, I can't tell you what's going on right now, but I need for you to come and get me out of jail."

I got out of the bed, got dressed, and went and got him out of jail. When I got there, of course, I had to ask him what was going on. He told me he and his wife got into this heated argument over her finding out that he was cheating on her. She called the police and told them that he hit her, and they took him to jail. I was like, Wow! And I couldn't believe this.

So I asked him, "Is it true?"

"No, of course I would never hit my wife!"

"What about the other part?"

"What about? Me cheating?"

"Yeah."

He dropped his head and said, "Yeah, I've been unfaithful to my wife."

Then as we sat there in my car for the next three hours, he explained to me how the spirit of pornography had completely taken over his life. He started out by telling me that he had always, even from his early teen years, struggled with pornography. He said he could remember as early as eleven or twelve years old masturbating to his father's stash of dirty magazines. He talked about how all throughout high school, he was very promiscuous, having at least twenty sexual partners. When he turned twenty, he knew the Lord was calling him to change his life and to do ministry full-time, so that's what he did. He accepted the calling and began to do ministry full-time at a small church in the local town where he lived. It was there that he would meet his wife, a beautiful virgin woman, who had never been married. His wife was totally different from him. Her father was a pastor, and she was raised very strictly, unlike my friend. Growing up, he was very wild, living a lifestyle where anything and everything was allowed in his house. They would get married one year after they met, and the following year, they would start a family.

My friend went on to say that the first five years were just as he had dreamed it would be. He had this beautiful virgin wife who knew nothing about sex except for what he taught her. He explained that the first couple of years were awesome, because everything he wanted his new bride to know about sex, and how to please him in bed, he would teach her, and she was willing to learn. One day, she told him she no longer wanted to be his sex slave, and if she couldn't be his wife and the mother of his children, without being abused in bed, then she was leaving him. He said now he had a problem, because regular, ordinary sex was boring to him because of his addiction to porn and his prior sexual relationships.

My friend confessed that the next ten years would be the most difficult time in his life—because now he had to find a way to satisfy his strong, and somewhat wicked, sexual desires without his wife knowing. This would lead him deeper and deeper into the underground world of porn. He said, "What people don't understand is that just because you get married doesn't mean you're no longer addicted to porn. It may slow it down for a little while, but it doesn't deliver you from it. So now that my wife wasn't interested in fulfilling my sexual fantasies any longer, I had to find someone who was. I started with the hardcore porn movies, waiting until everyone went to sleep, and then I would sneak into the living room and take care of my business on a daily basis.

"This was my routine for years, all the while raising four children, being the youth pastor of one of the largest Baptist churches in the state, and trying to provide for my ever-growing family. My kids got older and started staying up later so I had to change my venue. I began to use the computer in my wife's office, which was what led to me being arrested tonight."

He told me that one day, his wife came to him and asked him about some sex sites that someone at her office had been visiting, and wanted to know if it was him.

"Even though I knew it was me, I lost it and went off on her, but I didn't hit her. We hadn't spoken all week long until today, she said she wanted a divorce, I told her I wasn't giving her one because I hadn't done anything wrong, so we got to arguing about the divorce, and eventually, I pushed her to the floor, and she called the police on me. They came and took me to jail. I stayed here all day long, thinking of who I could call to get me out. And then I called you."

I told my friend I really didn't know what to say or what to do other than pray for him, and so I did. Within the next two years, my friend would lose his job, get a divorce, stop going to church, start drinking again, and become homeless for a period of time. The last time I saw my friend he was living with his girlfriend, with whom he had a baby by, in a one-bedroom apartment. Their life consisted of partying, partying, and more partying. As a tear rolled down my friend's face, he looked at me and said, "This pornography has ruined my life."

And as I looked at him, I saw a far cry from the man I met some ten years ago. The man who I myself envied because he had this beautiful virgin woman, four beautiful kids, a nice house, and a dream job, doing what he loved to do. Now, do I believe that my friend was ever saved? Absolutely! However, I believe this spirit of pornography was stronger than his salvation at that time. The struggle!

. . . .

Now most of you guys reading this book may not have had a struggle with porn on the level of my friend I mentioned in this chapter. As a matter of fact, you may not think you have a problem at all with porn addiction. However, I believe that most men have an issue with porn addiction of some kind, on some level. Why? Because we're made up of this thing called flesh. The Bible even tells us that there is no temptation taking us such as common to men. Meaning there are certain temptations that men from all, races, ethnic groups, religion, social status, and with all kinds of backgrounds are going to be subjected to. And pornography is one of those temptations.

I once read a book entitled *Every Man's Battle* by Steve Arterburn, Fred Stoeker and Mike Yorkey. When I first heard of the book, I thought, *Whatever they're talking about cannot be every man's battle.* I mean, how could it be, since every man is different? And this is true, but at least one of every man's battle is the same across the board, and that is the battle with pornography.

As a matter of fact, if any man says after reading this book that he does not struggle with some form of porn addiction, then not only does he struggle with porn, but he also struggles with lying. So here goes: Before we are able to realize that we may possibly struggle with pornography, we must understand what is and what is not considered pornography. At this time, we are going to take a little pop quiz. I am going to present a few different magazines, that we as men have more than likely encountered in our lives, and you are going to answer yes or no to whether you consider it to be porn or not. There is no pass or fail with this test. I'm just trying to get you to think outside the box for a minute. As I said before, most men think that since they don't have a problem with the obvious hardcore pornography (XXX-rated movies and XXX-rated magazines), they don't have a problem with pornography. However, I beg to differ. Pornography comes in all kinds of form, shape, and size these days. I mean if you think about it, do you think the devil could attack mankind and cause him to fall by the hundreds of thousands by using the same method on every single man? I don't think so. The devil is smarter than that. He knows exactly what to use on each man to cause him to fall to pornography.

Now let's take a look at three magazines, to see if they would be considered a form of pornography, based on the definition of the word. Any picture or writings, etc., with the intent to cause sexual arousal.

Sports Illustrated (Swimsuit Edition)

The way I determine if a magazine would be considered porn, or not would be to ask myself these two simple questions. Who is the target group of this particular magazine? Is it males or females? Of course, the answer to this question would be males. I plead guilty to this one myself. I used to subscribe to *Sports Illustrated* all year long, just to get the coveted swimsuit edition once a year. My mother used to tell me all the time that she knew I was going to be good in sports because I always got those issues of *Sports Illustrated*. In actuality, I wasn't even thinking about the sports. I just knew in order for me to get the swimsuit edition once a year, I had to subscribe year round; this would also cover me if my mother would have said anything about the swimsuit edition. I could have honestly explained to her, "Mom, I get this magazine every month—what's the big deal?" Question number 2: Is this particular magazine sexually arousing to its target group? The answer to this question would have to be yes. So here is my question to you, based on the definition of the word *pornography*. Is the *Sports Illustrated* Swimsuit Edition magazine a form of pornography or not?

• • • • • • • • • • • • • •

Maxim (The Ultimate Guys Guide)

This magazine was started in the UK in 1995; and in 1998, the United States received its first copy. *Maxim* is an international men's magazine targeted at adult males and based in New York, and prominent for its cheesecake pictorials of actresses, singers, and female models whose careers are at their current peak. Between 2010 and 2012, *Maxim* eliminated two issues, going from twelve issues a year to just ten, and decreased its circulation numbers by 20 percent, from a reported 2.5 million to only 2 million.

Now let's ask ourselves, What is the target group of this particular magazine? Of course, it would be men.

Question number 2: Is this particular magazine sexually arousing to its target group? The answer once again would have to be yes. So here's my question to you, based on the definition of the word *pornography*: Is *Maxim* a form of pornography or not?

• • • • • • • • • • • • • •

Stuff

This was first published in Britain in November 1996 by Dennis Publishing. It's a bimonthly title, and it followed the success of magazine such as *FML* and *Loaded* in being pitched toward a young male audience. Again, this particular magazine has had some of the most beautiful, most famous actresses to ever pose on the cover with a full pictorial on the inside.

Question number 1: What would be the target group for this particular magazine? Young men, of course.

Question number 2: Is the magazine sexually arousing to the target group? The answer, once again, would have to be yes.

So here's my question to you, based on the definition of the word *pornography*: Is *Stuff* a form of pornography or not?

• • • • • • • • • • • • • •

I'm sure there are other magazines that are questionable, regarding the definition of *pornography*, as to whether they would be considered porn; but these are just a few I always thought—based on the definition of pornography and not based on what people perceive pornography to be—would have to be a form of pornography.

I remember, about five years ago, a young lady was on the eleven o'clock local news, irate about her twelve-year-old son being suspended from middle school for bringing a *Sports Illustrated* Swimsuit Edition to school to show his friends the centerfold of the year. The centerfold model had on a G-string bikini. The magazine was confiscated, and the boy was sent home on a three-day suspension. His mom was beside herself with anger. For some ungodly reason, she didn't quite understand what the problem was, so she called the local news to help her figure it out.

Apparently, this middle school and its board of directors felt the same way I do about the whole *SI* Swimsuit Edition—which is that it is most definitely is a form of pornography; and we as fathers need to wake up, smell the coffee, and stop this magazine and ones like it from entering our homes and planting the seeds of pornography in our sons' minds. This is how the devil operates. He's very, very subtle. He doesn't do anything drastic and quick. No, that's not how he gets us; everything he does, he does slowly and over a long period of time. As I mentioned, he's a master at planting corrupt seeds in our minds and hearts. What I mean is this: the devil may not be able to bring a *Playboy*, *Penthouse*, or *Hustler* in our house and try to turn our young men into porn addicts, but he can quietly sneak a Victoria's Secret Catalogue, an *SI* Swimsuit Edition, or a *Maxim* magazine into our homes to fulfill the very same purpose.

How is this possible? Well, it's simple. You can purchase most of these magazines right over the counter without having to show any ID. The devil is smart; he knows that for most of us, he can't get us to fall with the obvious, so he trips us up with the not-so-obvious, which turns out to be just as effective. See, here's the deal the: *SI* Swimsuit Edition and *Playboy* are the same porn, the same spirit is behind both. It's just *Playboy* is a mature version of the *SI* Swimsuit Edition.

I heard a pastor once say, "Sin will take farther than you want to go, keep you longer than you want to stay, and cost you more than you want to pay." This is so true because sin always progresses, and you'll very seldom end up where you start out. Such was the case with me and my porn addiction.

Stage 3: My Victory:

A lot of people think that once they get saved, God saves everything about them, and takes every single sexual desire and ungodly thought away from them, so that their minds and their flesh will be in perfect harmony with their spirit so that they can do all that God has called them to do without interruption. Wrong! This is why the book of Romans 12:2 reads, "And be not conformed to this world; but be ye transformed by the renewing of your mind, that ye may prove what is that good, and acceptable and perfect, will of God." Isaiah 26:3 puts it like this: "Thou will keep him in perfect peace, whose mind is stayed on thee: because he trusteth in thee."

Everyone says that salvation is free, and they're absolutely right about the receiving part. But the retraining of the mind, and the keeping it stayed on Jesus—now that's hard work. After all, it's the mind that tells the flesh how to behave.

Anyway, as I was saying, the flesh still has needs to be fulfilled, even after I decided to completely follow the Lord; and now my dilemma was, how was I supposed to do that without a woman in my life? Now, I was no stranger to masturbation. I'd been doing it ever since I was twelve or thirteen years old. However, the same old pattern of masturbating at home, and alone had lost its appeal to me. And this left me looking for a new, creative way to satisfy my sexual desires while living a life that could not be spotted by the world.

It would not take me long to find one—one that would keep me bound for nineteen years during my walk with the Lord. It was something I would never have seen myself doing, even as a sinner, or even thought possible to do. But since I couldn't go out and satisfy my sexual desires the way I was accustomed to doing, I had to be creative and find a way to fulfill my sexual pleasures secretly, and in my mind, I had finally found the perfect way.

As I said before, masturbation can start out in the comfort of your bedroom, and could end up pretty much anywhere. In a bathroom stall, a movie theater, outside, in a classroom, in an office, on a bus, or even in a car. Such was the case with me.

Shortly after I decided to completely follow Jesus, I was riding home from work one spring afternoon when I came upon an accident on my regular route home. Unlike most people, I didn't have an alternate route home from work. I only knew one way, that was from point A to point B, so when I came up on this accident, I began to freak out because I had no idea how I was going to get home. The accident was so bad they had to shut the road down and detour the cars that were stuck in traffic.

I figured everyone in front of me was trying to get back onto the same road I was, so I just followed them. We all turned onto one back road after another, until eventually, we were driving right alongside a park. It was crazy! I'd never seen so many women half-dressed, jogging and walking their dogs. Now for me, springtime was always the worst time when it came to lusting over women. For some it may be summertime, but to be honest with you, by the time the summer comes around, I'm already immune to the skin. However, in springtime, you get the first peek of skin that's been covered up for a whole winter. You see women that you've seen all winter long, and when you see them in the springtime you'd be like, *Man, I did not know she looked like that.* That's because she's been wrapped up like a cocoon for five months, and now, suddenly, she's at the pool, half naked.

Let's get back to the detour. I drove down this road with all these beautiful, fine, voluptuous, toned females all over the place; and I thought, *This is nice.* Needless to say, this became my new route home from work from that day on. Every day I would ride by the park and think, *How can I use these beautiful women for my own sexual gratification?* Until one day it hit me: I would become a carjacker. No, I'm not talking about a person who holds someone up and robs them of their automobile—no, I'm talking about a person who drives around in their car masturbating.

And for the better part of the next two decades, that's exactly what I did. Of course, I wouldn't be confined to just this one park for the next nineteen years—oh no, I would travel thousands of miles and find myself in cities I had no business being in, carjacking. Of course, as it progressed, and the years went by, it got to the point where it didn't have to be a park anymore; and the women didn't have to be beautiful anymore. It had gotten to the point where all I had to be was in my car, and all they had to be was outside of it.

About four years after I started carjacking, I suffered the most humiliating day of my entire life. It was around this time that I felt the Lord speaking to me, telling me to come out of this lifestyle. Enough was enough. That's the thing about God: He will always warn you before he exposes you. He was constantly telling me it was time to trust him for deliverance and move on to the bigger and better things he had waiting for me. But because the pleasure of my sin, at that time, was more desirable than the promises of my God, I continued to indulge in what I was doing until one day, the crap hit the fan.

It was a beautiful September day, and I was on my way to my favorite department store to do shopping. I stopped by my sister's house to see if my nephew could come along with me because I really did not like to shop by myself; that was just no fun to me. But once I arrived at my sister's house to pick him up, my sister said they already had plans for the day, so I went on by myself. I went to the department store and did all my shopping; and while I was in the store, I saw this beautiful, long-legged, perfectly tanned young lady standing in line three people in back of where I was. I thought I would just check on out, go to my car, and wait for her to walk by so that I could get a good look at her, if you know what I mean.

It took a while, but she finally came out of the store and walked right in front of my car. I did my thing, but before I could start my car up and leave, a police officer walked up to my window and knocked on it and motioned for me to let the window down. I was totally freaking out, even though I knew he didn't see what I just did because of the tint on the windows. But it was obvious he was on to something.

I rolled the window down, and he said, "Son, what are you doing in here?"

I said, "Nothing, sir. Just getting ready to leave. I just got finished shopping, and I was making sure I had my receipt in case I have to return something."

He said, "That's not what the lady inside told me. She said that her daughter saw you out here masturbating in your car."

My heart sank, and as I tried to plead my case, the officer ordered me to get out of the car. He handcuffed me and placed me under arrest. He walked me in handcuffs all the way through the middle of the store to the manager's office in the very back. The whole time I was walking through this store in handcuffs, for the entire store to see, I was thinking about this one scripture I had read the year before. I cannot think of where it is in the Bible, but it goes something like this: "Those things that are done in the dark, God will bring to the light." This scripture is so true. That day I felt as though a huge spotlight was on me, revealing my darkest secret for everyone to see. You may think the walk of shame through the department store would have been the most humiliating thing to happen to me that day, but it wasn't. The most humiliating thing to happen to me came on the ride from the department store to jail.

As I sat in the back of that police car for the first time in my life, listening to the police officer call my arrest in to the headquarters, I experienced the lowest point in my life. When the dispatcher asked what I was charged with, the police officer said, "Man, I really couldn't tell you. We don't even have a code for it. Just a pervert jacking off in a car." Then they both began to laugh. I thought, *They are exactly right. I'm just a pervert who masturbates in cars, and I must be the only one in the world with this problem since the law doesn't even know what to call it.* Absolutely the lowest of the lows for me. I'd never felt such shame, embarrassment, and the hurt in my entire life.

I mean, you gotta understand, growing up, I was Mr. Popular with the ladies. There weren't too many that I wanted that I could not get. Now there I was, masturbating in cars to women I'd never met, and women who would never let me violate them in real life, the way I have violated them in my mind. How in the world did I get here! Now, one might think that this life-changing experience would have changed my life. Well, not exactly. As a matter of fact, it would take another decade for me to finally surrender this terrible stronghold to God and ask for help. However, as soon as I did, God stepped in and delivered me. I cried out to him on a Friday night, and Saturday morning, God gave me seven keys to freedom. And I've been free every since!

• • • • • • • • • • • • •

Stage 3: The Victory

Hindsight. It was almost as if God himself was waiting for me to finally get to my breaking point and reach out to him for help. I have applied these seven keys to freedom to my own life for the last four years, and let me tell you like the Lord told me.

If you work them into your day, every day, then they will work for you, 100 percent of the time! The Bible says let the redeemed of the Lord say so. This simply means if God has done anything for you, you should tell somebody. That's exactly what I'm about to do. I'm about to help someone gain their freedom from porn addiction, simply by sharing what the Lord shared with me over four years ago.

I am so very excited about sharing these seven keys to freedom with you guys, because for anyone who knows me, they'll tell you that I'm not a selfish person. If I have something worth sharing, I'm the first to share with someone in need. I'm the type of person who, if I found a way to make a million dollars, after I made mine, I would share whatever secret I have with all my friends.

Friend. That's what I call every man reading this book right now who may be struggling with porn addiction. Not only do I call you friend, but I also want to let you know you're not alone. Look, I don't care what form of pornography you struggle with, you're not alone. I don't care if it's private or public. Meaning it doesn't matter if you're home alone doing your thing, or if you have found yourself masturbating in public. You've heard my story, now what's yours? Believe me when I say, whatever your story is, it's not yours alone. Somebody shares it with you. Satan wants to isolate you and make you think you are the only person who struggles with whatever it is you struggle with, like he did to me in the back of that police car. He tried to make me think that I was the only person in the world who had a problem with public masturbation. He wanted me to think it was so rare they didn't even have a name for it. But the devil is a lie. I would estimate there are thousands, maybe even hundreds of thousands of men around the world who struggle with some form of public masturbation. So without further ado, let's jump right into these seven principals and get you on your way to a lifestyle of freedom.

• • • • • • • • • • • • • •

The Seven Keys to Freedom

1. Make a vow before the Lord.

    Job says, "I made a covenant with mine eyes, when then should I think upon a maid." (Job 31:1). Another translation puts it like this: "I made a covenant with my eyes that I might not look at a woman with lust." When I was growing up, my mother was always watching some pastor on television asking for money to build their ministry, and she would always make a vow to send them some. There were times when my mother wasn't even working, and still she would vow to send a certain amount of money to these pastors, having no idea where the money would come from.

    And when she did get her hands on the money, my sister and I would say, "Mom, we really need that money to pay bills around the house."

    And she would always answer, "I'm sorry, this is the Lord's money, not mine, so you better find what you need somewhere else."

    Then we would say, "Momma, the Lord will understand we need this money more than he does at the time. I mean, he has a cattle on a thousand hills or something like that, right? We don't have a cattle on one hill. We're broke."

    And my mother would always say this: "It's better to not make a vow than to make one and not keep it; "That's in the Bible somewhere. Years later, I would find out my mother was exactly right. It is in the Bible somewhere, and she's right. It is better not to make a vow to the Lord than to make one and not keep it. Because of my dear mother, today I take my vows to the Lord very seriously!

Every morning, when I get up I make a vow to the Lord. Why, because there is power in the words we speak. According to Proverbs 18:21, "Death and life are in the power of the tongue: and they that love it shall eat the fruit thereof."

My vow goes something like this: "Lord, I will not ————————fill in the blank with your struggle. (Of course mine was carjacking) today. Rather I'm going to love you with all my heart, mind, body, and soul!

Look, you can talk yourself out of an addiction, and you can talk yourself into one, because the tongue is just that powerful. That's why people are always saying, "Watch your mouth." And "Be careful what you say because once it's out there, you can't take it back." And "Once the damage is done, you can't repair it." So when I get up in the morning and I began to speak those words, and throughout the day as I continue to speak them, Satan begins to throw a temper tantrum, because he knows as long as I am speaking life to my situation, he cannot bring death to it. This principle will certainly work for you as well. Begin your day each morning telling Satan what you're not going to do, and declaring unto the Lord what you are going to do.

• • • • • • • • • • • • • •

2. Go straight to point A and straight back home.

This one is pretty much self-explanatory. Go straight to where you're going, and return straight home. I remember when I was growing up, my mother would always tell me this. My best friend lived directly across the street from us, and every time I would ask my mother to let me go over to his house, she would always say, "Now you go straight over to his house, and when I call you, you better come straight home."

Even though I totally understood what that meant, every time my mother would call for me to come home, it seemed as though I always made a detour, and she always made me pay for it. The same is true even today. As a grown man, every time I fail to go straight to point A and return straight home, it seems as though I end up paying for it. That's why every morning, when I pray, I ask the Lord to take me straight to work and bring me straight home. Nine times out of ten, when I make a detour on the way to, or coming home from work, I end up paying for it. Honestly, though, going to work is not a problem for me. However, coming home from work can be, from time to time.

I thank God for my wife, because she helps me with this without even knowing it. I call my wife every day when I leave work, and as soon as she picks up the phone to answer it, the clock begins to tick. You see, she has timed my return trip home on numerous occasions, and she knows it takes me only twenty-eight minutes to get home; so she usually gives me thirty before she calls and checks on me. As a result, I know from the time I call my wife until the time I should be arriving in the driveway, that it takes no more than thirty minutes tops.

In other words, once I call my wife and tell her I'm on my way home, I better be on my way home. There is no time for detours. And this principle will work for you as well. Use your wife or girlfriend as a silent accountability partner if you're having a problem with going straight to point A and returning straight home. Detours will only sidetrack you and get you off your course; and believe me, that's a dangerous place to be. Go straight to point A and return straight home.

• • • • • • • • • • • • • •

3. Be where you're supposed to be, when you're supposed to be there.

Every time I think about being where you're supposed to be, when you're supposed to be there, I think about this young lady who was in a terrible car accident her senior year in high school—an accident that left her clinging to life. It was Senior Skip Day, and her parents knew it; however, before she left for school that day, she assured her parents that she would not be participating in the Senior Skip Day. She would definitely be at school, she promised. But as soon as her friend arrived to pick her up, she jumped in the car, changed her clothes, and headed straight for the house where they all were planning on spending the day.

Everything was going perfect until she unexpectedly began her menstrual cycle. She totally freaked out because she had on white pants. So she borrowed her friend's car to drive home and change clothes. The young lady was speeding on the way to her house trying to get there before it was too late and she ruined her favorite pair of white pants, and without even knowing she had crossed the center lane and crashed head-on into an oncoming truck.

The impact was so severe it threw the young lady through the back windshield, breaking several bones, including her neck and her back. She actually died on the way to the hospital, but when they got her to the ER, they were able to save her life. However she would remain in a coma for three weeks, and when she came out, she was informed that she would be paralyzed from the neck down for the rest of her life.

I'll never forget the mother's response when the police came knocking on her door that afternoon to inform her that her daughter had been in a terrible car accident. "You can't be talking about my baby because she's at school!"

According to this young lady's mother, this was the first time her daughter had ever lied to her, and it would nearly cost the young lady her life. Be where you're supposed to be when you're supposed to be there. I have a good friend of mine who would always call me and say, "Stafford look down at your feet and tell me where you're standing." Nine times out of ten when we fall to sexual immorality our feet are somewhere they have no business being.

For example, if you're struggling with fornication, don't be somewhere having sex when you should be at your best friend's house watching the football game. Or if you're struggling with drugs, don't be somewhere getting high when you should be at work. Well, how about this one: If you're married and you're having a problem being faithful to your wife, don't be going out to dinner with a female coworker when your wife thinks you are working late. Statistics have shown that 75 percent of churchgoing men visit a pornographic website two to three times a week. If that's your struggle, don't be on your computer at two o'clock in the morning when you should be in bed asleep with your wife.

You get the point. You will all but eliminate your chances of falling into temptation if you will just be where you are supposed to be when you're supposed to be there.

• • • • • • • • • • • • •

4. Find an Accountability Partner:
    Ecclesiastes 4:9 reads, "Two are better than one; because they have a good reward for their labor." This one here can be kinda tricky because most men feel as though there's nothing that can happen to them in life that they cannot handle all by themselves. Even Jesus told

his disciples to travel in twos. Just in case one gets weak, the other could pick up the slack. The Bible also tells us, where two or more touch and agree I am in the midst of them, which tells me there must be some kind of awesome power in unity of more than one. Not only do I realize this, but so does Satan. That's why he is forever trying to isolate men and keep us away from people who can help bring us out of the bondage that we were in.

If you think about it, the first thing that the enemy does in an attack is disconnect allies' line of communication. The reason they do this is that they understand that when they attack the allies, if they don't have a way to call for help, then the battle is won. Satan uses the same method of attack on mankind today. When he attacks us, he wants us to think we are all alone. He wants us to think no one knows about us, and he wants us to think no one cares about us, because he knows if he can do that, the battle is won, and he will reign victorious.

I must say the hardest part about this whole accountability partner thing is finding the right one. I even had a problem with this one myself. About five years ago, when I was really going through this struggle with pornography, I heard a pastor talk about the importance of having an accountability partner. I thought, *I should find me one of these accountability partners because I could really use some help right about now.*

I had this best friend at the time who was a very strong Christian brother who loved to pray. Now don't get me wrong. I love to pray too, but this brother would pray all the time. I would call him up sometime and ask, "How's the weather?" And he would break out into a prayer. So I thought, Who could be better to have as an accountability partner than someone who loves the Lord and loves to pray? The next time I talked to my buddy, I said, "Look, man, I need an accountability partner. Would you be my accountability partner?"

He said, "Sure, brother, what's the problem?"

I told him what I was struggling with, and he said, "Let's pray." It was cool having someone to pray with me concerning my issue, but I never really felt connected to my buddy as an accountability partner. As a result, I stopped confiding in him. It would take years, but the Lord would finally reveal to me that you don't pick out an accountability partner. You pray for one. See, here's the deal: the best accountability partner is someone who is either in the same struggle or has just came out of the same struggle you're in.

For example, if someone is struggling with pornography, the best accountability partner for him may not be someone who cheats on his taxes. It's the commonality that makes the connection so powerful, because this person understands where you are and what you are going through, literally. Like I said, you don't pick out an accountability partner, you pray for one, and the Lord will send the perfect person for you. Such was the case with myself. I prayed to the Lord to send me an accountability partner. One who understands what I was going through and could relate to me on that level.

Within two weeks, the Lord sent another very good friend of mine to me. He and I were sitting in his apartment one day, just shooting the breeze when out of the blue, he began to tell me how he struggled with public masturbation. His struggle was masturbating at his work in the bathroom stalls. Every morning he would walk into the office and turn his heat-seeking eyes on to see what young lady was looking the best on that particular day. Then after he got the visual down in his mind, he would go into the restroom and masturbate to that particular young lady. And when he finished, he would come out of the restroom, find the young lady, smile, and shake her hand and walk off.

He explained the reason he did this was to thank her because in his mind, he had just had sex with her. I was really blown away by his confession because to look at this guy, you would think he had it all together; but on the other hand, I was relieved, because here's somebody who could really understand me and relate to me right where I was. So needless to say, we became accountability partners and have remained accountability partners until this very day. Glory be to God. We both have been delivered from our public masturbation bondage, and my accountability partner was delivered by using the same seven keys to freedom that I'm sharing with you in his book.

Two is better than one. With that being said, start seeking God for an accountability partner. Someone who knows what you're going through with your issue and can relate to you right where you are. I'm a witness that God has the perfect person waiting for you. I believe that your freedom is right around the corner, and I believe that your accountability partner is going to play a huge role in it. Get someone in your life who's going to hold you accountable.

• • • • • • • • • • • • •

5. Use them.

The accountability partner, that is.

I'm reminded of the story of the man who was drowning in a flood, and when God sent a life jacket, the man said, "No, thanks, I'm waiting for the Lord."

Then the Lord sent a boat, and the man said, "No, thanks. I'm waiting for the Lord."

Then finally, the Lord sent a helicopter with a rope hanging to scoop the man up and into safety, and the man looked at the rope and said, "No, thanks, I'm waiting for the Lord."

Needless to say, the man died and went to heaven. When he got there, he said, "Lord, I was waiting for you. Why didn't you save me?"

The Lord said, "I sent you a life jacket. You refused it. I sent you a boat, and you refused it. Then I sent a helicopter, and you refused it as well. Look, I tried to help you and sent you what you needed to survive the flood, but you simply refused them."

What I'm trying to say is this: It is better not to have an accountability partner than to have one and not use them. Such was the case with me. God sent me this awesome accountability partner—someone who could relate to me because we were in the same struggle together, and it still took me the better part of a year to call on him in times of struggle. For a while there, my accountability partner was used more like a Bounty paper towel than an accountability partner. What I mean by that is I was good about calling him after I fell, but terrible about calling him before I fell.

I would call him and say, "Man, I fell again. Can you pray for me?" And we would be praying for forgiveness for my sin. This would go on for quite some time until the Lord finally spoke to me and said, "I'm tired of being your Bounty quicker picker-upper." He said, "I'm tired of cleaning up your spills when I'm here to help prevent them."

Then I said, "Lord, you are right. Help me to call on my accountability partner before I fall, and give me strength to trust you to keep me from falling through them. He did just that. The truth of the matter is, every time we trip and not fall, we get stronger in our walk. These days, if I think I might be in a position to fall, I call my accountability partner right away, and we pray. Notice I said if I think

223

I might fall, not when I'm on the verge of it. I personally do believe there is a point of no return for the flesh. Now don't get me wrong. I know there's nowhere you can go, and no valley too deep that God cannot save you from it if you just call on him.

However, there is a place where you can get in the flesh, where your prayer changes from "Lord, please keep me from sinning," to "Lord, please forgive me for this sin I'm about to commit." For example, if you struggle with Internet pornography, you don't want to click on to the website at two in the morning when everyone else is asleep, and then start praying, "Lord, please help me." No, at that point in time, your prayer is probably going to be more like, "Lord, please forgive me for I have sinned against you." Or better yet, if you struggle with drugs, you don't want to have a pipe in your hands, about to light it up, and praying that God will keep you from hitting it. No, at this point and time, your prayer is going to be more like, "Lord, please forgive me, because I'm about to get high." Or say, "You're a married man, and you struggle with infidelity. You don't want to find yourself at your mistress's house in her bedroom praying that God will give you strength to get up and walk out of there."

No, at this point and time, your prayer is probably going to go something like this, "Lord, please forgive me for my sin because I have fire in my bosom, and there's no way I'm walking out of here without satisfying my fleshly desires." My point is simply this: Once you get to those places and the flesh is turned on like that, it's possible to get out of those situations, but not likely, because once your flesh gets turned on to that degree it's going to demand that you satisfy it. So, do like I do: If there is a hint that you may be tempted in an area that you struggle with, pick up the phone and call your accountability partner before you reach the point of no return.

I bet if I conducted a survey today of one hundred men who have been in church for at least five years, and asked them if they have an accountability partner, most of them would probably say "Yes." Then if I asked them if they use their accountability partner to hold them accountable in areas in their lives where they struggle the most, I bet the response would more than likely be, "No."

And if I asked them why, they would probably say "I don't know." Hey, if a millionaire came up to you and gave you a pin number to an account that had 10 million dollars in it, how long would it take you to go and claim your money? Not long, because if you're like most of us you could use a little extra cash. Not only that, because you have the pin number you have everything you'll need to receive your blessing.

The same is true with your accountability partner. We have access to someone, who has been appointed by God, to help us gain our freedom. However, we chose to continue to be a slave to sin. Men, as you read this book, whether you're a young man, a middle-aged man, or an older man, God desires for us to be free from bondage, so that we can do what he's called us to do. So if you don't have an accountability partner, pray for one, and once God sends him to you, use him, use him, use him!

• • • • • • • • • • • • • •

6. Stay Focused:
    This key is probably the most difficult of all for most men, because if you let the doctors tell us, we all have ADD. Seriously, it's been proven that it is more difficult for men to keep their focus than it is for the opposite sex. It is hard for men to stay focused in school. That's why the dropout rate for boys in high school is almost twice as high as it is for girls. If the young man does make it

to college, his chance graduating is three times less likely than that of a female counterpart. It's not only school; it's also hard for men to stay focused in sports, on our jobs, and even in relationships, unless it's a new one.

Guys, do you remember the first date you had with your new girlfriend, who would eventually become your wife? Can you remember her talking the whole time, and you watching every word that proceeded out of her mouth as if it was the most important thing you had ever heard? And every time she paused to ask you if you understood her, your answer was always "Yes, sweetheart, totally."

Do you remember how you would laugh at her not-so-funny jokes as if they were the funniest jokes you ever heard in your life? You would laugh so hard until your gut hurt. However, once she becomes your girlfriend, or wife, things change. All of a sudden, when she talks to you, you don't even look at her, not to mention her mouth; and it's obvious your mind is a million miles away. There was a song out a long time ago that said, "Your body's here with me / but your mind is on the other side of town." That's how it is for us men after we get our lady. It's true our body is there with her, in the same room, under the same roof, but our mind is totally somewhere else.

Has your wife or girlfriend ever been talking to you and asked you, "Did you hear me?" and you responded, "Of course," then she ask, "Well, what did I say?" and you think about it for a minute, and you think, *Should I try and guess at what she said, or should I just tell her I don't know?* Neither one is going to sit well with her because you're totally busted! I believe the reason it is difficult for men to stay focused on a task is because our makeup is totally different from that of a woman. I don't believe that all men have ADD, I believe all men are just men.

Staying focused is definitely a hard one for most men, especially if you're struggling with pornography and trying to be free from it. Such was the case with me. Sometime ago, when I was having a really difficult time with pornography, I read a book called *Every Man's Battle*. In the book, the authors introduced me to what they called "Bouncing eyes." Bouncing eyes is simply this: When you see an attractive woman, teach your eyes to bounce off of her onto something else. I tried this technique for about two months, and it never did work for me. Then one day I realized what it was I was doing wrong. I was bouncing my eyes off an attractive woman, but as long as I stayed in the same place, eventually they would bounce right back onto her again. It's just like bouncing a basketball in the same spot for a long time. If you stay there long enough, you are more than likely going to bounce the ball in the same spot more than once.

The same is true with bouncing your eyes. If you bounce your eyes without moving your feet, eventually, your eyes will find themselves right back to where they started. So the Lord spoke to me and said, You need to teach your eyes to flee! Go, get gone, scat, run! See, here's the deal: If your eyes stay, your heart stays. If your heart stays, your mind stays; and if your mind stays, your feet ain't going nowhere.

The Bible says out of the heart flows adultery. Have you ever thought about how adultery enters into the heart? One way is through the eye gate. This is why it is so very important for us men to be careful with what we allow our eyes to consume. Fleeing eyes. It works like this. You see a beautiful woman you look, you admire, and then you leave the scene. When I say leave the scene, I mean immediately. Run if you have to. Don't hang around long enough for the second look, which is usually where we mess up. Look here, the way I see it, God wouldn't take the time to fashion the woman into such a beautiful creature if he didn't want us to look at them.

I truly believe it is possible for men to look at women without lusting. See, it's not a sin to look at a woman; however, it is a sin to look at a woman with lust in your heart (Matthew 5:28). I know you're probably thinking to yourself, *Man, it's not even possible for me to look at an attractive woman and not lust.* Of course, it is, and I'll tell you why I believe so. Ephesians 4:26, reads, "Be ye angry, and sin not: let not the sun go down upon your wrath:" Wow, be ye angry and sin not—is that possible? According to our God, it is. So check this out: If it's possible for us to get mad enough to knock someone's block off and not sin, then it's possible for us to look at an attractive woman and not lust. I believe God made woman so doggone beautiful for our admiration, and not for our sexual gratification.

I believe a beautiful woman is like any other wonder of this world. She is to be admired, and complimented. My wife doesn't know this, but I have admired women before, and I've even told them. If they have a nice hairdo or dress really nice, I might go up to them and say, Hey, I like your hair. That's really cute. Or I might say something like, "You dress very nice," and then I keep it moving, as my good friend Bernard Tucker would say. I don't see anything wrong with that. After all, if God didn't want us to look at and admire the opposite sex, then who does he want us to look at and admire? As soon as we adapt fleeing eyes, we begin to find it easier and easier to look at a beautiful, attractive woman without lusting. Fleeing eyes have definitely helped me to stay focused on my deliverance.

· · · · · · · · · · · · ·

After teaching one Saturday morning on sexual purity, a young man came up to me and asked me if I had a minute to talk. I said, "Of course."

He said, "Man, I've got this problem."

I said, "What is it?"

"All that stuff you were talking about being pure, and not even having thoughts of sexual immorality sound good, but it's impossible for me because of my work environment." Look, I'm a twenty-five-year-old man, and I work for an accounting firm. Besides two other guys, I am the only man there among about thirty women, twenty-five of whom should be movie stars—they're just that fine.

As a result of this, I am tempted with sex all day long. I just can't help it. I thought about what the young man said, and then I asked him a series of questions. First of all, I asked him, "Again, how many women work in your office?" he said. "About thirty, but like I said, at least twenty-five of them should be movie stars."

I said, "Yeah, I got that part, but look here: Out of the twenty-five movie stars, how many of them know your name?"

"Probably about eighteen or twenty, 'cause I'm pretty popular up in here, if you know what I mean."

I said, "Yeah, I got you, player. But check this out: Out of the twenty or so that know your name, how many of them have you had lunch with?"

"'Bout ten of them because we all get together and go to lunch sometimes."

I said, "Look, out of the ten you've lunched with, how many have you had one-on-one lunch with? Just the two of you?"

"None."

"Better yet, how many of the ten have ever cornered you in the break room and said, 'Hey, look, I know you're married, and so am I, but I just cannot stop thinking about us having sex. Come on, do me right now in the break room.'"

"Man, are you crazy? None of them would ever say that!"

I said, "My point exactly. Look, temptation is not temptation, until the one you want, wants you back. We've got to teach our eyes to flee if we are going to stay focused and do what God has called us to do as men."

Speaking of real temptation, I'm reminded of a young lady I met some time ago out on my route as a driver for UPS. She was a very shy young lady who hardly spoke at all, until one day, being the sociable man that I am, I went out of my way to speak to her. She worked at the counter where I made my daily pickups. I would go in day after day to make my pickups, and she would smile at me, since I'm a smiler myself, after a while, I begin to smile back at her. Pretty soon, we begin to have small talk on a daily basis when I would come in to make my pickup.

After a couple of months, she finally asked me if I was married. I said, "Yes, and happily?"

She said, "Okay, just checking."

A couple months went by with hardly any conversation at all between the two of us, until one day I came in to make my daily pickup, and she came over to me and held her hand out like she had something to give me. I reached out my hand and said, "What is it?"

She gave me a key and said, "I finally got my own place. It's on your route, and this is your key." She went on to say, "You can stop by on your lunch break. Your wife will never know. You wouldn't have to leave for work any earlier. Neither would you have to get home to your family any later. I'm here for your convenience. You can stop by whenever you want, and that's your key." When I looked at her and saw how serious she was, I dropped the key and ran out of the store. Not only did I leave the key on the floor, but I also left my pickup. See, here's the deal: this young woman was *fine*. She was exactly my type back in the day—young, nice butt, flat stomach, and as sexy as she wanted to be. With that being said, I knew I had to drop that key and get out of there in a hurry, because if I had kept the key, I would have used it. Like she said, it would've been very convenient for me, and my wife may not have ever known. But God would have! Real temptation is when the one you want, wants you back! Stay focused.

The last thing I do when it comes to helping me to stay focused on my deliverance is I take a photograph of my family everywhere I go. This helps me to stay focused because every time I get tempted, I take out the photo and I begin to ask myself, starting with my wife, *What has this beautiful woman ever done to me to deserve the hurt, the shame, and the pain that an affair will bring to her life?* Now my wife is not perfect, but she's very close, and I can't think of one thing she's done to me since I've known her that would justify me breaking her heart like that.

Then I look at my six-year-old who thinks his daddy is the best thing since sliced bread. He worships the ground I walk on, and when he grows up, he wants to be just like me. In his eyes, I can do no wrong, and to him, I'm perfect in every way. What has he ever done to me to cause him all the shame, hurt, and embarrassment, that an affair would bring to his young life? I can see his classmates taunting him and picking on him, saying evil things about his daddy, and him fighting every day taking up for me. What has he ever done to deserve that?

Then I look at my nineteen-month-old. He's not old enough to understand what would be going on; but one day he will be, and he too will have to go through all the hurt, shame, and embarrassment that I've caused my family by having an affair. Then there's my oldest son, who is twenty this year with a fiancée and a kid of his own. Now our story is a typical one. I'm his stepfather, and for years, we didn't get along.

As a matter of fact, the whole time he stayed with us, we were at each other's throats. However, now that he's out on his own, with his own child, he understands that everything I tried to do for him was for his own good, and today we have a great relationship. He even let me be a part of his proposal to his fiancée, which I thought was pretty cool. My son never really met his biological father, and I'm the only father he's ever known. So I ask myself, What has he ever done to me that was so terrible that I would want to bring disappointment to him for having an affair and being unfaithful to his mother. Men, we must learn how to stay focused on the big picture and not get derailed by the snapshots. Psalm 119:37 reads: "Turn away mines eyes from beholding vanity: and quicken thou me in thy way."

Teach your eyes to flee and allow your mind and feet to follow, and you will be able to stay sexually clean in a very dirty world.

• • • • • • • • • • • • • •

7. Have a well-made-up mind.

The mind is a tricky thing. The word *mind* has thirty-eight different meanings in Webster, it's mentioned ninety-five times in the Bible, and it's even part of one of the most famous slogans in history: "The mind is a terrible thing to waste." The reason the mind is so complex is that it can be anything and everything, all at the same time. It can be violent, it can be peaceful. It can be strong, and it can be weak. It can be intelligent, and it can be not so intelligent. It can be loving, and it can be hateful. It can be considerate, and it can be inconsiderate. However, the one thing it cannot be is easily changed once it's made up. Have you ever been around someone with a well-made-up mind? It's almost like they're possessed or something, and their level of focus is amazing. They seem to have this uncanny ability to do whatever it takes to achieve great things.

I'm reminded of three people right off the bat who, because of a well-made-up mind, was able to stay focused and change the world we live in today. The first is a woman by the name of Mother Teresa. Mother Teresa was born August 26, 1910, died September 5, 1997. Mother Teresa founded the Missionaries of Charity, a Roman Catholic religious congregation, which in 2012 consisted of over 4,500 sisters and is active in 133 countries. They run hospices and homes for people with HIV/AIDS, leprosy, and tuberculosis; soup kitchens; children and family counseling programs; orphanages; and schools.

Mother Teresa was the recipient of numerous honors, including the 1979 Nobel Peace Prize. I believe it was Mother Teresa's well-made-up mind that helped her to stay focused to do what God had called her to do, right up until the day she passed away. Then there's the legendary Billy Graham. William Franklin "Billy" Graham Jr. was born November 7, 1918. Graham was a spiritual adviser to several presidents. He was particularly close to Dwight D Eisenhower and Richard Nixon. During the civil rights movement, he began to support integrated seating for his revival and crusades. In 1957, he invited Martin Luther King Jr. to preach jointly at a revival in New York City. Graham bailed King out of jail in the 1960s when he was arrested in demonstrations.

Graham operates a variety of media and publishing outlets. According to his staff, more than 3.2 million people have responded to the invitation at Billy Graham's crusades to accept Jesus Christ as their personal Savior. As of 2008, Graham's estimated lifetime audience, including radio and television broadcast, topped 2.2 billion. Graham has repeatedly been on Gallup's list of the most admired men and women. He has appeared on the list fifty-five times since 1955 (including forty-nine consecutive years) more than any other individual in the world. However, the most impressive of all, to me, when it comes to Billy Graham, is the statement he made when he turned ninety-five years old. When asked in an interview what he thinks the world needs right now? He made this statement, "The world needs a revival." Here's this man who is ninety-five years old, and he's still trying to revive God's people. What a legacy.

Once again, I believe because of a well-made-up mind, Billy Graham was able to stay focused on what God had called him to do here on earth even until this present day. Last, but certainly not least, is one of my all-time favorite heroes, Martin Luther King Jr. I've already talked about Martin Luther King Jr. earlier in the book, so I won't go through his biography again. However, I would like to say I believe Martin's mind was so well made up and his focus was so intense, to point that he would be willing to die for his cause. And he did just that.

Not even death threats could change his mind and break his focus to the point where he would walk away from doing what God had called him to do. One woman and two men with such incredible strong minds and intense focus were able to totally change the world we live in today. See, the thing about having a well-made-up mind is it will cause you to do the other six. For example, if you have a well-made-up mind, it will cause you to make a vow to The Lord every day, go straight to point A and return straight home, to be where you're supposed to be when you're supposed to be there, you seek out an accountability partner and use him.

For example, do you remember the young lady I told you about who offered me a key to her place and an open door straight to hell? Well, I didn't tell you how the story ended. As I said before, she placed the key in my hand, and I dropped it to the floor and ran out of the store as fast as my little legs would carry me. I got back out to my truck, jumped in the cab, and was shaking like a leaf. It took me a minute, but I finally settled down long enough to start my truck up and go to my next stop.

I also remember this intense burning sensation within my skin as if I had literally stepped into hell and jumped right back out. I got to my next stop, and the Lord spoke to me and told me to call a good friend of mine by the name of Kenny. Now Kenny and I had been in ministry together for several years. He was older than me, and I really looked up to him as a spiritual big brother.

Having no idea why God told me to call Kenny, I was a little hesitant to do so; but out of obedience, I called. I pulled my cell phone out, found his number, and called him up. He answered the phone, and I began to tell him everything that just took place. "Kenny, man, you're not going to believe what just happened to me."

He said, "What happened? Are you all right?"

"Yeah, I'm fine. Speaking of fine, I just had this really fine young woman out on my route try to give me a key to her place."

"I could come over anytime I wanted to, and she would take care of me."

My friend Kenny said, "Jonathan, give the key back."

I told him I never did take it, that I dropped it in the store and took off running.

He said, "Good job."

"But, Kenny, you don't understand. This girl was nice. She had the body, the smile, and the sex appeal—all in one." And she made it clear—that I could have her whenever I wanted her, however I wanted her."

He said, "Jonathan, listen to me, brother. You do not want to go there!"

I said, "How would you know? You have no idea what I'm going through right about now."

He said, "Oh yes, I do, brother."

"How would you know? You've never cheated on your wife."

He paused for a moment and then said, "Yes, I have."

I was like, "What! I couldn't believe my ears."

Kenny was unfaithful to his wife." Now it made sense why God had me call Kenny instead of my accountability partner. I went on to ask him, "Was it before or after you got saved? Because I knew Kenny was a gangsta before he came to Christ.

He said, "It was after I got saved."

Now I'm really blown away. The man that I look up to as a spiritual big brother had an affair, was unfaithful to his beautiful wife. He went on to tell me the entire story about how it all took place. He told me he was out of town on a Christian function that his wife was unable to attend. It was a weekend event, with him and four other brothers from the church. He said they all went out to eat one night and the waitress was overly nice to him. The next day, he decided to eat there again, this time by himself. He walked in and sat at her table, and she waited on him. They begin to flirt a little bit, and one thing led to another; and before he left the restaurant she had found out where he was staying.

He said later that night, he was in his room getting ready for bed when he heard a knock on the door. He said he had forgotten all about the young lady at the restaurant, so he got up and answered the door. There she stood in the doorway, with nothing on but a trench coat, asking to come in. He said his heart stopped because he knew he was in a very bad situation. He realized that all day long, he'd been talking trash and saying stuff that he shouldn't have been saying, and now he was going to have to put up or shut up. Disregarding the warnings of the Holy Spirit, he let the young lady come in. He told her he was happily married. She said, "Good for you, but I'm not here to marry you." He said she laid him back on the bed, and he just closed his eyes and asked the Lord to forgive him as she did what she did.

After she finished, she got up and, without saying a word, left the room. He said, "Jonathan, as I lay there thinking about my wife and my kids, let me tell you what I felt, because it's the same thing you're going to feel if you ever cross that line. "I felt guilty. I felt ashamed, and I felt empty."

His testimony was one of the most powerful testimonies I had ever heard in my life, and I'll tell you why. This was the first time someone told me exactly how I would feel after I had committed sin. Someone who could tell me what the end result was going to be like before I fell. See, Satan doesn't want you to know what the end of sin looks like, sounds like, or feels like, because if we knew that, we would be less likely to fall into his trap. I would love to say it was my loving wife and wonderful kids alone who kept me from falling that day, but it wasn't. It was me having a well-made-up mind and telling myself time and time again, *I wouldn't sin against my God, and I will not be unfaithful to my wife.* God, knowing that my mind was well made up, sent me an immediate accountability partner who would help me to stay faithful and true to my wife.

And last, but not least, having a well-made-up mind causes you to stay focused on your calling, your promises, and your purpose in life. It's a lot easier to stay focused when your mind is in the right place. The mind is a terrible thing to waste and a powerful thing to misplace. As a matter of fact, as soon as you make up your mind to live a life of sexual purity, God will remove people, places, and things out of your way that may cause you to stumble and fall. I kid you not. I've seen God relocate employees on my behalf. Women that may have caused me to stumble, and maybe even fall, God would simply cause them to get a promotion and a transfer, all in the same week. Places that once upon a time would draw me to them, God would shut them down for good, overnight.

What about things? I'm glad you asked. The week after I got serious with the Lord about living a life of sexual purity and made it clear to him that I would do anything I had to do to remain free from the sexual bondage that once had me bound; I was on my way to work, and wouldn't you know it, I passed by my favorite billboard "Hooters." Now this billboard was directly on my path to work each day. Even if I took the long way to work, I still had to pass it on the way into my job.

That Monday when I saw the billboard on the way to work, I thought, *This is going to be difficult. That billboard is what used to get my flesh stirred up early in the morning, and it would stay that way throughout the entire day, so now, what was I going to do about this billboard?* Let me tell you something: When your mind is well made up, you don't have to worry about removing anything, because God has your back. That Wednesday, on my way to work, I rode by the spot where the sign was, and it had been replaced with an upcoming movie sign. Glory to God!

All you have to do is make up your mind, and I promise you, God will do the rest. I'm so very excited about sharing these seven keys to freedom with you guys, because I know someone's reading this book right now who's been thinking they would never be free from this bondage caused by porn addiction to live the life they've only dreamed of. A life completely free from pornography. You are probably thinking that you're going to die bound by your sin, and that you'll never be able to completely break free from it. If this is you, I have great news for you. You can be free from whatever it is you're struggling with starting today. If you apply these seven principles to your life daily, I promise they will work for you, and you will be free indeed from whatever bondage you may have.

Whether it's pornography, drugs, or alcohol, if you want to be free, you can be. I'm not telling you something I read in a best-selling book, or heard from some big-time pastor. I'm telling you what I know to be true. I myself was addicted to porn for the better part of two decades until I started using these seven principles on a daily basis, and they have kept me free from porn addiction for over four years. It all starts and ends with a well-made-up mind. We read in Isaiah 26:3, "Thou wilt keep him in perfect peace whose mind is stayed on thee: because he trust in thee.

Our Father

That if thou shalt confess with thy mouth the Lord Jesus, and shalt believe in thine heart that God hath raised him from the dead, thou shalt be saved. For with the heart man believeth unto righteousness; and with the mouth confession is made unto salvation.

—Romans 10:9–10

I opened this book with the question "Who's my daddy?" And I would like to close it with an invitation to meet the Father. This entire chapter is dedicated to those who are fatherless and are looking for a father. In chapter 2, we talked about the three big P's, as well as the three big Ws, and the best way to deal with each. In chapter 3, we talked about the process of initiation. In chapter 4, we talked about how to choose an authentic hero. In chapter 5, we talked about the eight responsibilities of the father. In chapter 6, we talked about the P-word and offered up the seven keys to freedom. And now as we come to the end of the book, it's only fitting that I offer you an open invitation to receive Our Father which art in heaven.

Regardless of whether you have ever met your biological dad or not, you can have the ultimate relationship with the Ultimate Father today. All you have to do is receive him. Unlike your biological dad, Our Father will never leave you nor forsake you (Psalm 27:9). When I think about salvation, I think about four words that start with the letter *R*. The first is *recognition*, the second is *repentance*, the third is *remission*, and the fourth is *reconstruction*.

. . . .

Step 1: Recognition

In order for you to receive Jesus in your life to fill a void, you must first recognize there is a void to be filled. I've heard many people give their testimony, and quite often, I will hear someone say, "I had it all. I had money, I had power, riches, and fame, but there was still something missing." I thought I could find it in women, but it was not found in them. I thought I could find it in drugs and alcohol, but it was not found in them either. I even thought I could find it in more money, more power, more riches, and more fame, and once again, it was not found in those things either. It wasn't until I recognized that the thing I was looking for was not an exterior but an interior thing—it wasn't hidden in a relationship that I already had; rather, it was hidden in a relationship I had not yet discovered.

You must understand that human beings are designed to have a relationship with the designer. We are creatures who have been created to be in relationship with our Creator (Genesis 1:26). With that being said, if you're not in a relationship with the One who made you, your heart will forever yearn for that relationship, and something will always be missing in your life. It's like a woman who cannot have children. She understands that her body was designed and made for that very purpose, and for her not to be able to bear children may leave her feeling somewhat empty, and live a life that is somewhat incomplete. The Bible says that every human being is a creation of the Almighty God himself. However, we don't become sons or daughters until we enter into a relationship with God through his son Jesus. I guess what I'm trying to say is this: If you don't recognize you need a Savior, then you probably won't go out looking for one.

For example, if your car is running perfectly fine, then you're probably not going to take it to the shop to get it fixed. Growing up, I was very shy and very poor. I was always chasing a dream, and usually, it was my mother's. She would always play the Ed McMahon sweepstakes, and every time we would get our numbers for the drawing, she would sit us down and tell each one of us what she was going to buy us when she won that million dollars. It was a very cool time for me, because even if it was only for ten minutes or so, I was able to dream, and dream big.

Two weeks later, the draw would take place; and of course, wouldn't win. As a matter of fact, we never won anything; but it was so much fun spending the money we never won, on stuff we could only dream about having. As I got older, I discovered alcohol—well, I shouldn't say I discovered alcohol. Both my parents drank, so I was practically raised with it, but it wasn't until I was a senior in high school that I started drinking myself, heavily.

As I said before, growing up, I was shy, and less fortunate (as my sister would call it). I often looked for ways to escape my life, to live life as someone else, and that was exactly what alcohol allowed me to do. When I was sober, I was very shy and had a hard time talking to the ladies. However, after a few beers, I had a hard time shutting up. It was as though I went from this shy, reserved young man to this all-out Romeo, and I loved it.

As you might have figured out, it didn't take long for me to become an alcoholic, which brings me to the night, the hour, the minute, the very second I recognized I needed a Savior. I've shared this before, and I'm going to share it again. It was a Saturday night, and I'd been out drinking all day and night. I got home that morning at about one o'clock. I tried to get up to go to the restroom, and I stumbled and fell on the floor. My chest began to tighten, and my breath began to shorten as if I was having a heart attack. All I could think about was how I didn't want to die in that one-bedroom apartment all alone.

In my dreams, I always passed away at a ripe old age, with my family surrounding me, not at twenty-six years old. I was raised in the church, and I had heard of God. However, I had never heard about a relationship with his son Jesus, but I knew enough about God to call on him this particular night. I called on the Lord, and he answered me. It was at that time that I recognized I needed a Savior in the form of a miracle. See, I was not able to get up and take myself to the hospital that morning. As a matter of fact, I couldn't get to the phone to call for help. It was just me and my prayer to my God, which went something like this: "Lord, if you save me, I will serve you."

He did, and I have been serving him ever since. As you can see, the first step in getting saved is recognizing you need a Savior, because if you feel there's nothing there to be saved, then more than likely, you will not seek the Savior.

• • • • • • • • • • • • • •

Step 2: Repentance

The definition of the word *repentance* is this: "deep sorrow compunction, or contrition for a past sin, wrongdoing, or error." Ezekiel 14:6 is a perfect example of what real repentance should look like: "Therefore say unto you the house of Israel, Thus saith the Lord of God; Repent, and turn yourselves from your idols, and turn away your faces from all your abominations."

See, a lot of people think that repentance simply means you ask God to forgive you for your sin, and then you continue to sin. However, real repentance is indeed asking God for forgiveness for sin, and also turning away from that sin and never doing it again. Repentance is twofold. Some people think it's like a get-out-of-jail-free card. In their minds, it goes something like this, *Oh, I've sinned. Let me ask for forgiveness so that my slate will be clean so I can go out and sin some more.* That's not how it works. The Bible says in Romans 6:1–2, "What shall we say then? Shall we continue in sin, that grace may abound? God forbid. How shall we that are dead to sin live any longer therein?"

What Paul is trying to say is this: How can we who have tasted the Lord and know that he is good continue to willfully sin against him? Once you get this thing the right way, and the Lord gets a hold of your heart the right way, those things you used to do, you will no longer have the desire to do them. Same with the places you used to go and the people you used to hang out with—all that will change. In a nutshell, real repentance is asking for forgiveness with a sorrowful heart, turning away from your sin, and never doing it again.

· · · · · · · · · · · · · · ·

Step 3: Remission

Acts 2:38 reads, "Then Peter said unto them, Repent, and be baptized every one of you in the name of Jesus Christ for the remission of sins and you shall receive the Gift of the Holy Ghost."

The remission of sin. There has to be a payment for our sin. Back in the Old Testament, animals were offered up as remission for sin. If one had sinned, he would take a goat or a bull to an altar and offer up the blood from that animal as remission for sin. Of course, in the New Testament, the ultimate sacrifice for our sins is Jesus Christ himself. He bled, suffered, and died for our sins. He did this so that we might have a right to eternal life, and the only way we can receive that life is through a relationship with the Father through his Son.

Some people look at the Holy Ghost as a curse instead of the gift the Bible proclaims. For this very reason, I think a lot of people are afraid to give their hearts to the Lord and be baptized. This, along with the many myths that surround salvation.

Let's look at a few of those myths.

. . . .

Myth number 1: Getting saved is for old folks, and I'll do it when I get older.

This is so not true. Salvation is for every age group, especially the young. If you don't believe me, check out this youth conference by the name of Forward, held each year in the state of Georgia, that hosts well over ten thousand young people. As a matter of fact, statistics has shown that the older a person gets, the less likely they will become Christians. Up to nineteen years of age, the likelihood of this person getting saved is somewhere between 75 to 85 percent. Once that same person hits twenty-five years of age, the likelihood drops to below 20 percent.

I guess what I'm trying to say is it's a lot easier to get saved when you're young. If the statistics are correct, with every decade, it gets harder and harder to give your life to Jesus.

. . . .

Myth number 2: Christian women are not attractive.

This is so not true. Christian women are some of the most beautiful women on the face of the earth. Unlike it was thirty or fourty years ago, when the Christian women dressed modest, when they wore the long dresses from neck to toe, with their hair up, no makeup on, and wore scarves around their necks.

I remember when I was about fifteen years old and this girl who was a year older had a crush on me. Her mom was the pastor of a small family-owned and family-operated church. She was very sweet, but her wardrobe was an eyesore. Not only were her clothes old and dated, but they were also loose and saggy. She was just not attractive at all. Her mother and my mother were best friends, and one day, they were over at our house for supper.

She pulled me to the side and said, "My daughter likes you."
I said, "Yeah, I know."

"She's a really good girl, and she would make you a wonderful wife one day."

I thought, *Oh no, she won't!* But I said out loud, "I've got a girlfriend. Sorry."

In retrospect, it had nothing to do with the young lady being a prize possession, but everything to do with the way that prize possession was packaged. See, even back then, the Christian women were beautiful women. They just did a very good job of keeping that beauty concealed for the only person who should know how beautiful they are—their husband. No, not today. If anything, today's Christian women reveal a little too much and leave very little to the imagination. To say the least, the Christian woman and her wardrobe has come a long way.

• • • • • • • • • • • • • •

Myth number 3: You have to be perfect to be saved.

This is so not true. The Bible says come as you are, because God will do all the cleaning up. As a matter of fact, you can't clean yourself up anyhow. If you could, you wouldn't need to come to him at all. It seems like most of us come to Jesus only out of desperation. When we've tried everything, and everybody, and all have failed, we decide to give Jesus a try. I mean, what do we have to lose, right?

Now this is fine for some people, because it may be the only way that God can get your attention. It seemed that way with me, but for others, it's not always necessary. For some of you, God has been tugging at your heart for years, and you're waiting until you get older to respond to the calling. My advice for you is this: Please don't ignore the voice of God. If God is calling you as a young man to give your life to him, then there's someone in your school that God is trying to reach through you, now! See, the only thing about waiting until you get older to get saved is that God needs you saved now to reach the people he wants you to reach.

· · · · · · · · · · · · · ·

Myth number 4: If I get saved, I'll have to give up everything I have right away.

This is so not true. I've been saved for almost twenty years, and I'm still giving up stuff, daily. God doesn't save you and then point a magic wand at you, and all of a sudden, all bad habits you have disappear, and you never have to deal with them again. No, sir, it doesn't work like that. I wish it did, but it doesn't. As a matter of fact, everything that God has delivered me from has come in stages.

There are certain things that God delivered me from right away, like cursing. Before I got saved, I used to curse like a sailor. I mean, I could not complete a sentence of any kind without cursing. However, on the morning after I repeated the salvation prayer that set me free, I woke up with no desire at all to curse, and I have not had a desire to curse for almost twenty years. God also took away my taste for alcohol and delivered me from drinking right away.

But there are also some things that would take years, and even decades, for God to say, "Okay, now it's time. Give it to me." So to think that if you do decide to get saved you're going to have to give everything up the day of salvation, that is so not true. Look, believe you me: God is patient, and he'll let you know when it's time to give something up and take a step forward with him.

· · · · · · · · · · · · · ·

Myth number 5: It's hard to make a living serving the Lord.

This is so not true. Again, back in the day, a mega church was about two hundred members, with about 2 percent of the membership tithing and providing a salary for their pastor. As a result, most pastors had regular jobs during the week, and they preached on the weekends. Not anymore. I do believe that the average pastor today in an average church can do quiet well for himself; and should not have to work a second job. That's on an average. I know pastors with mega churches today who drive Rolls-Royces, Bentleys, and Mercedes Benzes. They have private jets, and live in $2 and $3 million dollar homes.

Now don't get me wrong. Don't ever go into ministry for a paycheck, because ministry is hard enough for those of us who have been called. I truly believe it would be very difficult for those who are not. Here's the deal: In some ways, preaching is like any other occupation. If you're preaching good, and the anointing is on you, then you're eating good.

And for you singers who would love to sing for the Lord but feel you can't support your family singing praises unto our God, think again. Back in the day, if a Christian group, or artist, sold five hundred thousand copies of an album, it was considered to be a hit album. Not today. Today there are Christian artists who have sold 50, 60, and even 70 million CDs, and counting, and are making a lot of money while doing so. Look, my point is simply this: Whatever you're doing for the Lord, he's going to use it to make you prosper, and you'll never be in need of anything. Not only will he bless you with all of your needs, but he will bless you by fulfilling some of your desires as well. Which brings me to the next myth.

• • • • • • • • • • • • • •

Myth number 6: Aren't Christians supposed to be poor and humble?

This is so not true. Why do people always associate being poor with being humble? The two have nothing to do with each other. Who says you can't be rich and humble at the same time? God sure doesn't. Monetary riches are a social issues; humility is a heart issue. If Jesus wanted us to be poor here on earth, I do not believe he would have made heaven so rich. The Bible says the streets in heaven are made of gold, and everyone has a mansion. It doesn't sound like we're going to be broke when we get to heaven—not that it's going to matter anyway. And besides all that, ministry takes money.

I actually had to learn this one myself the hard way. In 2004, I started this ministry for young men called God's Posse Ministries, and our feature event each year is a 3-on-3 basketball tournament. We hosted this tournament the first year for the few members we had who had faithfully attended our meetings. The first year, we had six teams in attendance. The following year, it tripled to eighteen teams, so we had to change venues. The following year, which was our third year of holding the tournament, we thought, *If it triples, or even doubles this year, we're going to need somewhere pretty big to host our rapidly growing tournament.* So we stepped out on faith and rented one of the largest basketball venues in the county.

Now this is where the problem came. Up until this point, we had made this tournament free to all who attended it. My idea behind the tournament was outreach. After the first year, we knew we were on to something. The first year, there were more teams to show up at the tournament than we had members in the group at the time. I asked myself, *Where did all these people come from?* I asked some of the guys in our group where they got their players from. I don't remember seeing them at any of our meetings. They said, "These are guys from the neighborhood who love to play basketball. I just told them about the tournament and they said, 'Man, sign me up.'

And that's when it hit me: This could be an awesome outreach event. From that day on, we've been trying to reach every lost baller in our state through the game of basketball. That brings me back to my point: From day one, I wanted this tournament to be free to these young men, because believe it or not, even a $10 fee could turn a baller away—maybe even someone whom God himself was trying to reach through our tournament. So my mission was, and still is, to do whatever it takes for me not to have to charge these men a fee of any kind to participate in our tournament.

I called this very large facility to get a quote for a one-day rental, and the number the woman gave me blew my mind. It was so much I thought it was a misquote, so I called back the next day and asked to speak with the manager. I asked him the same question, and he gave me the same quote. I remember thinking, *There is no way in the world we can afford this venue with the money I have saved in my account.*

I called my crew together for an emergency meeting and told them about this unbelievable dollar figure to rent this large facility, and this was the first time I had ever heard of someone suggesting I charge a fee for the tournament to offset the cost. My right-hand man said, "Hey, Craig, have you ever thought about charging a small fee from each player or team to help you pay for the tournament?"

I quickly told him, "Absolutely not!" And I went on to explain why I didn't feel that was a good idea. They totally understood, and they went on to tell me why I should at least consider it. To make a long story short, I didn't charge a fee for the two years that we had our tournament there, and I'm still in debt because of it. However, I have no problem with it because we had thirty-two ballers to get saved in those two years, and that's what it's all about. It's God's money anyhow. He gives it, and he takes it away.

My point is this: It takes money to do ministry; and the bigger the ministry, the more money it takes. Whether or not you're in ministry, God does not want us to be broke as a joke and always having to depend on others for survival. The Bible says, "We are lenders not borrowers."

If the word of God is true, my question to you is this: How can you be a lender if you don't have anything to lend? Again, don't get me wrong. I do believe there are people of the faith who are abusing the financial blessing that the Lord has blessed them with. I personally do not believe that God wants us to be flashy or boastful with money or material things. We should make money; money should never make us. I remember when I was growing up, the old folks used to say, "Honey, money is the root of all evil."

Now you know when you're a child, and you don't know your Bible, you believe everything the old folks tell you. As a result, I always thought it was a sin to be rich; and for me, that was yet another reason for me to not get saved. I thought, *If I'm already poor, if getting saved isn't going to offer me any kind of hope from poverty, then why bother?*

Now that I'm older and have knowledge of the Bible, it's perfectly clear to me that scripture does not state the love of money is the root of all evil. In one story, Jesus asked a rich man to sell all his possessions and give the money to the poor "and follow Him. The rich man refused (Matthew 19:21–24).

Look, there's nothing wrong with having money, but when the money has you, it's a problem. Notice that God did not tell the man to give him all his money, because he shouldn't have money anyway. No, he gave him specific instructions on what to do with his riches. He told him to sell everything he owned, give the money to the poor, and follow him. The thing about God that the rich don't understand is that if he asks you to give up something, then what he has for you is much greater than what he's asking you to give up. See, this rich man thought he was giving up everything and he wasn't going to gain anything. So he hung on to what he had, dropped his head, and said to himself, *I just cannot do it.* He must have lived his life by the old saying, "A bird in the hand beats two in a bush."

In actuality, when you're dealing with God, his Word says, "It's better to give than receive" (Acts 20:35). So the more you hold on to what God has told you to let go of, the less you're going to have to hold on to. The Bible tells us God gives seed to the sower (2 Corinthains 9:10). What this means is that sometimes, when God blesses us with extra money, it's not always for our kingdom. Sometimes it's for his. What God will do from time to time is he will test you with a seed.

For example, he might bless you with a promotion on your job that will cause a significant increase to your income, and you automatically think it's for you. You would be like, Oh, it's on now. We can go out and get that huge house we always wanted for the kids. We can get that new Mercedes you've always wanted, and when springtime rolls around, I can go and get that fishing boat I've always wanted for myself. Yeah, things are really looking up for the Stafford family. Life is good! And while you're sitting there making all these plans to build your kingdom, God is saying, "It's not about building your kingdom this time. It's about building mine."

Now don't get me wrong. God doesn't mind us having nice stuff, and there will be times when he will indeed bless you, but there are also times when God will bless you financially so that you may be a blessing to others. Before I got saved, I was very, very stingy, or so my family says. They would ask me for $10, and even though I had it, I would lie and say I didn't have it. Nobody could squeeze a dime out of me—not even a girlfriend. When I took a date out, we always went to the dollar movies on Tuesday night, because it was half off; and when we would go out to eat, it was always at a restaurant that had a dollar menu. We ordered our food off the dollar menu and shared water.

Every year, around Christmastime, I made sure I didn't have a girlfriend, so I wouldn't have to buy her anything for Christmas. I dated this one girl for four years, and it wasn't until the fourth year that she figured out that every Thanksgiving I started an argument with her over nothing so we would break up, and stay broken up until the first day of the year. They called it stingy. I called it smart with my money.

However, after I got saved and gave my heart to the Lord, there was a change in the way I viewed money. Before I got saved, it was all my money to bless me, and only me with it. After I got saved, I realized that it all belongs to God. He's just allowing me to be a steward of his wealth while I'm here on earth.

I remember that shortly after I got saved, the Lord told me to give my sister $200. Without hesitation, I did so. I walked into her house and said, "Here you go, the Lord told me to give you this."

She looked at it and almost fainted, not because she had never seen two $100 bills before, but because she had never seen them come out of my pocket and go into hers. I will never forget what she said to me: "Boy, there must be a God, and he must have a hold on you." She went on to say, "As tight as you were with your money, for you to come and give it to me without me begging for it, there's got to be a God somewhere!"

See, what she didn't understand was that by this time, I had figured it out. God blessed me with a $5 pay raise in two years. With the raise, I was comfortable where I was, and I felt he was blessing me with the extra income to be a blessing to others. There was no better candidate at the time than my sister and her family. I even took the spiritual gifts test one time, and it confirmed that one of my spiritual gifts is giving. As a matter of fact, it's the second highest on my list, right under teaching.

God does not mind you having nice stuff and prospering financially, as long as you don't put your stuff before him. If he ever tells you sell it all, give the money to the poor, and follow him, obey him. In the words of Nike, "Just do it." And I promise you, what you give up will not compare to what you will gain.

• • • • • • • • • • • • • •

Myth number 7: Church folks are boring because they can't do anything or go anywhere.

This is so not true. Although I do understand this myth coming from a person who is not saved. However, I've been on both sides of the fence, and I can honestly say I've had ten times more fun as a Christian than I had as a nonbeliever. I promise you, and so will you!

I'm reminded once again of the daughter of one of my mom's best friends growing up. As I said before, her mother was the pastor of a small Pentecostal church in our neighborhood, and she had a little crush on me. One day she cornered me and asked me to be her boyfriend. At first, I thought, Wow, that was a bold move by this girl, considering I'd never even looked at her, let alone made any moves on her.

Up until this time, I always thought she was very shy. At first, I was just going to walk off like I didn't even hear her, but I thought, *I'm going to have a little fun with her for a minute.* So I asked her, "If I'll be your boyfriend, can I take you to the movies?"

She said, "No, I can't got to the movies."

"Okay, well, how about the football game Friday night?"

"No, I can't got to football games."

"Okay, well, how about a party? My best friend's having a party at his house next Saturday night. Can you go with me?"

She said, "Will there be alcohol there?"

"I'm sure there will be."

"I can't go. I can't be around alcohol."

"Look here, where can you go, and what can you do?"

"Well, we're going to another church service later on tonight. Would you like to go to that with me?"

"Is that all you do? Go to church?"

"Yes, pretty much."

"Thanks, but no, thanks!" I thought, *If all Christians do is go to church all day and all night, then I don't think I ever want to be one of them. They have to be the most boring people on earth.* I continued to think this way all the up until I myself got saved.

My second week of salvation, a group of Christian friends asked me if I wanted to go bowling. I said, "Sure." Now I'll be honest with you, I didn't really know what to expect, because I'd never been anywhere with a group of sober people; but I thought, *I might as well. I don't have anything else to do.* We went out that night and had a blast. It was awesome! I never thought I could ever have that much fun without being drunk. I will be totally honest with you: since I've been saved, there is nothing that I wanted to do, or nowhere that I wanted to go, that I have not done or gone to.

I also have way more fun because I've been sober. Look, it's a lot easier to have a good time when you're sober because you can enjoy whatever you're doing a whole lot more. After I went out with these guys the first night, I joined their group. Every Saturday night, we would go somewhere as a group of about fifteen or twenty believers. We would go to the movies—of course, we would have to screen the movie; we would go bowling, to the mall; to sporting events, cookouts, family get-togethers with unsaved family members. You name it, anywhere we wanted to go, we went and had a great time. I said all that to say this: Being a Christian today is the most exciting thing to be. If you don't believe me, join the Christian nation and become part of the movement.

• • • • • • • • • • • • • •

Myth number 8: Church folks are so judgmental.

This one is so true. Church folks can be judgmental, but Christians should never be. There is a difference between church folks and

Christians. Church folks are simply that—they are people who got to church on a somewhat regular basis and run around town criticizing the folks who don't. You know who they are; you see them at the family reunion telling Uncle Clyde he's going to hell if he doesn't put that liquor bottle down and come to church Sunday. Or you see them at your job walking through the office with the biggest Bible ever made by man, telling everyone who does not go to church that they're going straight to hell if they don't start going to church. We all know who the churchgoers are because that's all they do, and they have a bad habit of criticizing people who don't. As if they have a heaven or hell to put them in, and if they don't come to church with them, they're going to put them in hell.

It's the church folks who turn away the unchurched folks. I remember growing up. This one guy, whom I'll call Ricky, went to church every Sunday morning, every Wednesday night, and every revival that came his way. I remember my friends, and I thought this guy was the closest thing to God here on earth we'd ever seen. We even gave him the nickname Bible Boy, because he always had a Bible with him. He wore a big fat cross pendant around his neck and big fat smile on his face.

However, the only thing I didn't like about him was the fact that he always beat the unchurched folks over the head with his big old Bible. He would always say stuff like, "Man, you need Jesus. If you don't start going to church, you're going to die and go to hell." This has got to be the worst thing you can tell a nonbeliever, for two reasons.

First of all, they already know this; and secondly, they need encouragement—something that's going to lift them up, not tear them down. If a nonbeliever cannot see hope in a believer's life, then it's hopeless, and our salvation is in vain. Needless to say, Bible Boy's ministry didn't last very long. Two years out of high school, he got a young lady pregnant and moved in with her.

That's your church folks. A Christian, on the other hand, should be somewhat different.

The only thing the Christian and the church folks should have in common is that they both attend church; however, they do attend for two different reasons. The church folks attend church so that they can be seen by others and judge the people who don't go. The Christian, on the other hand, attends church to learn how to be more like Christ. After all, the definition of the word *Christian* is "someone who is striving to be like Christ," so this should be every Christian's purpose for attending church. If this is truly the Christian's purpose for attending church, then he or she should not be judgmental at all, because Jesus Christ himself was not, and neither did he allow anyone else to be (John 8: 7).

If you think about it, we were all one prayer away from being where the unbeliever is. Not only that, we were just as jacked up as they are regardless of what you may think about them. I know some of you might say, "I never did drugs, committed adultery, robbed a bank, got drunk, or raped someone." And the truth is, maybe you haven't but you have sinned; and a sin is a sin. The same blood that saved you, washed you, and made you whole is available to every sinner regardless of what they've done.

I guess what I'm trying to say is that Christians who have been set free by the power of the blood of Jesus Christ should have more important things to focus on than sit around judging other people who don't go to church. As a matter of fact, we should be on a mission to show every nonbeliever the love of Christ, which will draw them a lot quicker to the cross than anything we could ever say to them. So for the nonbeliever reading this book right about now, if you know someone who is always telling you you're going to hell if you don't start going to church, pay no attention to that person, because they are not the people you want leading you anywhere.

It's true, church folks can definitely lead you away from church; but a good old Christian can definitely lead you to church. Fret not over those who try to judge you. After all, there's only one person who can judge us, and only one person who can send us to heaven or hell, and that's the Almighty God himself.

My prayer for each one of you reading this book right now is that when you stand before God, he will say, "Well done, thou good and faithful servant," and not "Depart from me, I never knew you."

• • • • • • • • • • • • • •

Myth number 9: Church folks are just too happy for me.

They're always smiling and saying things like, "Praise the Lord." And when asked how they're doing, they always say stuff like, "I'm blessed" and "How are you?" (with a smile on their face). I just personally believe no one can be that happy all the time. Well, once again, this myth is so true. There is a place you can get in the Lord, where you literally draw your strength from his joy (Nehemiah 8:10).

Now don't get me wrong. There are some out there who are faking it, and there some out there who have figured it out. There are Christians who have figured out the key to happiness here on earth, which is the joy that's found only in Christ Jesus. Happiness comes and goes, and it's usually determined by our emotions. For example, if we have money in the bank, the bills are paid, our children are perfect, our house is big, our cars are nice, and we're very well respected in our community, then we may find it very easy to be happy.

Joy, on the other hand, is having no money in the bank, having your credit card maxed out, having bill collectors calling you, having your kids going astray, having your wife filing for divorce, your home under foreclosure, and the one car you do have just broke down—and through all this being able to smile and be glad in the Lord because you know there is a God who is able to fix your situation with one simple word.

Although your issues may be many, it doesn't take but one word from the Almighty God to fix everything. And there are people out there who call themselves Christians who actually live like this. Can you imagine that? It's like they've figured out the scripture that goes something like this: "Greater is he that is in me, than he that is in the world."

As a Christian, if you ever figure this one out, and it becomes real to you, then you too will be able to smile and give God the glory no matter what's going on in your life. The devil hates this type of Christian. I think he calls them radical, or something like that. Radical Christians are dangerous Christians, and Satan knows this. That's why he tries to keep the average churchgoer just that—an average churchgoer. The devil doesn't mind you going to church every Sunday, because he knows the average churchgoer has never done anything radical for Jesus Christ. The only thing the average churchgoer is good for is arguing over their favorite seats at the front of the church, requesting their favorite song every week, and getting upset when they arrive late and someone has already taken their favorite parking spot.

The devil doesn't mind this at all, because he knows that this type of so-called Christian will eventually bring division among the church and its people. But the real Christian (Christ follower) is a severe threat to the devil and his kingdom. You see, these Christ followers do something weird in times of trouble: They begin to call on the name of Jesus of Nazareth. And something amazing happens. The sea parts, the blind receives their sight, the lame walk, the deaf hear, the dumb speak, and the dead arise.

I know you're thinking, *That's Bible talk. What can this name of Jesus do for me today in my current situation?* I'm glad you asked. I know Christians who have called on the name of Jesus, and deliverance has taken place, the blind receive their sight, the deaf can hear, the addicted are set free, the broke become rich, and those without end up with plenty. I don't care if it was two thousand years ago in the Bible days or 2014—there is power in the name of Jesus to supply you with whatever it is you need. It is so awesome being a Christian because we understand there's nothing that the world can throw at us that God cannot handle if we just give it to him.

• • • • • • • • • • • • • •

Myth number 10: I would become a Christian, but I can't tell the difference between them and myself.

Unfortunately, this is so true. In today's society, it can be difficult to distinguish between a so-called Christian and a nonbeliever. Jesus says that we are in the world, but we are not of this world. Our problem today is that we have way too many so-called Christians who are in the world and of the world at the same time. And people cannot distinguish between the Christian and the nonbeliever.

Here's the deal: If I'm a nonbeliever, never had a relationship with the Lord, and don't know who Jesus is, and I'm hanging out at a party with this guy who is supposed to be saved and he's drinking more than I am and cursing up a storm, really, what am I supposed to think about the Christians? I call these Christian fence straddlers. They have one foot in the church and the rest of their body in the world. They do everything the Bible says as long as it doesn't conflict with what their flesh wants to do.

For example, the Bible tells us that we should not forsake the gathering of ourselves together (meaning we should come to church). This person may come to church every Sunday. The Bible also tells us we should give a tenth of our income to the Lord, and they might even do this. However, when it comes to something like thou shall not fornicate, or thou shall not be drunk with wine—now there's a problem. Another name for them are convenient Christians.

Christianity is cool as long as it's convenient for them at the time. The problem today is that true Christianity has been watered down to taste sweet in society's mouth. As Christians, we can no longer stand up for what we believe in and not be offensive to someone who has different beliefs. It's almost like the beliefs of certain groups are more powerful and more accepted in our society than that of the Christian. As a result, if we voice our opinion and they voice theirs, ours get shot down, and theirs get magnified.

Okay, enough about that. The sad reality is, there is hardly any difference at all between the so-called Christian and the nonbeliever. Some of them hang out at the same places, they date the same women, they party with the same group, they drink the same alcohol, they do the same drugs, and they even tell the same dirty jokes. There's hardly any difference at all. I'm not bragging or anything like that, but on my job, everybody knows I'm saved and I love the Lord. It's not because of what comes out of my mouth but because of the life I live before them.

For example, guys on my job like to talk about all the women they've slept with out on their routes. I remember this one particular guy who parks right next to me decided he would share his sex life with me one morning. He jumped into my truck and said, "Jonathan, you'll never guess who I slept with last week out on your route."

Before he could say another word, I put my hands over my ears like a little kid, and started shouting, "BFI! BFI! BFI!"

He finally said, "BFI—what in the world is that?"

I said, "I'm not going to allow you to dump trash in my head. BFI is a trash company. Go dump that junk onto their trucks—that's what they're made for." From that day until this one, when that same young man comes into my truck, he does so with the utmost respect for me.

If you take a stand for what you believe in, the people around you will believe in you. I no longer have to worry about my coworkers bringing trash of any kind around me because they know now that just because I'm in the world, I am definitely not of the world.

• • • • • • • • • • • • • •

Step 4: Reconstruction

2 Corinthians 5:17 says, "Therefore if any man be in Christ, he is a new creature; old things are passed away; behold, all things become new."

There are two words in this passage of scripture that really jump out at me. The first is the word *passed*. "Old things are passed away." This tells me that when you get saved, and you give your heart to the Lord, there are some things he will take away from you immediately, and then there are other things that you are going to have to pass along to him. For example, God took my foul mouth away immediately. It was like I just woke up one morning and could not curse anymore. God took that desire away quickly, and again, this was huge for me because I used to love to curse. I could not complete a sentence without cursing, but it was like I got saved and God said, "Okay, there's no way you're going to praise me and curse up a storm with the same mouth."

And then there were other issues I had that took years for me to get to the point where I said, "Okay, Lord, I'm ready to pass these issues on now." And the Lord said, "Okay, I'm ready to take them."

You see, God always has his hand out reaching for our sins. It's usually us who have a problem passing them on.

The other word that just jumps out at me every time I read this passage of scripture is the word *become*. All things become new. What I tell most young men who get saved, and I have the opportunity to minister to them about salvation, is this: Salvation is a work in progress, and we Christians are somewhere between a *mess* and a *message*.

My son and I went to see this cute little movie called *Frozen*. Upon arriving at the movie theater, an usher met us at the front of the building and informed us that the movie theater was under construction. He went on to say that they were in the middle of a complete makeover. I was curious, so I asked the young man, "How does something like this take place?"

He said, "Well, what happens is we remove everything from the inside of the theater and replace it. We remove the old chairs, carpet, and movie screens and replace them with new chairs, new carpets, and a new movie screen."

I said, "So you pretty much take out all the old and replace it with the new?"

"Exactly."

"Oh, okay, well, what do you do with the old stuff that you take out?"

"We throw that away. It's no longer any good."

"How about the sign outside, when does it get replaced?"

"Oh, the sign—we replace that last. Once we've reconstructed the inside completely, we replace the sign to let the people know on the outside that a change has taken place on the inside."

I thought, *This actually is a pretty good description of salvation.* After the change has taken place on the inside by the Almighty God himself, there will be signs on the outside that will let people know that there's been a change on the inside. Even though the building may look the same, it's been totally renovated on the inside. Just like salvation, this type of change happens from the inside out. When God changes us, he does it from the inside out. This helps to explain why once we get saved, we don't automatically lose weight, grow hair if we're bald, or become more attractive, because these are external changes. Now God is concerned about them, but not as much as he is with the internal changes. The internal changes I'm talking about consists of three parts: the heart, the spirit, and the mind. When God saves us, he changes our hearts, our spirits, and our minds.

• • • • • • • • • • • • • •

The Heart

First, let's take a look at the heart. In Ezekiel 36:26, God gives the believers a heart transplant, and it reads, "A new heart also will I give you, and a new spirit will I put within you: and I will take away a stony heart out of your flesh, and I will give you a heart of flesh." Basically, what the Word of God is saying here is, "I will take out that stone-cold heart of flesh that's insensitive to my voice, and I will replace it with a heart of flesh that's sensitive to the voice of God. This heart will be able to hear me when I speak to it."

I remember when I first noticed that God had given me a heart transplant. I'd been saved for about two months at the time, and I was down the street listening to some gospel music when a song came on that made me realize just how good God had been to me. I can't remember the title of the song, but I do remember the lyrics were something like, "I should have been dead and gone sleeping in my grave / but God saw fit to save me." And before I could say Big Mac and small fry, I was crying like a baby. I would later find out that I wasn't crying but weeping. However, at the time, I thought I was crying.

Anyway, whether I was weeping or crying, I had not done either one in over thirty years. I remember the last time I cried vividly—it was when my dear Big Moma passed away. My Big Moma was my heart, and when she passed away, my heart was broken, and I felt a pain I'd never felt before, and had not ever since. At my Big Moma's funeral my brother and I sat beside each other, looking at each other to see who would break down first; and of course, it was me. I started crying about fifteen minutes into the service, and I cried for two weeks straight after it was over. I remember I cried so hard for so long, and my head was killing me for about two days after I finally stopped crying.

Needless to say, for me to be crying, real tears flowing from eyes, was a huge deal for me. You also have to understand that growing up the way I did, in a house where men didn't show any affection of any kind for one another, to cry was to be a wimp.

My father never hugged me, kissed me, or anything like that. He told me he loved me one time in my entire life, and that was the year before he passed away, after I told him I loved him first. To all fathers reading this book, love your sons. Hug them, kiss them, and tell them you love them. Not only is this normal, but it's very necessary to produce a well-balanced young man.

I kiss my six-year-old at least three times a day and tell him I love him. I do it so often he's gotten to the point where he says, "Dad, you tell me this every day." And I say, "Yes, son, I know, because Daddy wants you to know that he loves you very, very, very much."

A new heart, one that's sensitive (it doesn't mind weeping, crying, whatever you want to call it), one that hurts, one that aches, and one that longs to be connected to the Father—this is the heart the Lord replaces your stony heart with.

The heart that is insensitive (that doesn't weep or cry), doesn't feel emotions of any kind, doesn't ache, and doesn't hurt, doesn't long to be connected to the Father. As a matter of fact, it's far, far away from him.

These days, it seems as though I can't even listen to a song, watch a movie, or hear somone's testimony without weeping. At times, I have to ask myself, *Man, what in the world is going on with you?* And then I remember: I had a heart transplant.

• • • • • • • • • • • • • •

The Spirit

The next thing the scripture talks about being placed in you is a new spirit. This is the one I personally have had the most problem with, because you've got to understand that when God saves you, he does not save your flesh. Look, I've said it before, and I'll say it a thousand times: Just because you're saved and have a new heart and a new spirit within you does not mean that your flesh doesn't still like what your flesh liked before.

So when God places this new you within you, there's this automatic battle that begins to take place between your ears—in the mind. I heard a friend once say, "There are two natures that lie between my breast—one is fouled, and one is blessed. One I love, and one I hate. The one I feed will dominate."

And it is so in Romans 7:14–24:

> For we know that the law is spiritual: but I am carnal, sold under sin. For that which I do I allow not: for what I would, that do I not; but what I hate, that I do. If then I do that which I would not, I consent unto the law that it is good. Now then it is no more I that do it, but sin that dwelleth in me. For I know that in me (that is in my flesh) dwelleth no good things: for to will is present with me; but how to perform that which is good I find not. For the good that I would I do not; but the evil which I would not, that I do. Now if I do that I would not, it is no more I that do it, but sin that dwelleth in me. I find then a law, that, when I would do good, evil is present with me. For I delight in the law of God after the inward man: But I see another law in my members, warring against the law of my mind, and bringing me into captivity to the law of sin which is in my members. O wretched man that I am! Who shall deliver me from the body of this death.

Have any of my Christian fathers ever felt like this—the things you want to do you can't, and the things you don't want to do you can't stop doing? I love this passage of scripture because it is so right on point with me. Being a Christian is a real struggle at times. See, before I got saved, there was no battle to fight at all.

I mean, I pretty much did what I wanted to do, how and when I wanted to do it, and there was no resistance to the flesh at all.

However, as soon as I got saved and God placed this new spirit in me, the battle for my soul began. For example, before I got saved, I could go to the club anytime I got ready. After I got saved, and caught myself trying to go to a club, the Holy Spirit would say, "Where do you think you're going?"

I would say, "Lord, I'm going to the club with the fellas to hang out for a while. I'm not going drink, though." He would say, "Yeah, you're not going to drink because you're not going, because the Holy Spirit doesn't do clubs."

Now I had a decision to make: Was I going to the club anyhow, regardless of what the Holy Spirit just told me, or was I going to have to give up the clubbing altogether? Of course, I gave up the clubbing altogether, but this is how it's been for the entire time I've been saved. I have had to consult with the Holy Spirit on everything, and I love it. It keeps me out of a lot of trouble if I obey him. That's not to say that I always do. I'm like any other child. I'm not perfect. Most of the time, I listen to the Holy Spirit; however, there are times when I didn't, and I paid a price for it, like the time when I bought a rental property that the Holy Spirit clearly told me to walk away from.

Once I graduated high school and knew for sure that I wasn't going to play in the NBA or the NFL, I began to ask myself, *How else can I make a million dollars?* And one day it hit me. I would become a real estate investor. I thought maybe I would get into buying and selling real estate, with my main focus being flipping homes. I started out strong with a couple of condos: buying them, fix them up, and selling them for a profit. At first, everything was great, until I made one very bad business decision, and it cost me dearly. The two condos I flipped made me a little money, but nothing to really brag about, so I started thinking to myself, I really need to make more money than this if I'm going to be a millionnaire by the age of forty-seven.

I came up with the age of forty-seven because I was twenty-two and just getting started at the company I currently worked for. When I first went to work for this particular company, I told myself I was only giving them twenty-five years of my life, and that was it—no more, no less. I'd watched my grandmother go to work every single day for forty-something years, and when she retired, she didn't receive anything. Not a watch, not a bracelet, not a necklace, not a check, not a pension. Nothing! Seeing this as a youngster really opened my eyes to society as a whole, and it made me think, *I'm not going to work myself to death for a company that doesn't even appreciate the work I've done.*

I kid you not, my grandmother had one paid vacation a year; and the rest of the time, Monday to Friday, she was at work. I never can recall her missing a day of work for any reason at all. This was the only thing she and my father had in common. Not only that, but in my mind, it didn't seem like my grandmother lived very long at all after she retired. It was as though she worked her entire adult life, retired, and then passed away. As a result, I made up my mind early on that I was going to retire early and enjoy more of my life as a retired man than as a workingman.

So anyway, back to my point here: I begin to look to invest in larger properties so that I could bring in larger profits, which brings me to the time when I totally ignored the voice of the Holy Spirit. I was out on my route one day, in my old neighborhood, when I rode up on a home that was very special to me. One of my few jobs in high school was that of a brick mason. A man whose wife used to keep me when I was a child gave me my first job ever as a brick mason. That job was by far, to this day, the hardest job I have ever had. Anyway, one the first homes we built was this house that he owned himself. It was kind of cool, seeing a house you helped build as a kid, with a man you admired as an adult, come up for sale and you're able to purchase it. So I went over to the house and called the daughter who was selling it and asked her to meet at the house to discuss details regarding the sale.

She was so excited to hear that it was me who was interested in buying her father's house. When we finally met up, she began to express to me how proud her father would have been of me for the man I had become, and that he would love for me to have this house, considering I helped build it. All that was fine and dandy, but all I wanted to know was how much money she was asking for it, and how much money I could make off of it. She gave me the asking price, I talked her down a few thousand, like I always do. Then it hit me: This house was in the hood, at the back of the hood, one way in and one way out. Now I had a buddy of mine who was already flipping houses on a much larger scale than I was. When I got started, I met with him, and he gave me a list of things to look for when finding the perfect house for flipping, and location was at the top of the list. The way he put it to me was like this: "Ask yourself, 'Would you live there?' If the answer is no, then stay away from it."

He said, "Here's what you have to look at with location. If it's in a bad place where you have to go through a bad neighborhood to get to it, you want to stay away from that because the location of the house will never change." Those words described this particular house I was looking at. It was at the back of the hood, meaning you had to ride through the hood to get to it, and you had to ride through the hood to get out. So I began to ask myself, *Can I really make money off of this house?* And the answer was no. However, I still wanted it. Then it hit me: *I'll rent it out. Section 8 (government assistance occupants)—that's right, Section 8. They're always looking for houses.*

So here's the deal: I would buy the house, rent it out section 8, make some good money off of it for a couple of years, and when I get tired of it, I'll just sell it and make money off of it again. What a perfect plan.

The next day, I called the agent for the daughter selling the house and told her I would like to buy the house. She said, "Great."

Within hours, she called me back with a closing date; and just like that, I was about to purchase my first rental property. Knowing nothing about being a landlord, I contacted another friend of mine who owned about forty or fifty homes at the time. I told him about my situation and the plan I had for Section 8 housing, and he thought it was a great idea. However, he informed me that with closing being in two weeks, I'd better call and get set up for Section 8 before I closed on the property.

I said, "All right, cool." The next day, I called to register my house with the people at Section 8, and the young lady I talked to said she would have to get someone to call me back. A week went by, and I hadn't heard anything from the people at Section 8. Finally, two days before I was to close on the house, they called me back and told me in so many words that there were more houses than people for section 8.

Now this was a shock to me because I had always heard there were more people looking for housing than there were houses for people. To the best of my knowledge, there was always a shortage of housing. I began to freak out, because this was a major problem. If I couldn't rent the house out on Section 8, and I didn't believe I could sell it for a profit, then what in the world was I going to do with it?

One day before closing, I called the daughter selling the house and told her I was backing out. This was the Holy Spirit talking, not me. As a matter of fact, he was screaming. Of course, she asked me what was wrong, and I told her the whole story about me wanting to rent the house out on Section 8 and not being able to, and then she began to tell me that I could rent that house out to anyone, it was a great house.

She was right about the house. It was a great house, but in a terrible location. Anyway, to make a long story short, she talked me into buying the house. It was the worse financial decision I've ever made, because I couldn't rent the house neither could I sell it.

Now let me clarify something: Just because your disobedience may get you into something doesn't mean that God won't get you out. This was nothing other than the Lord's work. This woman was relocating from Louisiana to Georgia after Hurricane Katrina hit. She saw the house on the website—from the outside; she had never seen the inside. When asked if she wanted to see the inside of the house, she said, "Nope. I saw the outside. It's all brick, so it doesn't matter what the inside looks like." She even gave me the asking price. What a blessing.

I said all that to say this: Once God changes your heart and makes it sensitive to the Holy Spirit, and it begins to speak to you, obey it! Because if you don't, there could be some long-lasting consequences.

· · · · · · · · · · · · · ·

The Mind

The last thing I want to talk about here is the mind. Romans 12:2 says, "And be not conformed to this world: but be ye transformed by the renewing of your mind, that ye may prove what is that good, and acceptable, and perfect, will of God." The mind, the mind, the mind, as I said before, it all starts and ends with the mind. We've talked about the mind already, so I'm not going to spend much time talking about it again. However, I would like to talk about the phrase "renewing the mind."

Exactly what does it mean to renew your mind? The word *renew* means "to revive, reestablish." According to the definition of the word, to renew the mind means to revive or reestablish your thoughts. This is a process that we must practice daily.

A lot of people think they can renew their minds overnight to get into a habit of thinking new thoughts. When they can't, they get frustrated. However, what you have to realize is that it took years for your mind to think, act, and react to certain things the way it does; and it's going to take quite some time for the same mind to be revived or reestablished to think, act, and react differently to certain things.

It's not an overnight process. It could literally take years. However, the process still must be done one day at a time, with consistency. There are things I am still reviving and reestablishing as I go through this process of daily renewing my mind. Nevertheless, the mind is a key part of this whole reconstruction process that each Christian must go through.

• • • • • • • • • • • • • • •

There you have it—the four steps to salvation: Recognition (realizing you're lost and you need a Savior), Repentance (asking for forgiveness of your sin and turning from it), Remission (receiving the payment for your sin, which is Jesus Christ), and Reconstruction (being made new).

Now my one remaining question for you is this: Are you ready to get saved?

I mean, are you sick and tired of being sick and tired? Do you believe deep down in your heart that there's more to this thing called life than you're experiencing? Do you feel that God has kept you here on earth for a reason but you have no idea what it is? Have you ever felt like giving up and giving in, but something keeps telling you it's going to get better? Are you ready for life, and life more abundantly? Let me just say this: If you don't know the Lord Jesus, you're not living life. You are merely existing here on earth. If you answered yes to any of the following questions, I would love to have the privilege to lead you to Christ right now.

I would like to share with you the same salvation prayer that I prayed when I got saved. It was actually from one of my favorite gospel CDs of all time. The name of the CD is *Show Up!* by Pastor John P. Kee and the New Life Community Choir, and the song is "I Surrender." The prayer goes something like this:

Lord, I surrender everything,

Father I want to thank you now for what you're doing in my life.

    If there's anything in me that's not like you, take it out right now.

    I've done wrong in this life, but right now, I surrender all to you.

    I acknowledge your son Jesus, and I ask him to come into my heart, my mind, my body, and my soul. Make me a new creature.

    Satan, take your ugly hands off me.

    I belong to God now. I belong to God right now.

    I confess with my mouth, and I believe with my heart that God raised Jesus from the dead for my sins, and now I know, that I'm saved.

If you said this prayer with all your heart, you are saved! Which means your past is forgiven, your present is empowered, and your future is secured. I'm so proud of you, and very excited about what God is going to do in your life.

Author's Note

Growing up without a father around, I know how it feels to figure out this thing called life on my own. I know how it feels to initiate yourself into manhood, because there is no man around to do it for you. I know how it feels to spend literally years looking for an authentic hero, because you want someone to identify with, to connect with, and to be associated with. I know how it feels to find your first porn magazine at an early age, and to struggle with pornography for nearly two decades. I guess what I'm trying to say is this: Regardless of where you are in life right now, I've been there, did that, got the T-shirt, and wish I could give it back! However, the good news for you is that no matter where you are, no matter what you're in, and no matter how long you've been in it, God can bring you out and save you. He can heal you, deliver you, and set you free. I hope you have as much fun reading this book as I did writing it. God bless you!

Bibliography

Arterburn, Stephen and Fred Stoeker. *Every Man's Battle: Winning the War on Sexual Temptation One Victory at a Time.* Colorado Springs: WaterBrook Press, 2009.

Dobson, James. *Bringing Up Boys: Practical Advice and Encouragement for Those Shaping the Next Generation of Men.* Wheaton: Tyndale House Publishers, 2001.

Eldredge, John. *Wild at Heart.* United States, Thomas Nelson Publishers, 2001.

King, Martin Luther Jr. "I Have a Dream." Speech, Washington, DC, August 28, 1963.

———. "I've Been to the Mountaintop." Speech, April 3, 1968.

Martin Luther King's Speeches and Life Website

www.biography.com/ people/ martin-Luther king-Jr. 9365086

www.brainyquote.com/quotes/authors/m/ martin-luther-king-jr.-5html

www.sheryl franklin.com/holidays/ml king.html

www.americanrhetoric.com/speeches/mll I've been to the mountaintop.html

Stanley, Charles. *Is There a Man in the House?* 1977. Victor Books a division of SP Publications Inc.Wheaton Illinois